Labor's Search for Political Order

Gary M Fink

LABOR'S SEARCH
FOR POLITICAL ORDER

THE POLITICAL BEHAVIOR OF THE

MISSOURI LABOR MOVEMENT

1890–1940

University of Missouri Press

The substance of the Conclusion originally appeared as "The Rejection of Voluntarism," in *Industrial and Labor Relations Review,* Vol. 26, No. 2, January, 1973.

In the Memory of
My Father

JOHN FINK
(1907–1962)

PREFACE

DURING the last quarter of the nineteenth century, the American Federation of Labor assumed the institutional structure that would characterize its organization for more than fifty years. The AFL was by far the largest and most influential labor organization in America and served as a central governmental agency over a highly decentralized confederation of sovereign international unions and a widespread network of state federations and city central unions. At the local and state level central bodies that were directly chartered and controlled by the AFL served much the same function as the national labor union.

These local central unions were the most politically oriented organizations in the American labor movement. In reality they were not labor organizations at all but political institutions that were ancillary to the trade union movement. Constitutional restrictions left them little economic power. They could neither call a strike, initiate a boycott, nor organize locals without authorization from international organizations that would be affected by their actions. The only area in which central unions had any degree of autonomy was in politics, and here they assumed the role of pressure groups, attempting to exert labor's influence on the local, state, and occasionally, the national level.

Despite the important political functions performed by these local central bodies, most students have virtually ignored them in their analyses of the political behavior of the American labor movement. Instead, conclusions are based on the applied practices of the AFL leadership and stated policy positions issued at annual conventions of the AFL. While valuable and enlightening, these studies accurately reflect the political behavior of only a very selective portion of the labor movement. Local central unions were allowed considerable latitude in evolving their own social and political objectives. As a result, differences of both attitude and behavior often separated the leadership of the AFL from leaders at the lower levels of the labor movement. This division was facilitated by the decentralized structure of the labor movement and the inherent difficulties an attempt to regulate such matters would have entailed.

In this study the political behavior of the Missouri labor movement has been analyzed in an effort to compare labor's political behavior on the state and local levels to that of the AFL nationally. More specifically, the attempt has been made to identify the political objectives of the labor movement, to analyze the environment in which it functioned, to describe the manner in which the labor movement sought to exercise its potential political power, and to measure the effectiveness with which it did so. In seeking answers to these questions, the newer methods of historical quantification have been used to supplement the more traditional methods of historical research. Although the results of the quantified analysis are reported separately from the text, this information has significantly influenced my interpretations throughout the study.

Because of the decentralized structure of the labor movement, a study of the political behavior of a state labor movement is not and should not be artificially limited to state and local history. To borrow the terminology of the economists, a microstudy should provide valuable insights into macrohistoriography; to ignore this potential would be to overlook the most significant contributions that such a study could make. It is in that spirit that the following study is presented. The objective is not the restricted study of the historical evolution of a single state labor movement, but rather it is to view the political behavior of organized labor in the twentieth century from a different perspective.

This study was initiated as a doctoral thesis at the University of Missouri under the direction of Richard S. Kirkendall, and I am especially indebted to Professor Kirkendall for his counsel, advice and constructive criticism. Professors David P. Thelen, University of Missouri; Harold D. Woodman, Purdue University; Donald G. Sofchalk, Mankato State College; and Merl E. Reed, Georgia State University, also have read the entire manuscript and made many useful suggestions. The directors and staffs of a number of libraries and historical societies have been very helpful, especially the personnel at the two state historical societies in Missouri and that in Wisconsin. Finally, I would like to acknowledge the efforts of Mary B. Fink who has participated in the study and made invaluable contributions from the initial research through the final revision of the manuscript.

G.M.F.
Georgia State University
September, 1972

Contents

Introduction

THE MISSOURI MILIEU

FIVE YEARS after the founding of the American Federation of Labor, twenty-one pioneer labor delegates from various Missouri cities and towns met in Kansas City in the spring of 1891 to organize the Missouri State Federation of Labor. Their action provided a climax to an activity that had begun in the 1820s when Missouri's first workingmen's societies and labor unions were organized. The Panic of 1837 and the depression that followed precipitated the growth of a short-lived central union in Saint Louis, but it was not until after the Civil War that a viable labor movement with permanent central bodies existed in various Missouri cities.[1]

Saint Louis was Missouri's oldest and largest city. It had a large immigrant population that consisted mainly of Germans but included substantial numbers of Eastern and Southern European peoples. There was little consensus in social and cultural values, political philosophy, or in the economic thought of its working class. The absence of homogeneity is strikingly illustrated in the development of the city's labor movement.

By the time the AFL was organized, Saint Louis had three central labor unions, the German *Arbeiter-Verband,* the Central Labor Union, and the Saint Louis Trades Assembly. Following the formation of the AFL, these three organizations merged into the Saint Louis Central Trades and Labor Union and requested an AFL charter. The Central Trades, the main body for all AFL affiliated unions in the area, was controlled by Socialists during a large portion of its early years. A vigorous and active organization, it enrolled a large percentage of the city's locals.[2]

The Central Trades typically carried on a rather uncomfortable relationship with the AFL officialdom. Conservative AFL leaders undoubtedly viewed the strength of the Socialists in the Saint Louis or-

1. For a discussion of the organization of the labor movement in the first half of the nineteenth century, see Halvor G. Melom, "The Economic Development of St. Louis, 1803–1846"; Walter R. Houf, "Fifty Years of Missouri Labor, 1820–1870"; Russell M. Nolen, "The Labor Movement in St. Louis prior to the Civil War"; Gary M Fink, "The Paradoxical Experiences of St. Louis Labor during the Depression of 1837."
2. Edwin J. Forsythe, "The St. Louis Central Trades and Labor Union, 1887–1945," pp. 16–18.

ganization with some misgivings. The discord was intensified when
the delegates from the Central Trades at AFL conventions voted in
favor of the collective ownership of the means of production and,
later, supported a resolution demanding the withdrawal of President
Gompers and other labor officials from the National Civic Federation. As a result of these tensions, the AFL president's threat to revoke the Central Trades' charter became an almost annual event during the early years of the century.[3]

The Central Trades' opposite number in St. Louis was the Building
Trades Council. Many of the city's building trade unions refused to
affiliate with the tightly controlled Council despite occasional pressure
from the AFL president.[4] Socialists had little influence with the leaders of the Council, who were among the strictest business unionists
in the city. The Council leadership often disagreed with the policies
of both the Central Trades and the State Federation of Labor; at
times, it carried its opposition to the point of seriously undermining
the local and state labor movements.

When the two Saint Louis labor organizations found it possible
to work together, they could exert considerable influence. Union
members were often elected to the city's board of aldermen, the Missouri House of Repesentatives, and at times, to the Missouri Senate
and the United States Congress. Organized labor also succeeded in
forming a number of useful alliances with various local civic and reform groups.[5]

The population of Missouri's second-largest city was not nearly
as diverse as that of Saint Louis. Although ethnic differences existed
in Kansas City, citizens of foreign birth seldom composed more than
6 per cent of the population. Largely a "mercantile and financial center with a large, native-born, middle class population,"[6] Kansas City's
environment was hardly conducive to the growth of a vigorous socialist movement, or to socialist influence in the local labor movement.
The absence of radical militancy in the political sphere, however, did
not characterize economic affairs. Businessmen in the city were well
organized and belligerently antiunion, and the struggles between labor
and capital were among the most volatile and violent in the state.

3. Nathan Fine, *Labor and Farmer Parties in the United States, 1828–1928,*
pp. 250, 261. Gary M Fink, "The Evolution of Social and Political Attitudes
in the Missouri Labor Movement, 1900–1940," pp. 9–11.

4. For example, Gompers to Maurice J. Cassidy, November 11, 1912,
Samuel Gompers, Letterbooks.

5. Owen Miller to Gompers, April 10, 1909; Gompers to Percy Pepoon,
October 29, 1910, American Federation of Labor, Papers, Series 117A, File
11A. *Official Manual of the State of Missouri for the Years 1913–1914,*
p. 46. Cited hereafter as *Official Manual* for the years indicated. Forsythe,
"St. Louis Central Trades," pp. 73, 74.

6. Lyle W. Dorsett, *The Pendergast Machine,* p. xii.

The two most important central bodies in Kansas City, the Industrial Council (later the Central Labor Union) and the Building Trades Council, followed both policies and leaders that were extremely pragmatic and opportunistic. Business agents who dominated the central bodies in Kansas City were able to erect a closely knit, highly oligarchical organization. Although these labor organizations rarely had problems with the AFL leadership, their hierarchical organization occasionally produced apathy among the rank and file. Kansas City labor leaders also seemed more susceptible to corruption than the union leadership of any other Missouri city.[7]

The labor movement in the smaller cities and towns of "outstate" Missouri was in some ways more dynamic than it was in either of the two metropolitan centers. With less centralization and fewer professional business agents, the labor unions in the smaller cities afforded the average member a larger role in union affairs. As a consequence, the union was more important to him. In the early years of the century, locals and federations of small cities seldom reflected the business unionism approach of the building trades or of the labor movement on the national level. Because railroad workers and miners were still numerous in these areas, their unions often showed sparks of nineteenth-century radicalism, mitigating the influence of the narrow bread-and-butter unionism of others. Furthermore, inhabitants of the smaller urban areas were often less antagonistic toward organized labor than those in the metropolitan centers and frequently permitted union labor to play a greater role in local affairs.[8]

The labor movement in Missouri was organized in an environment characterized by its economic diversity. When war broke out in Europe in 1914, agriculture was still Missouri's largest industry, but the production of boots, shoes, men's and women's clothing, processing plants for agricultural goods, and an infant automobile industry were becoming increasingly important to the state's economy. This industrial growth, accompanied by an expanding urban population, provided a great stimulus to the always important construction industry. The state was crisscrossed in all directions by a vast railroad network that directly provided employment for thousands of workers and indirectly provided the economic sustenance for numerous small towns and cities. Finally, Missouri produced significant quantities of such important mineral extracts as coal, iron, lead, zinc, and barytes.[9]

These industries provided the early focus of labor union activity.

7. The only available study of the labor movement in Kansas City is Wilford R. Sears, "The Kansas City Building Trades and Trade Unionism."

8. Cf. Herbert G. Gutman, "The Worker's Search for Power: Labor in the Guilded Age," pp. 38–63.

9. Missouri Bureau of Labor Statistics, *Missouri Red Book, 1914*, pp. 82–86, 170–94. Cited hereafter as *Missouri Red Book* for the years indicated.

In 1900 there were approximately 40,000 organized workers in Missouri, the great majority concentrated in the Saint Louis area. In the early years of the twentieth century, however, the labor movement throughout the state grew at a tremendous rate, more than doubling its membership. By 1914 there were 114,000 organized workers in Missouri, approximately 75 per cent of which were affiliated with the AFL. A little more than half of all organized workers lived in the Saint Louis area. Kansas City was second with about 16 per cent of the state's union labor force. The remaining third of the organized workers in Missouri was located in the smaller urban areas, in the towns along the railroad lines, and in the mining regions. Although the Missouri Labor Commissioner reported that 87.5 per cent of the trades in Missouri were organized, the depth of organization was very shallow. Missouri had a labor force of nearly 1.5 million in 1914, and fewer than 8 per cent of those workers belonged to labor organizations. Only one-fifth of the workers employed in or associated with the manufacturing and construction industries were union members. Of the quarter of a million women in the labor force, only a little more than 2 per cent were organized. Most of the organized women toilers were associated with either the garment or the boot and shoe industries that were located in the two metropolitan centers. Slightly more than 50 per cent of the state's miners and about 46 per cent of the railroad employees were union members. As was true elsewhere in the nation, the greatest degree of organization was among the skilled crafts and in the building trades.[10]

Nearly one-fifth of all union members in Missouri belonged to industrial unions. Two of the state's largest and most influential unions, the United Brewery Workmen and the United Mine Workers, were organized on an industrial basis. The principle of industrial organization also received support from labor leaders in the boot and shoe industry, the garment workers, and some officials of the carpenters' unions.[11]

It was in an effort to coordinate and guide the union labor activities of these various unions that the Missouri State Federation of Labor had been organized in 1891. In the early years of its existence, the State Federation was little more than an extension of the Saint Louis labor movement. A decade after its inception, two-thirds of the delegates to the annual convention of the State Federation still represented Saint Louis unions.[12] As the state labor movement grew,

10. *Ibid., 1902,* p. 148; *1914,* pp. 55, 58, 59, 124–233.
11. *Ibid.,* pp. 50–53. Forsythe, "St. Louis Central Trades," pp. 100–103. Although there is some evidence of activity in the mining areas of the state, the IWW was never a significant factor in Missouri's organized labor movement.
12. *Yearbook of the Missouri State Federation of Labor, 1899,* State Historical Society of Missouri, Columbia.

however, the State Federation became less dependent upon the Saint Louis unions that had played such a seminal role in its early history and grew increasingly important to smaller urban areas such as Saint Joseph, Springfield, Sedalia, and Hannibal. Because labor unions in these towns were dependent upon the state body for aid in organizing, assistance and leadership during strikes, and lobbying in the state legislature, they became the State Federation's most active and loyal constituency. The state central body received similar support from the various organizations of miners and railroad workers affiliated with the AFL. Labor in the larger metropolitan areas of Saint Louis and Kansas City was much less dependent upon the State Federation. Since they had sufficient resources and personnel to look after their own interests, union leaders in these cities were reluctant to delegate responsibility to an organization over which they had only limited control.

The major business of the State Federation was conducted at annual conventions where officers were elected, policies and programs enunciated, and a general sense of unity and solidarity fostered. The membership of the organization's two most important committees, the executive and legislative committees, was selected by the delegates of the convention. The executive committee, which varied in size from year to year, was responsible for conducting the affairs of the Federation between conventions. The executive committee could not contain more than two members of the same trade, and the Saint Louis and Kansas City labor movements were always represented. The legislative committee, which consisted of three members, coordinated the legislative efforts of labor bodies throughout the state. It assumed the responsibility for looking after organized labor's interests in the state legislature.[13]

The State Federation maintained two full-time, paid officials. The president, who presided over the annual conventions, was a standing member of the executive and legislative committees. He acted as a part-time organizer, assisted in strike activities, and when called upon, served as a mediator in jurisdictional disputes. The secretary–treasurer was responsible for receiving and spending the Federations' monies and maintaining a steady flow of communications between state organizations, city central bodies, and local unions throughout the state.[14]

One of the State Federation's most significant responsibilities, as it evolved and found its place in the state labor movement, was to speak for organized labor in the general areas of socioeconomic pol-

13. *Constitution, By-Laws and Rules of Order,* Missouri State Federation of Labor.
14. *Ibid.*

icy. Although directly chartered and controlled by the AFL, state and city federations were allowed considerable latitude in evolving their own social and political objectives and priorities. This function was facilitated by the decentralized structure of the labor movement and the inherent difficulties that an attempt to regulate such matters would entail. As a result not only did important differences develop within the state labor movement but also significant differences of opinion evolved between labor leaders in Missouri and the leadership of the AFL. Some Missouri labor leaders endorsed the AFL philosophy of pure and simple, craft-conscious trade unionism, an essentially exclusionist labor organization abdicating any responsibility to labor as a class and instead, in the words of Samuel Gompers, winning "more, more, more" for the relatively few workers of the specific trades that could successfully organize. Other labor leaders endorsed the Socialist party which, while it did accept the responsibility for uplifting the workers as a class, argued that this goal could only be accomplished through the overthrow of existing institutions and the substitution of the cooperative commonwealth.

The vast majority of Missouri trade unions and labor leaders, however, had no allegiance to either of these philosophies. Much of the early history of the Missouri labor movement was characterized by the search for an acceptable alternative. The search was not always conscious; more often it was the result of reluctant but necessary compromises. But whether conscious or unconscious, it became a necessity when a majority of Missouri trade unionists rejected the existing alternatives of socialism or business unionism.

In their quest for an alternative social and political philosophy, Missouri labor leaders borrowed selectively from a broad range of both foreign and domestic ideologies. The American interpreters and revisionists of Karl Marx, such as Victor Berger, Morris Hillquit, and Eugene Debs, had a lasting impact upon labor thought. Also influential in many ways was the example set by trade unionists in England. Indeed, the rhetoric of Missouri labor leaders sometimes leaves the impression that they were influenced as greatly by Labour Headquarters in London as by the AFL leadership in Washington when determining their political policies.

Two important native sources of Missouri labor's evolving social thought were the Knights of Labor and the Populist party. Perhaps the importance of these two organizations lies more in their recognition of the need for change than in the policies they pursued. On a more individual basis, the writings of Edward Bellamy and Henry George had a significant impact upon labor thought, and organizations bearing such titles as Bellamy Clubs or Students of Henry George were not uncommon in working-class districts.

As the foregoing suggests, the Missouri labor movement of the early twentieth century was, in many respects, physically and emotionally immature. But like a developing adolescent, it was vigorous, optimistic, and growing rapidly. Moreover, largely ignorant of its own strength and potentialities, it was constantly probing and testing in an effort to discover the extent and character of its potential social, economic, and political strength and influence.

Part One

DISILLUSIONMENT
WITH
NONPARTISANSHIP

The early years of the twentieth century were a time of trial and decision for the Missouri labor movement. Rejecting the antistatism of the national leadership of the American labor movement, Missouri labor leaders assumed that the trade union movement, by itself, had neither the resources nor the ability to assure the well-being of the entire working class. They believed that government had an obligation and a responsibility to insure a minimum level of security to the citizens it governed. As a result of this conviction, organized labor in Missouri placed a much greater emphasis upon the exercise of its potential political power and influence than did the national leadership of the labor movement. When labor leaders reached the conclusion that organized labor was not exercising the political influence to which its numbers and position in society entitled it, they began to question the nonpartisan policy espoused by the American Federation of Labor. Socialists offered one alternative to the apolitical, business unionism of the national organization, but despite the flirtation of many Missouri labor leaders with socialism, it captured neither the imagination nor loyalty of a majority of Missouri trade unionists. For many Missouri unionists, the organization of an independent labor party seemed the most viable alternative to nonpartisanship, but the AFL national leadership's adamant opposition to third-party politics along with the prevailing party loyalties of many union members and leaders were insurmountable obstacles. Consequently, Missouri trade unionists continued to practice the nonpartisan strategy but remained highly receptive to any alternative strategy that promised more effective results. Meanwhile, they sought to reform the political system in such a way that it would be more responsive to the needs and desires of the working class.

Chapter I

THE VAGARIES
OF NONPARTISANSHIP

THE Missouri State Federation of Labor, like other central bodies of labor organizations, soon found that politics was its most effective potential vehicle for promoting the interests of labor. Constitutional restrictions allowed it little flexibility to act or react in economic affairs; consequently, the State Federation's leadership devoted more and more of its energies and resources to political matters where the range of action and involvement was less restricted.

The State Federation's emphasis upon political action did not violate the spirit of the movement that had inspired its organization. Although Missouri unionists had always taken an active interest in politics, labor leaders had become convinced that despite some success, organized labor was not exerting the influence in state politics to which it was entitled. This assumption had been fundamentally important in the original movement to organize the Missouri State Federation of Labor. The anticipation of increased political effectiveness was clearly reflected in the Preamble and Declaration of Principles of the new labor central body:

> There is absolute need for such a central body. Such a Federation binds all the various labor organizations into closer bonds of fraternity, and is a powerful factor in obtaining needful remedial legislation. Indeed, labor legislation cannot be obtained without the active work and influence of a powerful state federation. The cause of one workingman is the cause of all. United they stand, divided they fall. How well the capitalist class understand this familiar axiom! Ah, how well they are banded together. As well might an army composed of separate, heterogeneous companies of soldiers, each company under its own supreme commander, without the formation into battalions, regiments, brigades and divisions, or control of such commanders, attempt to do battle with a well drilled, disciplined homogeneous army, organized under approved military rules. They could not stand for ten minutes, though equal in number, and would be swept like rubbish from the field.[1]

Despite its relative autonomy, however, the State Federation was in no way a politically free agent. Directly chartered and controlled

1. *Yearbook of the Missouri State Federation of Labor, 1899,* State Historical Society of Missouri, Columbia.

11

by the American Federation of Labor, state federations were responsible to the national labor federation for their actions. Moreover, the
AFL leadership had adopted a political strategy that, although passive and negative, its constituent assemblies were expected to carry
through.

The basic political philosophy of the AFL leadership was premised
upon the assumption that not only was labor's economic power more
important than its political power but also that political involvement
carried with it numerous dangers to the stability and survival of the
labor movement. As a result, the political strategy that emerged was
one that strived for neutrality in the political arena in order that organized labor could exercise its economic power with a minimum
of governmental interference. Under the tenets of this policy, which
soon came to be known as voluntarism, the workers were to rely
upon their trade unions for protecting and promoting their interests.
This function was to be accomplished through the exercise of labor's
primary economic weapons: collective bargaining, strikes, and boy-
cotts. Government assistance was not to be sought on either the administrative or legislative level because the power given to government to aid labor could also be used against labor.[2]

The AFL leadership, however, failed to pursue even its limited
and rather negative political strategy with any degree of urgency or
enthusiasm. Independent political action by labor groups or affiliation
with any particular political party, such as the Socialist party, were
firmly rejected as means of achieving political objectives. The basic
tactic adopted by the AFL was nonpartisanship. In Gompers's words,
workers had to be weaned "from being political followers of any
party by whatever name known."[3] The only political action the AFL
leadership wanted to take part in was the endorsement of those candidates who were favorable to the legislative objectives of the labor
movement.[4]

Almost from the beginning, the policies of the State Federation
of Labor reflected the Missouri labor movement's disagreement with
the basic political objectives and tactics of the AFL. Although there
were labor leaders in Missouri who endorsed and supported the ideals
of voluntarism, the attitude of most of the state's labor leaders and
union members evidences little commitment to the principle.[5] Mis-

2. David J. Saposs, "Voluntarism in the American Labor Movement."
George G. Higgins, *Voluntarism in Organized Labor in the United States,
1930–1940.*

3. Philip Taft, *The A. F. of L. in the Time of Gompers,* p. 291.

4. The best available study of the early political behavior of the AFL
is Marc Karson, *American Labor Unions and Politics, 1900–1918.*

5. This is one of the major conclusions of this study and is elaborated
upon in Chaps. 4 and 12.

souri labor leaders assumed that government had a legitimate role to play in the workings of the American economy. They exhibited no great fear of governmental power and did not hesitate to grant government increased power to deal with the social and economic problems that occurred because of the nation's escalating industrialism. Their aim was not for less government but rather for more power and influence for labor within government.

Missouri trade unionists, therefore, were never as convinced about what could be accomplished through purely economic means as was the leadership of the AFL. Missouri labor leaders did not debate the question of whether to stress their economic or their political strength but assumed that both were important. In its first Declaration of Principles, the State Federation listed a series of objectives upon which the political program of the state labor movement was built. Their program called for:

First—The enactment of a state law, and a provision for its rigid enforcement, making it obligatory for every child between the ages of six and fifteen years to attend school at least nine months of the year, and to still further make ample provision for the education of the masses we demand that the state municipalities shall furnish the necessary books free to every child.

Second—To secure to the toilers a proper share of the wealth they create.

Third—The abrogation of all laws that do not bear equally upon capital and labor.

Fourth—The enactment of all laws necessary to compel corporations or individuals to pay their employees weekly for labor performed the preceding week, and in lawful money.

Fifth—The abolition of the competition of convict labor with free labor.

Sixth—To secure for both sexes equal pay for equal work.

Seventh—The reduction of the hours of labor to eight per day.

Eighth—The taxation of land regardless of values.

Ninth—Prohibition of child labor under 15 years.

Tenth—Establishment of National Postal Savings Banks, and banks of discount and issue.

Eleventh—Adoption of a constitutional amendment requiring the election of President, Vice-President and United States Senators by the direct vote of the people.

Twelfth—Adoption of the initiative and the referendum, i.e., that all laws passed by legislative bodies be referred to a popular vote for ratification or rejection.[6]

At the same time that Missouri labor leaders disagreed with their AFL counterparts over the projected ends of political activity, they

6. *Yearbook of the Missouri State Federation of Labor, 1899.*

had serious reservations about the AFL's choice of means. They were less committed to the ideal of nonpartisanship than the national organization was and more predisposed to the idea of an independent labor party or any other alternative tactic that promised effective political action. Meanwhile, uncommitted to a definite alternative, they pushed the nonpartisan policy as vigorously as possible. The Missouri State Federation of Labor pioneered in the nonpartisan questioning of candidates for state office in the elections of 1902. Following the same tactic two years later, Missouri unions obtained pledges of support for the labor program from twelve of sixteen candidates elected to Congress. At that time the AFL also adopted the questioning technique.[7]

As a result of their own predisposition in political matters, Missouri labor leaders responded enthusiastically to the AFL executive council's announcement of a more activist political program in 1906. Officially communicated to central bodies and state federations in July, the new political program was preceded by a Labor's Bill of Grievances. The document, initially submitted to President Theodore Roosevelt and leaders of Congress, enumerated the grievances that provoked labor to assume a more active role in the political affairs of the nation. Among other requests, the AFL leadership wanted restriction of immigration, better administration of the eight-hour law for government employees, a law protecting seamen, better enforcement of antitrust and interstate commerce laws, less perverse use of the writ of injunction, more sympathetic appointees to the House labor committee, and the right of petition by government employees, which had been denied by presidential order.[8]

In a circular letter to central bodies and state federations of labor, AFL President Samuel Gompers recommended that local labor bodies immediately call a conference to formulate plans to implement the political program of national organization. Local labor leaders were instructed to work for the nomination of candidates who would unquestionably promote the enactment of progressive labor measures. Legislators sympathetic to the rights of labor were to receive generous support and hostile lawmakers given a "stinging rebuke." In the event that neither party nominated a candidate who was sympathetic to labor's legislative demands, labor leaders were instructed to run an independent labor candidate.[9]

Despite the flourish with which it was announced, the 1906 politi-

7. Philip S. Foner, *History of the Labor Movement in the United States,* pp. 302, 303.

8. *American Federationist,* 13:294–96, 529–31.

9. Gompers to Organized Labor, July 22, 1906, AFL, Papers, Series 117A, File 11A.

cal program did not actually represent a great change from the AFL's previous policy of nonpartisanship.[10] Philip Taft, an authority on the history of the AFL, argues that the program was a new departure, but he finds that it was the "concentration of energy and high-lighting of political demands" rather than any new policy or philosophy that was significant.[11]

Although the complaints enumerated in the Bill of Grievances generally have been accepted as the reason for the AFL's increased emphasis on politics, a few students of the politics of American labor have discerned some less obvious motivations for the AFL's political interest. The spectacular appearance of the Industrial Workers of the World, the growing and vigorous Socialist party, and a general decline in AFL membership and finances all appeared to challenge the adequacy of the existing leadership of the labor movement. The dramatic political activity provided a means of once again turning the spotlight on the activities of the AFL leadership.[12]

Early in the year, even prior to the 1906 session of Congress about which Gompers inveighed so bitterly, AFL officials had been discussing a political program that included an active campaign to be conducted by state federations along guidelines determined by the AFL leadership. Adolph Strasser first proposed such a program to an AFL organizer and relayed it to Frank Morrison, AFL secretary. In forwarding it to Gompers, Morrison commented that the plan was particularly appealing because it would "nullify much of the thunder which the Socialists use" and would "turn the public sentiment of members of trades unions in another channel, and have the effect of forcing the Socialist sentiment to a low ebb."[13]

Socialists in the early years of the twentieth century were presenting AFL "pure-and-simple" trade unionists with one of their most serious internal challenges. Criticism by Socialists of the inability of the AFL leadership to accomplish its legislative objectives was becoming increasingly effective with labor leaders at lower levels. Furthermore, both Socialist and non-Socialist labor leaders were watching with increasing envy the venture into politics by labor in England. Even Gompers found it impossible to ignore the election of more than fifty

10. Nathan Fine, *Labor and Farmer Parties in the United States, 1828–1928,* pp. 254, 255. Lewis Lorwin, *The American Federation of Labor: History, Policies, and Prospects,* pp. 88–91.

11. Taft, *The A. F. of L. in the Time of Gompers,* p. 295.

12. *Ibid.,* pp. 289–300. Lorwin, *The American Federation of Labor,* pp. 88–91. Bernard Mandel, *Samuel Gompers: A Biography,* pp. 284–97. Selig Perlman, *A History of Trade Unionism in the United States,* pp. 198–205. Fine, *Labor and Farmer Parties,* Chap. 8. Karson, *American Labor Unions and Politics,* p. 40.

13. Frank Morrison to Gompers, January 4, 1906, AFL, Papers, Series 117A, File 11A.

trade unionists to Parliament in 1906.[14] It was undoubtedly no mere coincidence that the new political action committee created by the AFL was given the same name as its English equivalent, the Labor Representation Committee. The name, however, was the only similarity between the two organizations. The AFL's Labor Representation Committee, which consisted of Gompers, Morrison, and Federation Vice-President James O'Connell, was largely a paper organization. It had no appropriated finances, and although it apparently held some meetings, it is impossible to separate its activities from those of the AFL office generally.

In Missouri the AFL's new "activist" political program consisted more of rhetoric than action. When AFL leaders did involve themselves, it was primarily in an effort to diminish the influence of Socialists in the labor movement or to provide a strong defense of the AFL's leadership and traditional political policies. Missouri labor leaders, nevertheless, obviously took Gompers's proclamation and rhetoric seriously and attempted to pursue the AFL's political program as vigorously as possible.

In Saint Louis a group of trade unionists formed an organization to run independent labor candidates in three Saint Louis congressional districts. The group was composed primarily of conservative trade unionists and firmly supported the AFL's announced political and legislative program. After examining the candidates of both major parties, it decided that third-party labor candidates should be nominated because the regular nominees were unacceptable to labor. Operating under the banner of the Union Workingmen's party, they immediately sought assistance from the AFL's Labor Representation Committee. They requested three speakers, including Gompers, campaign literature, and if possible, some financial assistance, although they felt that sufficient funds could be raised in Saint Louis. In response to these modest demands, Gompers, speaking for the Labor Representation Committee, declared that he was unable to make a trip to Saint Louis and ignored the other requests. Bewildered by Gompers's reply, sponsors of the political movement again wrote the AFL president asking why their requests had not been considered. The reply blithely referred to the previous correspondence. Several of the projected labor party's candidates also wrote Gompers requesting assistance, but they received no response from him or from the Labor Representation Committee.[15]

14. Fine, *Labor and Farmer Parties,* Chap. 8. Mandel, *Samuel Gompers,* pp. 323–33. Foner, *History of the Labor Movement,* Chap. 14. *American Federationist,* 13:319, 320.

15. Edward J. McCullen and James B. Conroy to Morrison, October 9, 1906; Gompers to McCullen, October 15, 1906; McCullen to Morrison, October 19, 1906; Morrison to McCullen, October 22, 1906; John Hanks to

In late October, after circulating petitions to get their candidates' names on the ballot, the leaders of the Saint Louis political movement decided to give up their venture. Edward McCullen, chairman of the Saint Louis group, wrote Frank Morrison that the failure of the Labor Representation Committee to give any assurance of assistance was the major reason for the termination of the project.[16]

The Saint Louis episode, along with other similar incidents, suggests that the AFL's leadership was not entirely sincere in its advocacy of an activist political program. Despite its proclamation that labor should nominate independent labor candidates when nominees of the two major parties were unsatisfactory, the AFL hierarchy seemed ill-disposed to encourage or support the candidacy of any independent nominee. Undoubtedly the officials were fearful that the nomination of labor candidates, especially if they should be elected, would increase the agitation within the AFL for independent political action.[17]

The experience of Congressman John T. Hunt, the Democratic representative from Missouri's Eleventh Congressional District, is illustrative. Hunt had a perfect voting record on labor measures and had to be considered one of labor's greatest friends in Congress. A member of the important House labor committee, he was the only congressman who held a union card and was credited by Gompers with forcing labor's eight-hour bill through the House labor committee where Republicans had attempted to block it. When Saint Louis Democrats refused to renominate him in 1906, Hunt entered the race as an independent, confidently expecting organized labor's "reward" during the campaign. Hunt's campaign manager, Thomas Brennan, wrote Gompers asking what assistance could be expected from the AFL and requesting that Gompers make a speech in the Eleventh District. Gompers casually replied that he was busy preparing his report for the forthcoming AFL convention and would not have time to aid the incumbent congressman's campaign. Gompers did assure Hunt, however, that he had his "best wishes for success."[18]

The response of the AFL leader was significantly different when

Gompers, October 16, 1906; Nat G. Eaton to Gompers, October 17, 1906; Jerry Burns to Gompers, October 17, 1906, AFL, Papers, Series 117A, File 11A.

16. McCullen to Morrison, October 26, 1906, *ibid.*

17. The experience in Missouri supports Philip Foner's argument that one of the reasons for Gompers's political activism was the attempt to undermine the growing agitation in the labor movement for independent political action in the form of a labor party. Foner, *History of the Labor Movement*, pp. 317, 318.

18. Charles Holton to Gompers, June 5, 1906; Thomas Brennan to Gompers, September 26, 1906, AFL, Papers, Series 117A, File 11A. Gompers to Brennan, October 8, 1906, Gompers, Letterbooks.

Democratic Congressman Champ Clark asked for assistance. In this case, Gompers immediately contacted the presidents of the United Mine Workers and several of the railroad brotherhoods requesting that they correspond with their locals in Clark's district in behalf of his candidacy. Gompers also dispatched Organizer Grant Hamilton to Clark's district with instructions to assist in any way possible during the campaign.[19]

Regardless of the reasons for which the AFL leadership chose to emphasize political activity in 1906, its proclamation on politics met with an enthusiastic response from Missouri labor leaders. While somewhat skeptical about the nonpartisan method to be employed, they generally agreed that the AFL had neglected politics for too long. In his report to the annual convention of the Missouri State Federation of Labor, President Thomas Sheridan reflected this attitude when he argued that the economic power of organized labor had failed to halt the inequitable concentration of wealth and power in the hands of the few. "Let us use our political power," he declared, "to again bring the institutions and laws of our common country under the control of the people and make this government in reality what it is in theory, a government of the people and by the people."[20]

Sheridan also proposed a program to reinvigorate the State Federation's political activity. He suggested that "independent political clubs should be organized in every town and city, and, acting in conjunction with the Legislative Committee appointed by the Federation, should pass upon the respective merit of candidates nominated. Whenever the candidates of the two old parties are simply hirelings of the machines, independent labor candidates should be put into the field."[21]

According to Sheridan's suggestions, the delegates to the State Federation convention outlined a ten-point political program to guide its officers. The program included questioning candidates for state and national office and appropriating funds for such items as campaign literature, questionnaires, and postage. Another appropriation was proposed to enable the legislative committee of the State Federation to secure legal advice and assistance in drafting and presenting measures to the legislature. The State Federation's officers also asked local unions and central bodies to appoint legislative committees to cooperate with the state committee to increase labor's political influence.[22]

19. Gompers to Champ Clark, October 8, 24, 1906; Gompers to L. W. Quick, October 8, 1906, Gompers, Letterbooks.

20. *Proceedings of the Missouri State Federation of Labor, 1906,* pp. 8, 9. Cited hereafter as MSFL, *Proceedings* for the years indicated.

21. *Ibid.*

22. *Ibid.,* p. 36.

The enthusiasm with which Missouri labor pursued its political endeavor is further evidenced in the volume of correspondence received by the AFL office from local and central bodies throughout the state. Correspondents asked about the voting records of Congressmen, described the political activities of local bodies, and sought endorsements for candidates. In Saint Joseph, for example, the Central Labor Union formed a local political organization called The Gompers' Political Club. In Hannibal the Trades and Labor Assembly developed an elaborate organization for political action and conducted a vigorous campaign. These local groups, like the state organization, were primarily interested in the enactment of legislation on the state level.[23]

It is difficult to evaluate the effectiveness of the 1906 political program of the AFL. Gompers argued that the reduction of the Republican majority in the House of Representatives from 112 members to 56 was a great victory for labor. In his report to the AFL convention, Gompers predicted that the political campaign waged by labor would bring "magical results," and that labor's "opponents will not be so arrogant toward the representatives of labor as they have been in the past." The Fifty-ninth Congress following the election of 1906, however, was as unresponsive to labor's demands as those that preceded it.[24]

Despite the inconclusive nature of its achievements, the leadership of the AFL was determined to restrict labor's involvement in politics at the same time that it hoped to reinforce the role of the AFL as the source of leadership for a labor movement in both the economic and political realm. Consequently, in the presidential election year of 1908, AFL leaders once again announced their intention to wage a vigorous campaign based upon the traditional nonpartisan policy. Gompers visited the Democratic and Republican conventions, and as a result of their responses to labor's demands, he denounced the Republican candidate and platform and endorsed the Democratic party and personally advocated and campaigned for the election of William Jennings Bryan.[25]

A number of Missouri labor leaders who were somewhat disillusioned by the AFL's efforts in 1906 questioned the wisdom of continuing the same tactic again in 1908. At a meeting of the Saint Louis Central Trades and Labor Union in August, correspondence was read from Gompers and other AFL leaders describing the response of the

23. *Ibid.*, p. 19. Charles W. Fear to Officers and Members of all Labor Organizations in Missouri, July 1, 1906, AFL, Papers, Series 117A, File 11A. Much of this correspondence is contained in Boxes 4 and 5.

24. Quoted in Foner, *History of the Labor Movement*, pp. 333, 334.

25. *Ibid.*, pp. 331–33. Taft, *The A. F. of L. in the Time of Gompers*, pp. 295–98. Karson, *American Labor Unions*, pp. 58–60.

two major parties to labor's legislative demands. The AFL leadership urged Missouri labor leaders to initiate immediate action along non-partisan lines. After some debate a committee was appointed to draft resolutions for discussion at the following meeting of the Central Trades.[26]

The committee presented a resolution in early September endorsing the political program of the AFL's executive council. Although the committee's proposal did not endorse Bryan, it did condemn Taft and the Republican party.[27] The central body, however, rejected the committee resolution and approved the following substitute:

> Whereas, There are numerous good reasons why Organized Labor cannot endorse the candidacy of William H. Taft for President on the Republican ticket; and,
> Whereas, The Democratic Party, as represented by the Hawes—Snake Kinney—Butler—Wells—Francis elements in St. Louis, and the Governor Comer Democracy in Alabama, or by the Tammany Hall Democracy in New York, is not a particle better than Mr. Taft and his party; therefore be it
> Resolved, That the Central Trades and Labor Union of St. Louis emphatically refuses to endorse the Democratic and Republican parties and candidates on either of the Capitalist Party tickets.[28]

Several conservative trade unionists in Saint Louis were convinced that a conspiracy by members of the Socialist party had caused the defeat of the AFL program. AFL organizer, Eugene Sarber, wrote Gompers, "It is not the expression of opinion of the majority of the delegates to the body, as you can see by the small vote cast, but it was a pre-arranged plan of the Socialists who led us to believe that they would support a resolution simply condemning Mr. Taft of the Republican Party."[29] Sarber was sure that at a future meeting the central body would reconsider the matter and endorse the AFL program. Nevertheless, he proposed that the AFL president and some members of the executive council attend the next meeting of the central union. Owen Miller, president of the Saint Louis Central Trades and Labor Union, agreed with Sarber's analysis. In reporting the affair to Gompers, he declared that the "Socialists caught us nap-

26. *St. Louis Labor*, September 19, 1908.

27. *Ibid.*

28. *Ibid.* The references are to Harry Hawes, Thomas Kinney, Edward Butler, Rolla Wells, and David Francis, all prominent Democrats in Saint Louis. The hostile reference to Governor Comer of Alabama was inspired by his use of the police power of the state to crush a United Mine Workers strike earlier in the year.

29. Eugene Sarber to Gompers, September 15, 1908, AFL, Papers, Series 117A, File 11A.

ping." Miller rationalized that the baseball season had detracted from attendance at the central body's Sunday afternoon meetings.[30]

In responding to this correspondence, Gompers declared that he expected the central body to accept the AFL policy, and he wanted the "tried and true trade unionists of St. Louis to do their duty." In a postscript he noted, "Some of our true trade unionists seem to prefer baseball to their duty to be on guard. Our enemies [evidently the Socialists] are not so negligent. Well! The seasons [sic] almost over."[31] Nevertheless, the central body twice refused to reconsider the matter.

During the 1908 campaign, AFL officials commissioned several additional organizers with the purported assignment of vigorously prosecuting the AFL's political program. Judging from the correspondence of these organizers with AFL headquarters, however, it appears that they were more active in internal union politics than they were in rewarding labor's friends and defeating its enemies. Most Missouri unions ultimately endorsed the AFL's program. Organizer P. E. Duffy reported that he expected the Central Labor Union in Kansas City to adopt resolutions declaring its loyalty to the AFL political program. The Saint Joseph Central Labor Council adopted resolutions endorsing the policy.[32] In Springfield, however, the AFL policy was challenged once again. The central body in that southwestern Missouri city returned the AFL president's correspondence with a cryptic message calling Gompers's attention "to the partiality shown in mentioning only two parties when there is another in the field which demands your attention and the attention of every man who labors for a living."[33]

The annual convention of the State Federation of Labor in 1908 became another testing ground for the AFL's nonpartisan program. Eugene Sarber, the AFL organizer who had fought unsuccessfully for the adoption of the AFL program in the Saint Louis central body, also led the fight at the State Federation convention; this time with more success. On the first day of the convention, Sarber sent a telegram to Gompers instructing him to wire fraternal greetings to Thomas Sheridan, president of the State Federation. Gompers immediately responded with an eloquent telegram reminding Missouri

30. *Ibid.* Owen Miller to Gompers, September 15, 1908, *ibid.*
31. Gompers to Sarber, September 24, 1908; Gompers to Miller, September 21, 1908, Gompers, Letterbooks.
32. P. E. Duffy to Morrison, October 21, 1908; John T. Smith to Gompers, October 20, 1908; C. L. Kennedy to Gompers, October 5, 1908, AFL, Papers, Series 117A, File 11A. Boxes 9 and 10 of Series 117A, File 11A, contain much of the correspondence between the special political organizers and AFL headquarters.
33. William H. Bush to Gompers, August 20, 1908, *ibid.*

labor of Gompers's martyrdom in the contempt proceedings growing
out of the boycott instituted against the Saint Louis Bucks Stove and
Range Company. The telegram had the desired effect. After Sheridan
read it, the delegates immediately demanded that a committee be appointed to draw up suitable resolutions praising Gompers and AFL
officials for "the brave fight they are making for the maintenance
of the liberties of the people."[34]

After establishing a positive tone in the convention, Sarber wrote
Gompers that he felt "confident of getting a favorable resolution
through. Also a delegate to the AFL convention at Denver who will
support the political policy of the Council." As requested, the resolutions committee submitted a statement commending the action of
President Gompers and the executive council of the AFL for the
stand taken to defend labor's rights. It was unanimously approved,
but a second resolution committing the state body to render all assistance possible to carry out the political program of the AFL was
more controversial. Delegate E. H. Behrens submitted a minority report condemning the AFL program and calling for "working class
political activity . . . independent and outside the economic movement, but clearly expressive of that movement." The minority report
lost by nearly a two-to-one margin, but among those who supported
it were a number of Missouri's most important future labor leaders.[35]

After the 1908 campaign, the results of which were even less satisfactory than two years earlier, AFL leaders lost interest in politics.[36]
Missouri labor leaders, however, did not share their attitude. These
men remained convinced that if the labor movement was to progress,
it had to exert its potential political influence more effectively. Many
Missouri labor leaders were beginning to suspect that the nonpartisan
political tactic was a fruitless exercise. Reuben Wood, the newly
elected president of the State Federation of Labor, clearly expressed
this sentiment in his first presidential report:

> Whenever it comes to a final line up in the fight between the
> organized working class and the Capitalist class, we find that the

34. Sarber to Gompers, September 21, 1908; Gompers to Thomas Sheridan,
September 21, 1908; Sheridan to Gompers, September 22, 1908, *ibid.* MSFL,
Proceedings, 1908, p. 53.

35. Sarber to Gompers, September 22, 1908, AFL, Papers, Series 117A,
File 11A. MSFL, *Proceedings, 1908,* p. 67. Among those who signed the
minority report were R. T. Wood, who was to head the State Federation
for more than forty years; D. A. Frampton, future president of District
25, United Mine Workers; Phil Hofher and Kindorf both held important
offices in the Saint Louis Central Trades; E. H. Behrens, past president of
the State Federation of Labor and future editor of the *Railway Federationist;*
and W. H. Brown, official of the Sedalia Central Trades Union.

36. Foner, *History of the Labor Movement,* pp. 364–66. Karson, *American
Labor Unions,* pp. 67, 68.

Capitalistic political organizations will line up on the side of capital against labor. I am aware of the fact that there are good men and honest men in all political parties . . . We have good men in the Democratic and Republican Parties who are doing their very best for organized labor, and I could mention a number of them by name. But no matter how good their intentions, their good work is limited by the Capitalist influence of the political parties that elected them to office. What is urgently needed in Missouri and in all other states is a powerful working class organization which will be a natural ally of the trade union movement . . . more than ever I am convinced that the organized working class should not place themselves in a position where they must beg and petition when they could elect their own representatives on their own working class platform.[37]

Although Wood, who was a Socialist, obviously had the Socialist party in mind, he was expressing a sentiment not uncommon among the state's labor leaders. While many of them did not agree with Wood's solution, they were searching for some alternative means of exercising labor's potential political influence. It was a search that would prove almost as frustrating and unrewarding as nonpartisanship.

37. MSFL, *Proceedings, 1913.*

Chapter II

ALTERNATIVES
TO NONPARTISANSHIP

IN their search for an effective substitute for political nonpartisanship, labor leaders in Missouri confronted two alternatives that were philosophically poles apart. One, an alliance with the Socialist party, theoretically involved an effort to overthrow the prevailing system; and the other, political reform, was built upon the principle of making the existing system work more effectively. As they were perceived by labor leaders, however, the first was neither as radical nor the latter as conservative as it appeared. Although these approaches to the problem seem contradictory, many labor leaders were advocates of both, assuming that either would favorably alter the prevailing living and working conditions of the laboring classes.

The Socialist Alternative

In the early years of the twentieth century, the Socialist alternative to the nonpartisan political strategy of the AFL appeared workable. The Missouri Socialist party was young, vigorous, and deeply committed to the trade union movement; moreover, it was predominantly a working-class party. A vast majority of Missouri Socialists were trade unionists, and the labor movement, in turn, provided the Socialists with their most important support.

Missouri Socialists clearly were committed more to a gradualist political policy than to syndicalism or violent revolution. The platform of the party in Missouri, like that of the national organization, always contained a long list of immediate demands to ameliorate living conditions of the workers while awaiting the eventual fulfillment of the cooperative commonwealth. Most of these immediate demands closely conformed to the objectives of the trade union movement. Nevertheless, such demands as the extension of the public domain to include mines, quarries, oil wells, forests, and water power, along with the collective ownership of land "whenever practicable" still marked the Missouri party as one that advocated radical change. Ultimately, the party stood "unqualifiedly for the abolition of the capitalist wage and profit system . . . [and] for the collective ownership of the means of production and distribution."[1]

1. *Official Manual, 1913–1914*, pp. 474–76.

24

Perhaps no Socialist state organization other than Wisconsin's made a more dedicated attempt to work within the established labor movement or was rewarded with as much influence. In the years preceding the outbreak of World War I, Socialists presided over two of the state's most influential labor organizations, the Missouri State Federation of Labor and the Saint Louis Central Trades and Labor Union. Socialists also firmly controlled the Springfield Trades and Labor Assembly and wielded considerable influence in the central bodies of other cities. Finally, the Socialists were highly influential in a number of unions of individual trades such as the machinists, cigarmakers, miners, brewers, carpenters, and bakers.[2]

Socialists had been a consistently strong influence in the State Federation of Labor from its beginning. Socialist delegates had helped to organize the State Federation in 1891, and it was a Saint Louis Socialist, David Kreyling, who served as its first president. Although usually in a minority, Socialists often were elected to high office in the state organization and received representation on important committees. Perhaps the Socialists' most important contribution to the State Federation in its formative years was an expanded social awareness and an appreciation for the importance of political action.

In Saint Louis the single most influential position of the Central Trades and Labor Union was that of secretary–organizer; it was the only paid, full-time office maintained by the central union. During the first three decades of the twentieth century, this office was held by Kreyling, a delegate from the cigarmakers' Local No. 44. In 1910 another influential Saint Louis Socialist, Louis Phillipi, was elected to the presidency of the Central Trades despite a vigorous campaign conducted against him by Owen Miller, a popular state labor leader and future president of the American Federation of Musicians.[3]

The buyers of stock in a Socialist-controlled, cooperative printing establishment provides a unique insight into the sources from which Socialists in Saint Louis received their support. Various unions affiliated with the brewing industry purchased nearly half the shares in the company. Large purchases of stock were also made by the United Brotherhood of Carpenters and Joiners, Local No. 4596, and by the Carpenters' District Council of Saint Louis. Lesser purchases of stock were made by unions of machinists, bakers, journeymen tailors, printers, and the poor but influential Local No. 44 of the Cigar

2. *St. Louis Labor,* March 5, 12, 19, 26, April 2, 9, June 11, 1910. William H. Bush to Gompers, August 20, 1908, AFL, Papers, Series 117A, File 11A.

3. MSFL, *Proceedings, 1941,* p. 22. *Missouri Socialist,* March 16, 1901. Edwin J. Forsythe, "The St. Louis Central Trades and Labor Union, 1887–1945," pp. 46, 47. *St. Louis Labor,* December 24, 1909; January 1, 1910.

Makers' International Union. A vast majority of the stock in this venture was subscribed by trade unions and trade unionists, which further evidences the working-class character of the party in Saint Louis.[4]

Socialists in Saint Louis had been very influential in the formation of the Socialist Party of America and played an important role in its early history. After the party was united in 1901, Saint Louis was chosen as the first national headquarters, and a trade unionist from the city, Leon Greenbaum, was the party's first national secretary. Because the National Committee, the executive body of the party, was chosen from the Local Quorum to which the national secretary belonged, prominent Saint Louis Socialists served as the party's first executive committee. They were ousted in 1903, because as trade unionists, they were reluctant to support or encourage the dual union activities of the American Labor Union.[5]

Missouri Socialists acquired their radical economic and political convictions in a variety of ways. Ethnically derived socialism was particularly important in Saint Louis, which had the largest and best-organized Socialist party in the state. The large German population that had migrated to that city carried not only many social and cultural customs but also political and economic traditions. The major Socialist newspaper, *St. Louis Labor,* published both German and English editions until the 1920s, and the leadership of the party bore such guttural names as Otto Pauls, Gottlieb Hoehn, and Otto Vierling.

Undoubtedly the single most influential member of the Socialist party in Saint Louis was Gottlieb A. Hoehn. Hoehn spent his early life in Baltimore where he worked as a custom shoemaker and became involved in the local shoemakers' union and the Baltimore trade union movement. He entered into a journalistic career almost by accident when asked by the editor of the nearly bankrupt *Baltimore Journal,* a daily newspaper published in German by the German Typographical Union, to write reports of a series of lectures delivered in Baltimore by Paul Grottkau, editor of the *Chicago Arbeiter-Zeitung.* Grottkau was so impressed by the journalistic flair of the young shoemaker that he later invited Hoehn to join his editorial staff. Hoehn served a three-year apprenticeship on the Chicago paper before moving to Saint Louis in 1891 to edit the *St. Louis Tageblatt,* a daily, German language, union labor paper. Two years later he joined another young journalist, Albert Sanderson, in the publication of an English language Socialist weekly, *St. Louis Labor.* Sanderson was later forced to resign because of poor health, and

4. *St. Louis Labor,* March 5, 12, 19, 26, April 2, 9, June 11, 1910.

5. Ira Kipnis, *The American Socialist Movement, 1897–1912,* pp. 144, 145ff. Nathan Fine, *Labor and Farmer Parties in the United States, 1828–1928,* pp. 276–78.

Hoehn assumed the responsibility for editing and publishing the paper. For nearly four decades he kept *St. Louis Labor* on the city's newsstands.[6]

Hoehn was a vigorous participant in the deliberations of the divided Socialist councils of the 1890s. He was one of the founders of the Social Democratic party and was a prominent proponent of the unity conferences between the Social Democrats and the Rochester faction of the Socialist Labor party in 1900. He served on the first National Committee of the Socialist party when party headquarters were located in Saint Louis. Later he was placed on a slate of candidates for national committeeman by Victor Berger's Wisconsin party organization but was not elected. The Socialist editor, who served in a number of important positions in the state Socialist party, was also a frequent candidate for various public offices in Saint Louis. Hoehn, however, always considered himself as much a trade unionist as a Socialist, and the columns of his paper vigorously supported the trade union movement in Saint Louis.[7]

Outside that city, Socialists were found in a variety of places during the early years of the century. In almost all railroad towns, small Socialist organizations sprouted and thrived. One of the important roots of radicalism along the railroad lines of Missouri was the Knights of Labor, which earlier had organized many of the state's railroad workers and had a spectacular career in Missouri.[8] The machinists were the most important railroad trade unionists to espouse socialism, and most of the brotherhoods contained Socialists or Socialist sympathizers.

One of the more prominent railroad Socialists was E. T. Behrens of Sedalia. Behrens held several important positions in the trade unions, including AFL organizer, official of the Sedalia Central Labor Trades, and president of the State Federation of Labor from 1901 to 1905. Later, he became the editor of the *Railway Federationist*, the major railroad labor paper in the state. He was an equally important official in the state Socialist party. In 1906 he represented Missouri on the National Committee and at various other times, the Seventh District of Missouri on the Socialist State Central Committee. He was a candidate for office on the Socialist ticket as often as he would allow his name to be used. Perhaps of most importance was his 1904 nomination as the Socialist candidate for governor.

6. Hoehn to Francis English, March 4, 1945, Gottlieb A. Hoehn, Papers.

7. Fine, *Labor and Farmer Parties,* pp. 195, 203. Kipnis, *American Socialist Movement,* p. 187. Leon Greenbaum to Frank Morrison, December 3, 1901, AFL, Papers, Series 117A, File 11A.

8. Missouri members of the Knights of Labor played an important role in the Knights' successful strike against Jay Gould's Wabash Railroad. See Foster Rhea Dulles, *Labor in America,* pp. 139, 140.

The mining areas provided other important strongholds for the Socialist party in Missouri. Socialists were very influential in the two major miners' organizations in the state, the United Mine Workers and the Western Federation of Miners. Moreover, the state's two most important officials of the miners' unions, Arch Helm and D. A. Frampton, were professed Socialists. The best example of the Socialist appeal in the mining areas is Jasper County, which produced large quantities of coal, lead, and Socialist votes.

The Socialist party also received votes but little organizational support from predominantly agricultural areas that had previously backed the Populist party. This transition is illustrated in the Bootheel area in the southeastern corner of the state. In 1910 this area contributed more than 10 per cent of the state's total Socialist vote, and in 1912 Eugene Debs ran second only to Woodrow Wilson in some Bootheel counties. These rural Socialists, like their urban counterparts, were more committed to reform than to revolution. Socialism in the rural areas, however, was capricious and never was deeply entrenched.[9]

Finally, the Socialist message often was carried by the cigarmakers wherever they organized. The cigarmakers' union was particularly important in Saint Louis socialism, because it provided much of the leadership, not only for the party, but also for the trade union movement. The cigarmakers were almost as influential in the Springfield union movement. Here they followed the able leadership of H. A. W. Juneman who had been associated with Samuel Gompers in organizing the cigarmakers in New York City. Unlike Gompers, Juneman never rejected the radical idealism engendered by his belief in socialism and was acknowledged by many Missouri labor leaders as their intellectual counselor and teacher.[10]

Cigarmakers in Missouri had been introduced to socialism in a variety of ways. In Saint Louis the fact that the large German element was associated with the cigarmakers' union suggests that socialism was part of their ethnic background. Missouri cigarmakers were also associated with the Knights of Labor, and many were members of Bellamy Clubs, both of which advocated a form of native radicalism very important to the American socialist movement. It would be difficult to overestimate the importance of these trade union Socialists in the Missouri labor movement. An inordinate number of Missouri's major labor leaders were contributed by the various cigarmakers' unions, and while not all of them were, or remained, Socialists, few lost the social consciousness that the union inspired. The

9. Leon P. Ogilvie, "The Development of the Southeast Missouri Lowlands," pp. 354–74.
10. MSFL, *Proceedings, 1928,* pp. 53, 54. *The Springfield Laborer,* September 1, 1916. *St. Louis Labor,* August 2, 1930.

Socialist alternative that Missouri trade unionists had to the non-partisan political policy of the AFL was, then, a "constructive" So-cialist party with a deep commitment not only to political action but also to trade unionism, a Socialist party dedicated to the defense of the established labor movement and fundamentally hostile to dual unionism.

Missouri trade unionists seemed interested and increasingly sus-ceptible to Socialist propaganda. The Socialist vote grew steadily, party membership increased, and trade unions continued to choose Socialists for leadership. Moreover, the Socialists were fundamentally important in the formulation of a political program. A large portion of the reform proposals that the labor movement came to advocate as its own first appeared as immediate demands of the Missouri So-cialist party. In 1906, for example, the Socialists advocated such re-forms as municipal ownership of public utilities, municipal home rule, abolition of child labor, a legal eight-hour day, old-age pensions, em-ployer liability laws, compulsory education and free text books, equality of the sexes, and several proposals relating directly to the affairs of organized labor.[11] By the time the United States entered World War I, these Socialist objectives were firmly established as goals of the Missouri labor movement.

The greatest threat to the Socialist party was the growing hostility of the AFL officialdom. As the Socialist movement grew stronger and more popular among local labor units, the opposition of Gompers became more dogmatic and adamant. This animosity was dramatic-ally illustrated in 1903 when he declared:

> I want to tell you Socialists that I have studied your philosophy; read your works upon economics, and not the meanest of them; studied your standard works, both in English and in German— have not only read, but studied them . . . And I want to say that I am not only at variance with your doctrines, but with your philosophy. Economically, you are unsound; socially, you are wrong; industrially, you are an impossibility.[12]

As a consequence of his dislike and distrust of the Socialists, Gompers naturally was annoyed by their influence in the Missouri labor movement, especially in the Saint Louis Central Trades and Labor Union and in the Missouri State Federation of Labor. As a result, Gompers launched an attack upon the Socialists along with the announcement of his new political program in 1906. The most obvious way to strike at the Socialists in Saint Louis would be to revoke the charter of Federal Labor Union No. 6482. The federal union had been chartered in 1893 and contained many prominent

11. *St. Louis Labor,* January 6, 1906.
12. Quoted in Henry Pelling, *American Labor,* p. 115.

Saint Louis Socialists, including the influential editor of *St. Louis Labor,* G. A. Hoehn. Charges against the union were initiated by James Shanessy, the secretary of Local No. 102 of the barbers' union and future president of the Journeymen Barbers' International Union. The charge was obviously contrived, since it alleged merely that the Socialist-controlled federal union was not holding regular meetings. Actually, Gompers and Shanessy had been corresponding for nearly eighteen months prior to the attack on the Socialist union. During the course of that correspondence, Shanessy had informed the AFL leader of criticism of his leadership voiced by "some officers of the St. Louis central body," which undoubtedly influenced the thin-skinned labor leader's decision to pursue the matter. In turn, Gompers had pointedly warned Shanessy that one of the greatest threats to the labor movement was its "secret enemies . . . who appeal under the pretense of friendship."[13]

Charges against the federal union were also made in the Saint Louis Central Trades and Labor Union. It was alleged that the union contained political officeholders, a violation of the central body's constitution. An investigating committee appointed by the Central Trades returned a report concluding that the representatives of the Socialist local were not political officeholders, and that it was a bona fide labor union. After a vigorous debate, the committee's report was upheld by the central body by a vote of 146 to 33. Undaunted by this defeat, the antagonists, the barbers' union, continued their assault this defeat, the antagonists of the Socialist local, the barber's union, continued their assault through the AFL hierarchy where they expected and received a more sympathetic hearing.[14]

Upon receipt of Shanessy's charges against the federal union, Gompers immediately ordered AFL organizer Grant Hamilton to look into the matter. In fact, Hamilton had been sent to Saint Louis several weeks earlier with the confidential assignment to "investigate the St. Louis situation" and undoubtedly had been instrumental in the formulation of the original charges. Hamilton's report predictably condemned the federal local and Gompers ordered that the charter and seal of the organization be returned to AFL headquarters.[15]

Many members of the Saint Louis central body deeply resented the AFL's "highhanded" action. One delegate asked why the report of an individual "holding a little organizership by the grace of the

13. Gompers to James Shanessy, February 13, 1906, Gompers, Letterbooks. Gompers to Shanessy, October 4, 1906, AFL, Papers, Series 117A, File 11A. Boxes 2 and 3 of the AFL, Papers, Series 117A, File 11A, contain this series of correspondence between Gompers and Shanessy.

14. Gompers to Shanessy, April 21, 1906, AFL, Papers, Series 117A, File 11A. *St. Louis Labor,* March 3, 1906.

15. *St. Louis Labor,* July 7, 1906. Gompers to M. Grant Hamilton, May 14, June 25, June 29, 1906, Gompers, Letterbooks.

AFL President, is endowed with more wisdom and power than the old, solid bona fide Central Trades and Labor Union. If the charter of the Federal Labor Union has been revoked simply because the members are Socialists, we want to know it." Complaints also were made regarding the secrecy with which Hamilton's investigation was conducted and about his failure to inform the officers of the Central Trades about his mission. "Everyone connected with the Federal Labor Union is entitled to fair treatment," another member commented. "As far as I have learned there was no hearing in the Federal Labor question. A square deal is what we want, and we ought to insist on it."[16]

After a lengthy and acrimonious debate, the Saint Louis central union finally declared vacant the seats held by the delegates from Federal Labor Union No. 6482. In an editorial concerning the action, G. A. Hoehn reasoned that the Central Trades had acted wisely. He argued that one of the objectives of those officials who attacked the federal union was the revocation of the central union's charter, thus making possible a "radical reorganization" that would bring the Central Trades "in line with the other central bodies throughout the country." The Socialist editor gained some solace from the conclusion that the Saint Louis union would "remain what it has been in the past a fearless, progressive central body."[17]

In an acrid letter to Gompers, Hoehn wrote that, even though Gompers's "paper-written power" could put the editor outside the AFL, it could not put him outside the labor movement. Hoehn vowed to continue supporting the Saint Louis trade union movement as he had during the preceding twenty years. "You may allow your anti-Socialist feelings (which, to a great extent I always recognized as justified, in view of the vile DeLeonite attacks and misrepresentations) to get the upper hand in dealing with a little union composed of Socialists," Hoehn wrote Gompers, "but I assure you that I shall not act likewise toward you or the AFL."[18]

With an air of injured innocence, Gompers replied that he had not even attended the executive council session in which the matter was taken up. He told Hoehn that he had "shot entirely wide of the mark" in assuming that "antisocialist feeling" had been responsible for the decision. A letter Gompers wrote Shanessy somewhat later, however, leaves little doubt that the charter of the Federal Labor Union was revoked primarily because it was a Socialist-controlled federal labor union over which the AFL had complete authority. "I feel confident," Gompers wrote, "that as we have eliminated from

16. *St. Louis Labor,* July 14, 1906. *The St. Louis Republic,* July 9, 1906.
17. *St. Louis Labor,* July 14, 1906.
18. Hoehn to Gompers, July 2, 1906, Gompers, Letterbooks.

the St. Louis movement much of the friction caused by the representatives of the old Federal Labor Union, it has given an opportunity to the true and tried trade unionists to come to the front and be recognized as the real directors in the bonafide labor movement of our country."[19]

The editors of the conservative St. Louis Globe-Democrat correctly concluded that the assault on the federal local was an attack on Saint Louis Socialists in general and Hoehn in particular. They believed Hoehn to be a very influential figure in the Saint Louis central body and declared that his "talks on any proposition were usually effective, and any measure he advocated or opposed was almost certain to be decided as he wished." The editorial concluded with the observation that Hoehn's downfall was precipitated by his promulgation of socialistic ideas.[20]

The Saint Louis central body membership voted to ask President Gompers for a statement of charges against the federal union and for an explanation of the reasons for revoking the charter. Gompers responded with a long letter in which his conclusions were drawn largely from his correspondence with Shanessy and Hamilton. Later the Central Trades again requested a review of the case, but the charter was never restored.[21]

Despite the assault against them by the more conservative elements in the labor movement, the Socialists continued to exert considerable influence among trade unionists. Moreover, the Socialist vote in Missouri continued to increase steadily as it had since the turn of the century. In the Saint Louis municipal elections of 1911, the Socialists came within twelve votes of electing a Socialist alderman, and they ran ahead of the Democrats in several wards. In a citywide election to fill a vacancy on the city council later in the year, the Socialist candidate, William Brandt, ran two thousand votes ahead of the Democratic candidate and came within a thousand votes of being elected.[22]

As a result of their growing strength at the polls, Missouri Socialists prepared for the general elections of 1912 with an air of expectant optimism. While they had no illusions about electing a Socialist administration, they hoped for a large Socialist vote. The 1912 vote for Debs did reflect a significant increase over 1908 but was a disappointment since the state's vote did not match the 6 per cent

19. Gompers to Hoehn, July 20, 1906; Gompers to Shanessy, February 19, 1907, ibid.

20. St. Louis Globe-Democrat, July 9, 1906.

21. Gompers to David Kreyling, July 19, October 4, 1906, Gompers, Letterbooks.

22. St. Louis Post-Dispatch, April 5, 1911. St. Louis Labor, November 18, 1911.

that Debs received nationally. The only source of solace reflected in the election returns was that most Missourians voting for Debs voted a straight Socialist party ticket. A comparison of the number of votes Debs received to the numbers of the other statewide Socialist candidates shows a variance of less than 1 per cent of the nearly thirty thousand votes cast for the Socialist ticket.[23]

The strength of the Socialists in Missouri steadily declined after 1912. The party's chances of success within the state, of course, were closely linked to the fortunes of the party nationally; nevertheless, Missouri Socialists undermined their own appeal by making costly tactical errors. Paradoxically, Missouri Socialists were both too dogmatic and too flexible. By placing too much emphasis on reform, the party lost its legitimacy as a radical alternative to the existing party system.[24] As the established parties began to adopt many of the reforms advocated by the Socialists, the Socialist party became a less and less viable alternative to the existing political system. Although they exhibited excessive flexibility in the matter of ideology, the Socialists were extremely dogmatic about their political strategy. They resolutely opposed all efforts to organize an independent labor party and insisted instead that labor support the Socialist party. This position alienated those elements within labor that were genuinely interested in an independent political movement but did not want to be affiliated with the Socialist party.[25]

The Alternative of Political Reform

Whatever the reasons, the labor movement rejected the Socialist alternative more through neglect than conscious decision. Rejection of the Socialists, dissatisfaction with the nonpartisan tactic, and the apparent impracticality of independent political action, however, left the labor movement in a state of political limbo. Such a situation might have rendered the labor movement politically helpless but for the faith of many state labor leaders in the opportunities for constructive political reform. They still believed that if the established political system were reformed, it would become more responsive to the needs and desires of the working class.

Like many other elements of Missouri society, organized labor was

23. *Official Manual, 1913–1914,* pp. 755–66.
24. The most convincing argument for this theory as it affected the socialist movement nationally is Kipnis, *American Socialist Movement.* Cf. James Weinstein, *The Decline of Socialism in America, 1912–1925,* and John H. M. Laslett, *Labor and the Left: A Study of Socialism and Radical Influences in the American Labor Movement, 1881–1924.*
25. For accounts of the Socialists' refusal to join the movement to form a labor party, see *Missouri Socialist,* March 9, 16, June 22, 1901; *St. Louis Labor,* May 26, June 23, 1906.

convinced that a small class of businessmen had usurped the powers of government and was exploiting that power in pursuit of personal interests. Thomas Sheridan, president of the Missouri State Federation of Labor, expressed this view:

> In view of the fact that there are over one hundred thousand wage earners in Missouri, it is evident that we do not exert the influence over legislation that our numbers would justify. This is due in a measure to our defective political system. It is also due to the fact that Organized Labor has neglected the political aspect of the labor problem. We have permitted the political parties, which were intended to be agencies through which people would express their will through legislation, to pass under the control of special interests that dictate the laws of the state and prevent the legislature from enacting laws in the interests of the people.[26]

Throughout Saint Louis the term *Big Cinch* became synonymous with business control of the municipal government. It was generally assumed that a small group of unscrupulous businessmen and bipartisan politicians had banded together against the general interests of the citizenry for the purpose of enriching themselves through the manipulation of the granting of public utility franchises and the issuance of city contracts. Although not as graphically identified, the same condition was alleged to exist in a number of other Missouri cities.

Organized labor's solution to these problems entailed democratizing the political system. This reform was to be achieved by provisions for direct legislation, recalling elected officials, direct primaries, direct election of senators, and woman suffrage. Labor leaders had an amazing faith in the adage that "the cure for democracy is more democracy," and they were not easily disabused of that notion.

Of all the political reforms in which they expressed an interest, labor leaders were most enamored with the possibilities of the initiative and referendum. They saw in these provisions for direct legislation the opportunity not only to reform the political system but also to virtually revolutionize it. In a speech before an assembly of Saint Louis trade unionists, Sheridan commented upon the need for such reforms and projected the change that such measures would produce:

> The demand upon which we should concentrate our efforts and strength because of its significance is the "Initiative and Referendum" in state affairs. This measure in my judgment is second to none in importance for the reason that it enables the people

26. *St. Louis Labor,* April 14, 1906.

to propose and initiate laws independently of the state legislature. A small percentage of the voters can, by petition, propose a law, and it is imperative upon the Secretary of State to submit such law to a referendum vote of the people. If the proposed law is adopted by the majority of the people, it becomes a part of the statutory laws of the state, as constitutional amendments are now made a part of the constitution. Through the referendum the people can pass upon and reject any act of their representatives that does not meet with their approval. This change makes the will of the people supreme, and makes the acts of their representatives conform to and carry out their will. While the adoption of the initiative and referendum simply affects a change in our methods of making statutory laws, yet it is the key to progress. It will open the door for other reforms.

With its adoption we can secure an effective law against child labor, and protect our children from the greed and selfishness of employers. We can secure an extension of the 8 hour law by applying it to different trades and occupations in the state. The adoption of the initiative and referendum in municipal affairs will enable the voters to apply the 8 hour work day to all city work. We can secure a law abolishing the competition of convict labor with that of free labor, releasing men unfortunate enough to commit crimes against the state from rapacious greed of contractors who contract with the state for their labor at so much per head. To abolish the competition of the products of prison contract shops with those of fair manufactories will enable Organized Labor in the trades affected to secure improvement in their condition that justice and fair play demand. We can secure the taxation of land values irrespective of improvements by exempting personal property and landed improvements from taxes and increasing the rate of land values. This reform will abolish speculation in land and speculation in rents. It will break up the private monopolies of Missouri's natural resources, and give to labor opportunities for self-employment. It will lessen the power of employers by relieving the labor market of the unemployed and cause economic forces to tend to elevate wages to their normal level, according to the wealth produced. We can obtain legislation granting towns and cities home rule and local self-government, permitting them to conduct their municipal affairs in their own way, and enabling them to own and operate local public utilities and regulate municipal corporations and raise local revenues in the manner that appeals to them as just and equitable without interference from the state. In fact, the Initiative and Referendum makes it possible to secure every reform that appeals to the conscience and intelligence of American voters.[27]

Stimulated by both the Populists and Socialists, the labor movement had adopted direct legislation as one of its major objectives

27. *Ibid.*

by the turn of the century. This concern was directly evidenced in 1900 when Missouri's labor commissioner sent a questionnaire to state labor organizations asking what measures would best promote the interests of Missouri labor. The commissioner reported that by far the greatest number of responses referred to the adoption of direct legislation as a means of securing better conditions for the wage earners of the state. Two years later the delegates to the annual convention of the State Federation ordered its legislative committee to question the candidates for Congress and the state legislature regarding their attitude on direct legislation. After complying with these instructions, the legislative committee reported that a majority of those elected to the state legislature indicated they would vote for such a measure. The legislature did pass a constitutional amendment providing for the establishment of initiative and referendum, but the amendment was defeated in the general elections of 1904.[28]

A few years later, delegates attending the annual convention of the State Federation voted to renew the campaign for direct legislation. They once again ordered the legislative committee to draft a bill providing for a constitutional amendment permitting the enactment of the initiative and referendum procedures. Introduced during the 1907 session of the General Assembly, the members of the legislative committee defended their bill in committee hearings, lobbied individual legislators, and generally guided the bill through the General Assembly. The amendment finally received the approval of the General Assembly and was submitted to the electorate for approval in 1908. Prior to the election, organized labor again waged a vigorous campaign for the amendment, and it received the approval of a large majority of the voters.[29] Initiative and referendum became operative in Missouri the following year when legislation governing its provisions and explaining its operation was enacted.

Although organized labor was largely responsible for the implementation of this reform, it had the support of important allies in other areas. Socialists had advocated such reforms since the 1890s, and, although their political influence in the state legislature was minimal, they did continue to use their force within the labor movement, where they had more authority. Labor's greatest support, however, came from a variety of Single-Tax Leagues and Henry George Clubs. The single-taxers realized that the state legislature was unlikely to endorse their particular panacea and concluded that their program would have its best chance for success only if the initiative procedure were adopted. The single-taxers, like the Socialists, had a great deal of influence in the labor movement, and many of the state's important

28. *Missouri Red Book, 1901,* p. 342. MSFL, *Proceedings, 1903,* p. 15.
29. Anson E. Van Eaton, "The Initiative and Referendum in Missouri," pp. 4–10. Fred R. Graham, "A History of the Missouri Federation of Labor," pp. 135–37. *Missouri Red Book, 1907,* pp. 694, 695.

trade union leaders were single-taxers. To other groups that advocated the principle of direct democracy, the Missouri Referendum League and the Farmer's Union, played an important role in the enactment of direct legislation at both the local and state level.[30]

After their success in getting direct legislation at the state level, labor leaders immediately began a campaign for similar provisions locally. The 1910 convention of the State Federation ordered the legislative committee to draft and have introduced into the General Assembly a constitutional amendment granting the privilege of initiative, referendum, and recall to all Missouri counties, cities, towns, and villages. Agitation for direct democracy at the local level was vigorously supported by labor leaders in Saint Louis and Kansas City. When efforts to obtain the initiative and referendum were frustrated, the Industrial Council of Kansas City, in the autumn of 1912, vowed to oppose every bond issue in Kansas City until such reforms were accepted.[31]

Socialists and labor leaders in Saint Louis had urged the enactment of direct legislation on the local level since before the turn of the century. Seeing an opportunity to achieve such reforms when the movement for a new city charter began in the latter half of 1908, the labor movement readily joined a large number of civic organizations to form a Joint Conference on Charter Revision. The executive board of the Joint Conference agreed upon a slate of twenty-six citizens who were recommended for election to the new Board of Freeholders, which would have the responsibility for drawing up the new charter, subject to the approval of Saint Louis voters. Among those recommended by the Joint Conference were Gottlieb Hoehn and Owen Miller.[32]

Agitation for charter reform was successful, and Miller, running as a Democrat, was elected to the Board of Freeholders. The legislative committee of the Central Trades then was ordered by its delegates to attend the public hearings of the board to urge the incorporation of provisions for initiative, referendum, and recall in the new charter.[33]

It was nearly eighteen months before the Board of Freeholders submitted its proposed charter, and the Saint Louis labor movement quickly expressed its opposition to the document. Not only had no provisions been made for direct legislation, but also, under the prospective new city charter, the mayor's power was greatly increased, and the number of elective offices reduced. Furthermore,

---

30. *Missouri Red Book, 1907*, pp. 694, 695. Norman L. Crockett, "The 1912 Single Tax Campaign in Missouri," pp. 42, 43. Van Eaton, "Initiative and Referendum," pp. 1–11. *St. Louis Labor*, April 14, 1906.

31. *Missouri Red Book, 1910*, p. 391. *The Labor Herald*, November 29, 1912.

32. *St. Louis Labor*, February 20, 1909.

33. *Ibid.*, May 15, 1909.

the proposed charter provided for a small unicameral legislative body to replace the larger two-house legislature. Labor leaders concluded that, under the new charter, government would be even less democratic and more susceptible to control by special interests than it was under the old charter.[34]

Although many of labor's allies in the Joint Conference on Charter Revision were disappointed with the proposed charter, most of them recommended its approval. Owen Miller at first attempted to defend the new charter before labor organizations, but realizing labor overwhelmingly opposed the proposed charter, he ultimately refused to sign the document and campaigned against it.[35]

Two important supporters of the original movement for charter reform, the Civic League and the *St. Louis Post-Dispatch,* both endorsed the new charter, as did most other civic organizations. The principal opponents of the proposed charter were the Central Trades and Labor Union, the Building Trades Council, and several small Progressive associations including the Missouri Referendum League. The legislative committee of the Central Trades banded most of these organizations together into a labor-dominated Peoples' League, which led opposition to the charter. When the voters overwhelmingly voted against the proposal, organized labor took full credit for its defeat.[36]

The following spring the Civic League invited the Central Trades to join in a second effort to campaign for a new city charter. This time the Central Trades declined, commenting that in the previous campaign the Civic League had sold out to the Big Cinch interests when it supported the proposed charter. The labor body instead vowed that it would work through the Peoples' League to reform the charter.[37] Consequently, in the fall of 1912, the legislative committee of the Central Trades cooperated with the representatives of the Peoples' League and the Socialist party to draft an amendment to the city charter providing for initiative and referendum. After a vigorous campaign, they succeeded in getting the amendment on the ballot where it received the approval of a large majority of the electorate.

With these reforms achieved, Saint Louis labor leaders opposed further efforts toward charter revision until the potential for reform through direct legislation could be tested. The movement for charter revision, however, was vigorously pushed by several civil organizations; and in 1914, Saint Louis voters again were given the opportunity to vote on a new city charter. By adding provisions for

34. *Ibid.,* January 14, 1911.
35. *Ibid.,* January 28, 1911.
36. *Ibid.,* February 4, 25, 1911. *St. Louis Post-Dispatch,* January 29, 30, 31, 1911. Louis Phillipi to Austin Biggs, n.d., in *Missouri Red Book, 1911,* pp. 7, 8.
37. *St. Louis Labor,* May 4, 1912.

initiative, referendum, and recall, the authors of the new charter hoped to quell much of the opposition that the previous charter had aroused. They also courted the support of organized labor by including in the charter a provision for an eight-hour day for city employees and an increase from fifty cents to three dollars a day in the rate at which fines were worked off in the city jail. Nevertheless, organized labor strongly opposed the new charter proposal. They objected to the reduction in the number of elective offices and, as before, to the provision for a small unicameral legislature that failed to give effective representation at the ward level.[38]

The new charter passed narrowly with a 3 per cent margin, but only thirteen of the city's twenty-eight wards voted for the proposal. Wards along the river that were dominated by laborers and the three German, Socialist wards provided the largest vote against the charter, while the largest positive vote came from the wealthy west end.[39] The new city charter represented a successful attempt by the affluent suburban areas to reduce the power of the city central areas in municipal government; labor leaders had recognized this fact and had opposed the charter's implementation. This time, however, they had few allies, and their efforts were not as successful.

After it had successfully sponsored the provisions for direct legislation, the labor movement maintained a constant vigil in the defense of these laws. In 1913 the opponents of initiative and referendum pushed a constitutional amendment through the state legislature making the utilization of the procedures more difficult. They increased both the required number of signatures on petitions and of congressional districts in which names for such petitions had to be secured. Although the labor lobby failed to prevent the passage of this amendment in the General Assembly, before the 1914 general elections, it successfully conducted a campaign against the measure among the voters. Another attempt in 1915 to emasculate the law was defeated in both houses of the legislature. The attitude of organized labor toward these activities was reflected in a statement by the Industrial Council of Kansas City, which described any effort to change the laws as "specific and deliberate acts of unfriendliness toward the working class of the state."[40]

The motivation for organized labor's initial and continuing devotion to the principle of direct democracy is somewhat obscure, but judging from the rhetoric of labor leaders, they assumed such devices

38. *Ibid.*, February 25, 1911; November 16, 1912. Curtis Hunter Porter, "Charter Reform in St. Louis, 1900–1914," pp. 49, 50.

39. Porter, "Charter Reform in St. Louis," pp. 41, 42, 49, 50.

40. *The Labor Herald,* January 31, February 14, 1913; September 18, 1914. *Official Manual, 1915–1916,* pp. 570, 571. Graham, "History of the State Federation," p. 137.

as initiative, referendum, and recall would force legislators and administrators to be more responsive to the general will of the people. They theorized that direct democracy would serve both a positive and negative function. It provided a means by which the normal legislative process could be bypassed if legislators failed to enact desired measures, and conversely, it served as a constant check on the conduct of elected officials and their activities in office. For example, labor leaders felt that the referendum would be a powerful weapon for public control of the policy of granting public utility franchises; if public officials knew their decisions could be subjected to a referendum, they would be less likely to act irresponsibly, and if they did act irresponsibly, their decisions could be repudiated.[41]

Organized labor had no formal legislative program that it planned to propose immediately after the initiative was achieved, but because of the availability of the initiative alternative, labor leaders assumed that state and local legislative assemblies would become more responsive to the demands for reform. There can be little doubt that the labor movement greatly overestimated the reform possibilities of direct legislation. Gov. Herbert Hadley gave a much more realistic appraisal of the system, "This new departure in the work of legislation will not prove to be the general panacea for public evils that its advocates have claimed for it, nor will it prove . . . to be the dangerous and cumbersome procedure that its opponents have feared it would be."[42]

Despite labor's enthusiasm for direct legislation, it used the method most infrequently, especially at the state level. Even though the Missouri law was quite liberal with respect to the requirements for signatures, the use of the initiative and referendum was very expensive to the relatively insolvent state labor movement. Furthermore, because of its success in defeating undesirable legislation in the state legislature, organized labor found little use for the referendum. Indeed, the referendum became a formidable weapon against labor. The labor movement soon found some of its most desired legislative goals, such as a full-crew law for railroad trains and workmen's compensation, referred to the electorate and defeated.[43]

On the other hand, labor leaders discovered that Missouri voters usually opposed initiative measures. Only a massive educational campaign throughout the state, for which the labor movement had insufficient funds, could overcome this anti-initiative bias.[44] Although or-

41. *St. Louis Labor,* April 14, 1906.
42. *Messages and Proclamations of the Governors of the State of Missouri,* Vol. X, pp. 15, 16.
43. *Official Manual, 1915–1916,* pp. 570–75. Workmen's compensation is more completely discussed in later chapters of this book.
44. Van Eaton, "Initiative and Referendum," see especially Chaps. 3 and 4.

ganized labor frequently supported the efforts of other groups invoking the initiative procedure, it was not until 1924 that the labor movement, essentially through its own efforts, initiated a measure for the approval of Missouri voters. That effort failed and so did a similar attempt several years later. Thus, in the first three decades after the enactment of direct legislation, not a single labor reform was achieved on the state level through the initiative procedure.

Labor used initiative and referendum more frequently and effectively at the local level. In Saint Louis and Kansas City labor groups often successfully invoked the referendum to oppose franchise grants.[45] At neither level of government, however, did these provisions for direct democracy have the reforming qualities that labor leaders had anticipated.

The labor movement was equally disappointed with the results of other political reforms. The direct primary did not significantly change the General Assembly's responsiveness to the labor lobby, and it did not greatly alter the relationship between labor leaders and elected officials in the state government. Proposals for urban reform, such as the commission plan, often resulted in the numerical reduction of elective officials which, if anything, lessened labor's influence in city government.

Thus, despite high expectations and considerable success in achieving desired changes in the political process, political reform proved no more viable a substitute for nonpartisanship than the Socialist party. Consequently, the labor movement continued to practice the policy of nonpartisanship, although it remained highly receptive to any alternative strategy that promised more effective results.

45. For examples, see *St. Louis Labor,* November 2, 1912; *The Labor Herald,* June 26, 1914.

Chapter III

THE LABOR LOBBY
IN THE PROGRESSIVE ERA

THE two chambers of the state legislature and the various administrative offices of the state government provided the ultimate proving ground for the political effectiveness of the state labor movement. Because many Missouri labor leaders assumed their organization had failed to function effectively in this political arena, they questioned the wisdom of continuing the nonpartisan political policy. The convening of the Missouri General Assembly for its biennial sessions at the State Capitol in Jefferson City, of course, greatly interested the state labor movement. There legislation vitally concerning both the organized and unorganized workers of the state became or failed to become law; there the political program of the state labor movement was either adopted or rejected.

The Organization and Operation of the Labor Lobby

Anticipation of greater labor influence in the state legislature had been a major consideration in the original movement to organize the State Federation of Labor. The labor leaders assumed that the union movement failed to exercise the influence in the General Assembly to which it was entitled and hoped the coordination of labor's lobbying activities under a more centralized agency would prove advantageous. Nevertheless, as organized under the State Federation's legislative committee, the labor lobby failed to provide coordination in lobbying activities. Consequently, in January, 1907, State Federation officials called a general meeting of all labor representatives attending the Forty-fourth General Assembly in Jefferson City. After a lengthy discussion, they organized a Joint Labor Legislative Board to coordinate the efforts of all labor lobbyists at the State Capitol and appointed a conference committee to draw a general plan to guide the activities of the new labor lobby.[1]

The core of the reorganized labor pressure group consisted of three legislative representatives from the State Federation in addition to the representatives of various railroad brotherhoods. This group was supplemented by lobbyists that were sent by city central bodies, building trades' councils, the United Mine Workers, and various locals. The additional lobbyists assisted the State Federation's legisla-

---

1. *Joint Labor Legislative Committee Report, 1907.*

tive committee and worked for special legislative items. Ten labor representatives were usually in Jefferson City during a session of the General Assembly, and often there were as many as twenty or thirty lobbyists.[2]

During the average legislative session, members of the Joint Labor Legislative Board met a few days prior to the convening of the General Assembly. Establishing headquarters in a rented office located near the State Capitol, they hired a stenographer and established a regular office routine to facilitate their lobbying activities. They then began to review the legislation they wanted to have introduced and the legislative items that had been forwarded to them by various unions throughout the state. They also analyzed the composition of the General Assembly and planned their over-all strategy for the session. Once the legislative session began, the Joint Board met each evening at eight o'clock to review the day's work and to outline the work and assignments for the following day.[3]

The labor representatives' first task during a session was to attempt to influence the selection of officials in both houses of the legislature. They were especially interested in the election of the speaker of the House and in appointments to the Committee on Labor, the Committee on Railroads, and any *ad hoc* committees created to deal with special legislation of concern to organized labor. After the election of the speaker, the labor lobby provided him with a list of the legislators it favored for appointment to these committees.[4]

During the legislative session, the labor lobby operated much like any other pressure group. It carefully selected legislators in the House and Senate to introduce various measures. The choice of a sponsor was extremely important, and the labor representatives sought legislators who would not only introduce a bill but also actively work for its enactment. When they found such a sponsor, the labor lobbyists encouraged unions in the home district of that legislator to write the lawmaker or visit the Capitol to express their appreciation for his efforts on labor's behalf. The selection of a legislator who was essentially indifferent or hostile to the desired measure could be disastrous. Such a legislator might introduce a bill "by request" and forget it, fail to call the bill for its third reading, or make no effort to get the bill out of committee where it would die at the end of the session.[5]

.2. *Ibid. Missouri Red Book, 1908,* p. 774. MSFL, *Proceedings, 1906,* pp. 9, 10. *The Saint Joseph Union,* June 9, 1916. *The Labor Herald,* January 15, 29, 1915; January 10, February 14, 1919.

3. *Joint Labor Legislative Committee Report, 1907.*

4. These activities are evidenced in the various reports of the Joint Labor Legislative Board published in the *Missouri Red Book* and the MSFL, *Proceedings.*

5. See, for example, Mark McGruder to Phillips, December 6, 1918; Phillips to Reuben Wood, December 14, 1918, Alroy S. Phillips, Papers.

Once a bill was introduced, the labor lobbyists testified before the committee to which it had been referred, lobbied individual legislators, sought allies among other special-interest groups, and generally attempted to shepherd the bill through the legislative process. On measures that were considered especially vital, labor lobbyists operated through a structure of legislative representatives from various central bodies and local unions to initiate a letter-writing campaign designed to favorably influence the General Assembly. At times they also called for visits to the capital by labor delegations from the home district of key legislators.[6]

The Joint Labor Board's negative function of carefully studying the various bills that were making their way through the General Assembly in order to search out those measures threatening the interests of the working class and the labor movement was as important as promoting favorable measures. When it discovered this type of legislation, the labor lobby immediately launched a campaign against it. Its major objective was to acquaint legislators with labor's objections to the legislation. Lobbyists followed much the same procedure to defeat a bill as they did to promote one. During an ordinary session of the General Assembly, labor representatives devoted nearly as much time to lobbying against bills as lobbying for them.

The labor lobby usually practiced the "art of the possible." No matter how desirable a particular piece of legislation was, unless the labor representatives believed it could possibly be enacted, they assigned it a relatively low priority. Such opportunism, however, was often unpopular among those elements of the state labor movement that had different legislative priorities or a different view of what was possible than the Joint Labor Board. The lobby took special care to avoid such divisions among its constituency, because it found its influence in the General Assembly, at times, seriously compromised when factions within the labor movement who disagreed with the lobby's policies aired their grievances publicly. In an effort to prevent such conflicts, a "preferred list" of legislative goals was instituted by the executive council and annual conventions of the State Federation.

Although it supported a broad range of reform legislation during the Progressive Era, labor's primary legislative objectives, as revealed by the State Federation's preferred list, included the enactment of the initiative and referendum procedures, a reformed convict labor system, and the establishment of a system of compensation for injured workmen. Labor's efforts on behalf of the initiative and referendum had resulted in constitutional amendments enacted in both

6. For examples, see MSFL, *Proceedings, 1906,* p. 9; *1921,* pp. 112, 113; Charles W. Fear to "Officers and Members of all Labor Organizations of Missouri," July 1, 1906, AFL, Papers, Series 117A. File 11A; *The Missouri Trades Unionist,* March 3, 1915; *St. Louis Labor,* February 12, 1927.

the 1905 and 1909 sessions of the General Assembly; the latter received the approval of the state electorate in the general elections of 1910. Labor's lobbying efforts in support of convict labor reform and workmen's compensation accomplished much less.

Convict Labor Reform

Labor's effort to abolish the state's system of contract prison labor had always been on the list of preferred items. The convicts, who were leased to private contractors at low rates and who worked long hours, produced marketable items that were priced at a great competitive advantage over the products of free labor. Organized workers in affected industries found it almost impossible to maintain an adequate wage scale, and organization itself was seriously retarded. By 1897 private firms operated eight factories within the state penitentiary. The state received compensation of only fifty cents a day for the manual labor performed by the convicts in these factories. Such competition especially suppressed boot and shoe workers, harness makers, garmentworkers, broommakers, and various woodworkers.[7]

The State Federation advocated the "state-use system" as the most desirable reform. Under this system, pioneered in New York, the state penal institution made only articles that could be used by other state institutions. Since no articles were produced for public sale, the plan completely abolished the system of leasing prisoners to private contractors. Labor's interest in reforming the use of prison labor was primarily economic, but labor leaders also expressed humanitarian reasons for encouraging the change. The New York system, they argued, would be advantageous not only to free labor but also to the prisoner. Collis Lovely of the Saint Louis branch of the Boot and Shoe Workers of America clearly reflected this line of thought when arguing:

> Of the persons sent to prison now, seventy per cent go back the second time; and of those who serve the second time, sixty-five per cent go back the third time. The Lease system and the Contract system do not reform. The prisoners are made slaves to the men who hire their labor, and they are mistreated in every way. Politicians are opposed to the New York convict law because it prevents them from working graft. The New York law provides that all goods made by the prisoners shall be used in state institutions only and that no goods shall be sold. It will probably be hard to get this law passed in Missouri, as the State has made as high as forty thousand dollars a year out of its contract system.[8]

7. Fred R. Graham, "A History of the Missouri State Federation of Labor," pp. 58, 59. *Missouri Red Book, 1910*, p. 259.
8. Quoted in Graham, "History of the State Federation," pp. 59, 60. Owen Miller to J. C. A. Hiller, December 10, 1909, in *Missouri Red Book, 1909*, pp. 462, 463.

Lovely's prophecies were accurate; despite the combined efforts of the labor movement, injured manufacturers, and humanitarian reformers, prison contractors clung to their source of cheap labor with amazing tenacity. Organized labor cannot be blamed for failure in this area. Actually, labor did score significant legislative victories only to see them undermined by the disingenuous efforts of state legislators, administrators, and prison contractors.

Labor leaders were reassured when a Senate committee was appointed in 1907 to collect facts and statistics to inform the General Assembly concerning the need for effective convict labor legislation, but the investigation produced few tangible results. As often happened in the General Assembly, the appointment of an investigating committee was merely a delaying tactic designed to alleviate immediate pressure for reform. A year later the State Federation's legislative committee prevailed upon Gov. Joseph Folk to include in his legislative program for a special session of the state legislature a recommendation that the prison leasing system be abolished. The resulting measure was passed in the Democratic Senate but failed in the Republican-controlled House, even though both parties had condemned the prison labor system in their state platforms.[9]

Shortly after taking office in 1909, Gov. Herbert Hadley publicly criticized the low rates at which prison labor was being leased and the long period for which contracts were let. The officers of the State Federation were always sensitive to a potential ally and immediately called upon the Governor to urge him to disapprove any contract that called for compensation of less than one dollar a day. They hoped this action would temporarily relieve the distress caused by cheap convict labor until a new law could be passed. Hadley explained that, while he agreed in principle, he had no authority in the matter; moreover, he informed the labor representatives that the board of prison inspectors had already awarded the contracts at a rate of seventy-five cents a day.[10]

In 1911 labor achieved one of its illusory victories when the General Assembly enacted legislation designed eventually to abolish the contract labor system. The law provided that each year a few hundred additional convicts would be put to work manufacturing products for use in state institutions, and in this way, the leasing system would be completely abolished in a few years. It was seriously handicapped, however, by the failure of the legislature to appropriate enough money to implement its provisions.[11] Nevertheless, prison

9. *Missouri Red Book, 1907*, pp. 694, 695; *1909*, p. 457; *1910*, p. 259.

10. William M. Holman to Herbert Hadley, November 9, 1909; Hadley to Holman, November 15, 1909, *Missouri Red Book, 1910*, p. 255.

11. Graham, "History of the State Federation," p. 63. *The Labor Herald*, March 17, 1911.

officials who were attempting to comply with the law withdrew three hundred convicts from the leasing system on April 1, 1912. Whereupon prison contractors immediately instituted injunction proceedings to prevent the withdrawal. The rationale behind the injunction proceedings quickly became apparent. When hearings were held on the injunction, the state was accommodatingly unrepresented and a judgment favorable to the prison contractors rendered by default. The Prison Warden publicly protested to the Attorney General, and the judgment by default was set aside, but the case was carried over until the autumn term of the court. Through such tactics, the law was on the statute books for nearly twenty months before it was put into effect at the end of 1912.[12]

When labor lobbyists arrived at Jefferson City for the 1913 session of the General Assembly, they vowed to strengthen the law and to ensure that the legislature appropriate enough funds to make it effective. Their attempt soon failed at the hands of legislators who not only refused to appropriate the necessary funds to put the new system into effect, but also ignored earlier legislation and extended the prison labor contracts through 1915.[13]

An angry group of State Federation of Labor delegates convened in Springfield in September, 1913, and pledged to defeat all candidates who did not commit themselves to the abolition of the contract labor system. The legislative committee of the State Federation later sent questionnaires to all candidates for the legislature to ascertain their views on the prison labor system. The committee reported receiving more than three hundred replies, and, although some respondents were uncertain about the prospect of the state going into business, they all expressed opposition to the existing system.[14]

Organized labor's efforts in the campaign seemingly paid important dividends when the 1915 session of the state legislature passed a measure abolishing the leasing system and appropriating $250,000 to establish the state-use system. Furthermore, the legislation provided that one-half of the prisoners be relieved from contract work immediately and employed at the task of producing articles for use by the state.[15]

When little progress was made in carrying out the provisions of the law, President Reuben T. Wood of the State Federation went to the Capitol to investigate. Interviews with members of the prison board provided little enlightenment. One member, John P. Gordon, dismissed the subject with the comment that he had been too busy with other matters to look after prison affairs. Another member,

12. Graham, "History of the State Federation," p. 64.
13. *Ibid.*, p. 65.
14. *Ibid.*
15. *Ibid.*, p. 66. *Missouri Red Book, 1915*, p. 184.

John T. Barker, explained that the Governor's cut in the appropriation made it extremely difficult to carry out the intent of the legislation. Wood then attempted to contact the Superintendent of State Factories, the state official responsible for instituting the new system. When this proved impossible, he discussed the matter with the Superintendent's chief clerk, who admitted that the only factory that had been started was a garment factory employing two or three hundred prisoners. Despite Wood's insistent questioning, he failed to learn how goods produced in this factory were distributed.[16]

It soon became obvious that little was being done to carry out the provisions of the law, and despite labor's constant badgering, little was likely to be done. Thus as the nation prepared to enter the hostilities in Europe, the legislative committee of the State Federation prepared for yet another battle in the state legislature. Prospects improved, however, when Governor-elect Frederick D. Gardner committed his administration to the enactment of an effective law. The 1917 session of the state legislature finally enacted a strengthened convict labor law, carrying with it a $600,000 appropriation to put the state-use system into effect, but, as had been true of previous legislation, labor leaders soon discovered that little effort would be made to carry out the intent of the law.[17]

In the two decades the state labor body had fought for effective prison labor reform, it had scored a number of legislative victories only to see them disintegrate because of bureaucratic caprice. Such experiences constantly eroded the confidence many labor leaders had in the capacity of the major parties to implement reform, so they were increasingly amenable to any third-party movement offering hopes for success. Disillusionment intensified when labor's efforts to create a system of compensation for injured workmen were equally frustrating.

Workmen's Compensation

Agitation for workmen's compensation legislation grew from earlier attempts to clarify and broaden the area of employers' liability for injuries occurring while a person was working. The major objective was the elimination of traditional common law practices which forced the injured worker to prove that he was not guilty of contributory negligence, that the injury did not result from the negligence of a fellow employee, and that he had no knowledge of the risks involved in his particular job.

Organized labor made some gains in its efforts to strengthen the

16. Graham, "History of the State Federation," pp. 66, 67.
17. *Ibid.,* pp. 67–69.

provisions of emplyers' liability. In 1907 the labor lobby secured the enactment of a law defining the liability of mine operators and explicitly identifying a fellow servant in the operation of mines. During a special session of the General Assembly in the same year, Governor Folk, in response to pressure from labor organizations, added a fellow-servant law to the legislative agenda, and the General Assembly passed an act permitting recovery of $10,000 damages for contributory negligence in cases of death.[18]

Although organized labor quickly moved to assume leadership in the agitation for a workmen's compensation system, Gov. Herbert Hadley first advocated such legislation. To supplement his knowledge of industrial accident insurance, the Governor opened correspondence with Edwin Krauthoff and John P. Andrews of the American Association for Labor Legislation during the summer of 1910. Andrews suggested that the Governor obtain the temporary services of Reuben McKittrick, who had been trained to deal with this type of legislation in Charles McCarthy's Wisconsin Legislative Reference Library. Krauthoff, secretary of the association, agreed to serve on Hadley's proposed commission. John Mitchell of the National Civic Federation, with whom the Governor also corresponded, declined to serve but furnished Hadley with information and the names of several prominent Missouri labor leaders the Governor might choose to consult.[19]

Hadley took his compensation proposal to the annual convention of the State Federation of Labor in the fall of 1910 and announced that he would appoint an investigative commission composed of representatives of labor, capital, and the general public. Convention delegates received the suggestion enthusiastically and immediately passed a resolution endorsing the proposal but, deciding to give priority to the enactment of a new employers' liability law, approved a bill prepared by the Industrial Council of Kansas City for introduction in the General Assembly.[20]

The Governor followed his speech to the labor convention by canvassing state labor organizations asking them to recommend appointees for the proposed commission. Ultimately, eight members of organized labor served on the commission of thirty. Hadley presided

18. *Missouri Red Book, 1907,* p. 694. *Messages and Proclamations of the Governors of the State of Missouri,* Vol. IX, p. 509. Louis G. Geiger, *Joseph W. Folk of Missouri,* p. 117.

19. John P. Andrews to Hadley, n.d.; Edwin Krauthoff to Hadley, June 6, August 8, 1910; John Mitchell to Hadley, August 10, 1910, August 26, 1911, Herbert S. Hadley, Papers.

20. Ruth W. Towne, "The Movement for Workmen's Compensation Legislation in Missouri, 1910–1925," p. 12. *Missouri Red Book, 1910,* pp. 304, 389, 401. *The Kansas City Star,* September 20, 1910.

over the first meeting held in the Jefferson Hotel in Saint Louis on December 2, 1910, and augmented the duties of the commission by adding for consideration the questions of child labor, factory inspection, and women's labor.[21]

John T. Barker, a future attorney general of Missouri, was elected chairman; John T. Smith, secretary of the State Federation of Labor, vice-president; and J. Lionberger Davis, a prominent Saint Louis progressive, secretary. Although the 1911 General Assembly was urged by Hadley to draw up a measure for presentation, commission members reported that they believed the problem of injury compensation was too important and complex for such precipitant action. Instead the commission recommended that the General Assembly create a new committee that had sufficient time to make a thorough study of the issue.[22]

In compliance with Hadley's request, the forty-sixth session of the state legislature created a new commission to investigate employers' liability and workmen's compensation insurance. The new commission consisted of fifteen members; the House, Senate, and Governor each appointed five commissioners. Hadley selected two members to represent the employers in the state, and by request of labor leaders, he named George Manual of the United Mine Workers and Charles G. Brittingham of the Brotherhood of Locomotive Engineers to represent labor. Hadley's final appointment went to a representative of the insurance industry.[23] The new commission held hearings in Kansas City and Saint Louis to obtain opinions of both labor and management concerning the type of legislation that should be proposed. Meanwhile, Hadley's successor, Elliott Major, bolstered the drive for a compensation act by endorsing the principle in his inaugural address and promising to work for the enactment of a compensation system. Although a consensus of opinion existed regarding the desirability of a compensation law, numerous disagreements remained as to the most desirable type of law. Labor and employers differed over questions such as state insurance, automatic compensation, em-

21. Folder 401 of the Herbert S. Hadley, Papers contains a good deal of this correspondence. Hadley to Hiller, November 14, 28, 1910, in *Missouri Red Book, 1910.* (The minutes of the meeting are also printed on these pages.)

22. Hadley expanded the scope of the commission in response to a request by Cynthelia Knefler, president of the Saint Louis Women's Trade Union League, who suggested that the Governor appoint a commission to investigate the need for a number of progressive measures. Knefler to Hadley, August 8, 1910, Herbert S. Hadley, Papers.

23. Towne, "Movement for Workmen's Compensation," pp. 13–17. *Missouri Red Book, 1911,* p. 240. Folders 401–410 of the Herbert S. Hadley, Papers contain a large volume of correspondence relative to the appointment of commission members.

ployee contributions to the insurance fund, rates of compensation, and whether the system should be elective or mandatory.[24]

The draft legislation that the commission submitted in 1913 followed the employers' inclinations in most of these matters and was unacceptable to state labor leaders. Rates of compensation were low, the use of private insurance companies was proposed, and the employers' system of elective insurance advocated. The Saint Louis Central Trades and Labor Union, the Kansas City Industrial Council, the Building Trades Councils of both cities, and the Missouri State Federation of Labor all opposed the bill. Federation President Reuben Wood declared that while labor wanted a compensation act, it did not want this one. He argued that compensation rates were too low, and because of several loopholes in the bill, workers would still need a lawyer to collect.[25]

Besides the commission bill, a number of other compensation acts were introduced at the 1913 session of the state legislature. It soon became apparent that the issue was too controversial to permit the passage of any measure. Labor leaders finally called a conference of legislative representatives of state labor unions at the capital in March to consider amendments that would make the commission bill acceptable. Their action came too late, however, and hopes for passage of a compensation measure during the session died. Legislators instead decided to appoint yet another commission to reconcile the differences between employers and labor. Meanwhile, the delegates at the State Federation convention meeting in September decided to appoint their own special committee to prepare compensation legislation for introduction at the Forty-eighth General Assembly.[26]

During the sessions of the General Assembly in 1915, a number of measures concerning industrial injuries were introduced. Representatives of organized labor sponsored one bill, business groups proposed two, and the Senate commission that had been appointed during the preceding session of the General Assembly introduced another. Much of the debate during the session focused on the Senate commission's bill, which provided more liberal benefits than the legislation introduced by the Senate committee two years earlier. Compensation rates under the proposed measure were relatively high, and adequate medical benefits were provided, but the bill was still elective, and state insurance was rejected. The commission bill repre-

24. *Report of Missouri Commission on Employers' Liability and Workmen's Compensation to the Governor and the Forty-seventh General Assembly.*
25. *Ibid. St. Louis Post-Dispatch,* February 26, 1913. *The Kansas City Star,* February 10, 14, 1913.
26. Towne, "Movement for Workmen's Compensation," p. 35. *Missouri Red Book, 1913,* p. 647.

sented a compromise between the legislation desired by employers and the type of bill that labor leaders envisioned.[27]

State Sen. Alroy Phillips of Saint Louis, a member of the Senate commission and shortly to become the State Federation's chief legal counsel, wrote the commission bill and took a draft of it to the Hannibal convention of the State Federation in September, 1914. Unimpressed by the Phillips bill, the labor body voted instead to endorse a liability act prepared by its own legislative committee.[28]

A large segment of the business community also opposed the commission bill. The Kansas City Commercial Club and Manufacturers Association, the Saint Louis Business Men's League, and the Associated Employers of Missouri all expressed opposition. These groups cooperated in drafting a third measure for introduction in the state legislature. The employers' bill provided limited benefits and extremely low rates of compensation, and it included minimal medical payments. The insurance interests were among business groups most opposed to the commission bill. Mutual companies, led by Metropolitan Life, were especially hostile. Dismissing Senator Phillips's arguments that the bill would ultimately benefit their interests, these companies contended that it would force them out of the liability insurance business in Missouri.[29]

Despite its earlier opposition, organized labor had reversed its position and strongly endorsed the Senate commission bill by the time the Forty-eighth General Assembly convened in January, 1915. Little evidence exists to explain this change, but some alterations were probably made to quell labor's objections. Moreover, labor leaders, possibly concluding that they could best ensure the defeat of the employer bill by supporting the commission measure, began to seek backing for their endeavors from various labor organizations throughout the state. In Saint Louis and Kansas City, the central bodies and the building trades councils endorsed the commission bill. Reuben Wood wrote to the Joplin Trades Assembly urging its leaders to lobby local representatives and senators in support of the commission bill. The Kansas City Industrial Council even sent its legislative committee to the capital to aid the efforts being made by the State Federation's legislative committee.[30]

Despite the strong campaign waged by organized labor, the commission bill failed, due in part to an equally strong opposition campaign conducted by employer associations and insurance companies. Actually, the legislation had little chance for passage anyway, because

27. Towne, "Movement for Workmen's Compensation," p. 38.
28. *Ibid.,* p. 39.
29. *Ibid.,* pp. 41, 42, 43.
30. Wood to the Joplin Trades Assembly in *Missouri Trades Unionist,* March 3, 1915. *The Labor Herald,* January 15, 29, February 19, 1915.

the 1915 session of the General Assembly, which was deeply divided over prohibition, spent most of its time debating that emotional issue.[31]

By the time the United States entered World War I, Missouri remained one of the few industrial states without a workmen's compensation program. The only other major legislative objectives they had satisfactorily achieved were the initiative and referendum laws. Although limited reforms had been enacted pertaining to employer liability, the agitation for convict labor reform produced laws that were evaded, undermined, and unenforced.

General Labor and Social Reforms

The labor lobby experienced mixed results with other measures it promoted during the period. Proposed legislation directly involving the activities of organized labor failed completely, and so did a series of measures concerned with employer–employee practices. As a result, employers could continue legally to discharge workers for union membership, to employ private detective agencies for spying and strikebreaking activities, to advertise for strikebreakers, and to transport strikebreakers through intrastate commerce. The labor lobby also failed to curb the issuance of injunctions in labor disputes. On the other hand, labor successfully sponsored a State Board of Arbitration in 1907 and had limited success in establishing the eight-hour day in selected trades, but labor failed to get a comprehensive eight-hour law for all workers in the state.[32]

The labor lobby seemed to accomplish more when it supported reform legislation of a more inclusive nature. Labor representatives successfully sponsored a measure to restrict the employment of women to fifty-four hours per week, although a minimum wage law for women failed. The Missouri labor movement had also written and lobbied for the child labor laws enacted in 1897 and 1907 but later failed in attempts to strengthen and expand the laws. Always concerned about education, Missouri labor advocated and got a program for compulsory school attendance, free textbooks for children in the public schools, and a Children's Code Commission to supervise the various laws involved with the protection and well-being of children. In a similar vein, the state labor movement contributed to the successful efforts to provide pensions for the needy blind and for widowed mothers with minor children. The labor movement was less successful in its efforts to legislate an old-age pension system and a program of health and sickness insurance.[33]

31. Towne, "Movement for Workmen's Compensation," pp. 44, 45.
32. Gary M Fink, "The Evolution of Social and Political Attitudes in the Missouri Labor Movement, 1900–1940," Chap. 3.
33. *Ibid.*, Chap. 4. Jack D. Muraskin, "Missouri Politics during the Progressive Era, 1896–1916," pp. 258–60.

The reform with which labor had the least sympathy was prohibition. Labor in Missouri advocated temperance and supported the strict regulation and control of the liquor traffic but considered prohibition a violation of personal liberty that could lead to the establishment of a public "morality police." Organized labor, of course, also opposed prohibition because of its potential effects on a large number of brewery workers and such related occupations as cigarmakers, musicians, bartenders, cooks, and waiters.[34]

Labor first exhibited concern over the growing agitation for prohibition in 1907 during a State Federation meeting at Sedalia. When the Women's Christian Temperance Union, meeting in Sedalia at the same time, sent a delegation to extend fraternal greetings to the labor movement, a Saint Louis brewery workers' union delegate objected to receiving the women of the WCTU. While the convention preserved chivalry and overruled the brewery delegate's objections the incident undoubtedly alerted the unions to the far-reaching consequences that prohibition would have for their movement.[35]

The following year, President Sheridan told the State Federation convention that the time had come for labor to take a stand on prohibition. Shortly thereafter, a resolution bearing the signatures of almost every influential labor leader in the state expressed organized labor's adamant hostility to prohibition in "whatever form advocated." Organized labor joined with other antiprohibitionists in 1910 to defeat a constitutional amendment placed on the ballot by initiative petition that called for the prohibition of the manufacture and sale of all intoxicating liquors in the state. Similar amendments were defeated in 1913 and again in 1916. Public opinion on prohibition, however, was drastically shifting. By 1916, every major city in the state voted in favor of it except Saint Louis, whose vote defeated the proposal. Impressed with the growing threat of prohibition, the Trades Union Liberty League of Missouri was formed during the 1915 convention of the State Federation to make labor's opposition more effective. The league was composed primarily of brewery workers and was supported by trade unionists in related industries and by officers of the State Federation who played a prominent role in the new organization. The league, which held annual conventions immediately following those of the State Federation, was formed, according to its first president, Joseph Hauser, "to devise ways and means to combat county option, state and national prohibition, as well as such other legislation that may be detrimental to Organized Labor or the personal liberty of the working class."[36]

34. Graham, "History of the State Federation of Labor," pp. 133, 134. MSFL, *Proceedings, 1908,* p. 13.

35. Graham, "History of the State Federation of Labor," p. 134.

36. MSFL, *Proceedings, 1908,* pp. 13, 52. *Missouri Red Book, 1911,* p. 19. Graham, "History of the State Federation of Labor," pp. 134, 135. See

In its opposition to prohibition, labor's concern with the denial of civil liberties can be considered simply a tactic that was used to protect economic and personal interests, but Missouri labor periodically expressed concern over infringements of other types of civil liberties. Saint Louis labor, for example, fought against a proposal for movie censorship that was introduced at a meeting of the Saint Louis Board of Aldermen. The State Federation opposed a similar effort to create a state board of censors with arbitrary powers to permit or prohibit the public showing of motion pictures.[37]

At best, organized labor's concern with personal liberty and civil rights remained selective, however. An ingrained nativism, reflecting contemporary Missouri society, prevailed in the labor movement. Labor's concern over immigration reflected one manifestation of this implicit nativism. While understandable (if misconceived) economic concerns motivated labor's demands for destricted immigration, labor framed its opposition to unrestricted immigration in both racial and economic terms.[38] Missouri's labor newspapers contain numerous examples of racial prejudice toward Oriental immigrants. Despite the relatively insignificant number of Asian immigrants in the state, the "Yellow Peril" was pictured as a constant threat to white workers.[39] Furthermore, racial identification was not limited to Asian immigrants. "Unionists should protest against compelling workers possessing American ideals to compete indefinitely with the illiterate of southern and eastern Europe," proclaimed the respected editor of the *Labor Herald*. Similarly, a speaker at a State Federation convention reportedly "brought down the house" when referring in ethnically derogatory terms to Jews and their small clothing factories.[40] Both economic and nativistic motivations are evident in a bill which the legislative committee of the State Federation advocated in 1909 making it illegal for any manager, superintendent, firm, or corporation to employ aliens for more than 10 per cent of their work force. Perhaps nothing better evidences organized labor's nativism than its fervent support of the Brunett Immigration Bills of 1915 and 1917 with their obviously discriminatory provisions in the form of literacy tests.[41]

The labor movement's indifference toward the problems of black

also Muraskin, "Missouri Politics," *passim. The Labor Herald,* October 8, 1915. *The Saint Joseph Union,* September 22, 1916. *St. Louis Labor,* September 30, 1916.

37. *St. Louis Labor,* January 15, 1916. MSFL, *Proceedings, 1916,* p. 112.

38. Selig Perlman, *A Theory of the Labor Movement,* pp. 168, 169. Cf. Isaac Hourwich, *Immigration and Labor.*

39. For example, MSFL, *Proceedings, 1906,* p. 43. *The Labor Herald,* May 23, 1913.

40. *The Labor Herald,* September 26, 1913; February 18, 1916.

41. *Missouri Red Book, 1909,* p. 457. *The Labor Herald,* February 18, 1916. *The Saint Joseph Union,* February 25, 1916.

Americans was even more misguided. Missouri labor could have made a significant contribution to a reformed society in the area of racial understanding. Instead of accepting this challenge, as labor had done in many other areas, the labor movement submitted to the racist impulse. Labor leaders sometimes even exploited racial prejudice to serve their own purposes. To be sure, labor leaders recognized that a large, unorganized Afro-American labor force represented a constant threat to the wage scale of union workers, and they did make some attempts to organize black workers. Organization, however, usually involved the chartering of Jim Crow unions. This method of organizing black workers was dictated to some extent by the policies of international unions, many of which excluded Afro-American membership either by practice or by constitutional provision.[42]

The largest number of black workers lived in Saint Louis, and on the surface, it would appear that labor in Saint Louis was as liberal concerning the race issue as conditions would allow. When international unions permitted it, black workers usually could join existing union locals, and black delegates sat in the Central Trades and Labor Union. Moreover, the officers of the Central Trades expressed a re-occurring interest in the organization of black workers and made their services readily available to any group interested in organizing.[43] Unfortunately, offenses of omission and commission severely qualified Saint Louis labor's apparent liberalism on the race issue. No evidence exists that local labor leaders expressed objections or attempted to alter the racist policies of international unions. Even worse, when Saint Louis labor had an opportunity in 1916 to express its views forcefully, it failed to act against a proposal to segregate Saint Louis into defined black ghettos. Although labor usually took special interest in such referendum elections, neither the Saint Louis Central Trades nor the Building Trades Council recognized the existence of the segregation issue. Gottlieb Hoehn spoke out against the proposal in the columns of his Socialist newspaper, but his was "a voice in the wilderness" in the Saint Louis labor movement.[44]

42. Edwin J. Forsythe, "The St. Louis Central Trades and Labor Union, 1887–1945," pp. 162, 163. Philip Taft, *The A. F. of L. in the Time of Gompers,* pp. 302–19.

43. Forsythe, "St. Louis Central Trades," pp. 162, 163. William A. Crossland, *Industrial Conditions Among Negroes in St. Louis,* p. 71.

44. *St. Louis Labor,* February 12, 19, 1916. Although there was considerable interaction between black workers and the trade union movement in the economic realm, there is little evidence to indicate that the black worker had any substantial impact on organized labor's political behavior. Even the East Saint Louis Race Riot of 1917 does not appear to have had any effect on the political policies of the labor movement. For a further discussion of the relationship between black workers and organized labor, see Fink, "The Missouri Labor Movement," pp. 119–23, 278–81.

Black workers faced similar prejudices and discriminations in other Missouri cities and towns.

Summary: The Labor Lobby in the Progressive Era

In comparative terms, the labor lobby experienced its greatest success during the Progressive period. Nothing comparable would follow in either the 1920s or the 1930s. Although Democrats in the General Assembly generally supported labor more consistently than Republicans, legislators from both parties supported the goals of the labor movement. Moreover, it was a Republican governor, Herbert Hadley, who many labor leaders considered most responsive to the goals and objectives of the labor movement. The key to whatever success the labor lobby achieved was its ability to gain the support of significant numbers of rural legislators. Many of these sons of rural America, apparently still holding Populist views against big business, seemed inclined to find some mutuality of interest between the workers on the farm and the laborer in the factory.[45]

Despite the comparative success, however, labor leaders remained dissatisfied with their lobbying efforts. They failed to gain effective legislation on many of the issues they considered most vital. Convinced that a popular majority, if not a legislative majority, supported their proposals, they believed that the prevailing party system not only frustrated the labor movement but also thwarted the popular will.

Near the end of the Progressive Era, the attention of labor leaders was increasingly drawn to events over which they had no control but that were significantly affecting the lives of workers and the stability of the labor movement. The outbreak of war in Europe and the changes it precipitated in the United States brought a temporary deemphasis of political action as the labor movement devoted most of its energy and resources to militant activity in the economic realm.

45. See Chap. 7 and Appendix A.

Part Two

EXPERIMENTING
WITH
THIRD-PARTY POLITICS

An expanded sense of militancy and class consciousness gripped the steadily growing Missouri labor movement during World War I. This posture, along with the problems organized labor confronted during and immediately following the war, strengthened the resolve of many Missouri labor leaders to break with the political tactics of the past and to attempt a radically different approach. Yet, in many ways, the wartime experiences of organized labor had been paradoxical: the beneficial possibilities of positive government intervention in economic affairs became apparent, but labor's limitations and weaknesses in the realm of politics were starkly exposed. Although "politics as usual" was suspended during the war period, politics remained vitally important. It was not electoral politics or legislative lobbying, however, that consumed the time and energies of labor leaders but the politics of bureaucracy. Since it was assumed they were failing to function effectively in this area, they were more thoroughly convinced than ever that they were pursuing a faulty political strategy. Consequently, when the Conference for Progressive Political Action organized a third-party movement, it found in the Missouri labor movement an enthusiastic and loyal following.

Chapter IV

WORLD CONFLICT
AND LABOR MILITANCY

ORGANIZED labor in Missouri reacted to the news of a general war in Europe with horror and disgust. Like most other labor movements in the United States, Missouri labor had an antimilitaristic bias that had its origins in a long tradition of opposition to imperialism and an assumption that military organization and standing armies were antithetical to democracy. Missouri labor quickly registered its opinion of the war in unqualified terms. The Saint Louis Central Trades adopted a Socialist-inspired resolution condemning all aspects of the war.[1] A few months later at the September convention of the State Federation of Labor, President Reuben Wood recommended that the convention make a formal statement regarding its disapproval of the war. Wood concluded his remarks with the observation that "If General Sherman was justified in saying, 'War is hell!' the workingmen of the world are as justified in adding, 'To hell with war!' "[2] The convention delegates later adopted resolutions severely denouncing the war.[3]

The labor movement in Missouri favored neutrality, and until the formal declaration of war, it opposed the preparedness campaign. In June, 1916, the Industrial Council of Kansas City declared itself "unalterably opposed" to a preparedness parade and requested that no Kansas City labor organization participate.[4] At about the same time, the Saint Louis Central Trades voted 133 to 42 against participating in a preparedness parade. The leadership of the Central Trades believed that the preparedness campaign was advocated primarily for the benefit of munition makers. Somewhat later the Central Trades instructed its State Federation delegation to introduce motions requesting the legislative committee to follow carefully the coming sessions of the state legislature in order to prevent the enactment of preparedness legislation. In a similar vein, the Saint Joseph Central

1. Lewis Lorwin, *The American Federation of Labor: History, Policies and Prospects,* pp. 136, 137. Philip Taft, *The A. F. of L. in the Time of Gompers,* pp. 342, 343. *St. Louis Labor,* August 12, 1914.
2. *The Labor Herald,* September 18, 1914.
3. *Ibid.,* September 25, 1914.
4. *Ibid.,* June 2, 1916.

Labor Council opposed any declaration of war until the proposition could be referred to the general electorate for a referendum vote.[5]

Prior to America's entry into the war, Missouri labor spokesmen interpreted the causes of the war in censorious terms. Autocratic governments, armament manufacturers, and industrial capitalists were all roundly condemned as perpetrators of the war.[6] In discussing the war in his annual report to the State Federation, President Wood emphasized the latter: "Let us not forget, that this world war is nothing else but a capitalist business war between the ruling classes of Europe, and the tremendously powerful war machines operated by modern militarism are simply the police power of those ruling classes in the several war countries."[7]

The Labor Movement Before American Intervention

The outbreak of war in Europe affected the lives of workers in Missouri long before the United States actively entered the struggle. Orders for American munitions and supplies from Europe stimulated business and created an inflationary spiral that had repercussions throughout the economy. Wages rose steadily; so did the cost of living, and in many cases, real wages actually declined. By the end of 1916 the laborer's position in the economy of the state was rapidly deteriorating. His wages had risen 18.4 per cent during the preceding decade, but his cost of living, as measured by the cost of food, went up 33 per cent. A workingman who made $3 a day working 10 hours in 1907, earned $3.48 in 1916 for a working day of 9 hours and 36 minutes; but he spent $4.17 to buy the same quantity of food his $3 bought in 1907. Using 1913 as the base year, wages in Saint Louis had risen 49 per cent by 1919; but during the same period, the cost of the most common food products rose 92 per cent. The plight of workers in Kansas City and in Missouri's other major cities was only slightly less serious.[8]

The failure of wages to keep pace with the constant pressure of inflation produced one of the greatest periods of class consciousness and militancy in the twentieth-century history of the Missouri labor movement. The number of strikes in Missouri increased sharply in 1916, and militant strike activity continued for several years.[9]

5. Edwin J. Forsythe, "The St. Louis Central Trades and Labor Union, 1887–1945," p. 130. *St. Louis Labor,* July 29, 1916. *The Saint Joseph Union,* February 16, 1917.

6. Forsythe, "St. Louis Central Trades," pp. 125–27, 131.

7. MSFL, *Proceedings, 1916,* p. 43.

8. *Missouri Red Book, 1917,* p. 380. United States Bureau of Labor Statistics, *Bulletin No. 274,* p. 24; *Bulletin No. 270,* pp. 47–49.

9. *Missouri Red Book, 1917,* pp. 233–39.

Reuben Wood expressed the feelings of many Missouri labor leaders when he concluded that the industrial unrest could be

> attributed to the general condition of unrest which has been brought on by a class of people whom we may justly designate as industrial pirates and commercial vampires, who considered the unprecedented food speculation their highest ideal of life. They took advantage of the unfortunate war situation and succeeded in amassing fabulous fortunes by forcing up the cost of living to such an extent that even those of our fellow-workers who enjoy the protection of a solid and influential labor union are today unable to buy back enough of the products they produce to keep their families in a condition approaching a respectable living.[10]

During these years of labor militancy and class consciousness, the labor movement in Missouri made more significant gains in membership than it had since the early years of its history. The membership curve of the state labor movement had reached an early peak in 1904 and remained fairly stable for several years. It turned upward again in 1912 and rose sharply from 1916 to 1920. There were eighty thousand organized workers in Missouri in 1912, and by 1920 this figure had more than doubled (Figures 1 and 2).[11]

It has usually been assumed that the large increase in union membership during this period resulted primarily from sympathetic government policies. Judging from the experience of organized labor in Missouri, however, the importance of government in stimulating these membership gains has been exaggerated. Nearly 50 per cent of the increase in union membership between 1912 and 1920 occurred before the establishment of federal war agencies.[12] Furthermore, the government at no time during the war either seriously encouraged or effectively supported the organization of workers in Missouri. Or-

10. *Ibid.,* pp. 205, 206.
11. Figures taken from the *Missouri Red Book, 1912–1921.*
12. *Ibid.*

Figure 1. Membership of Missouri labor unions, 1900–1930.

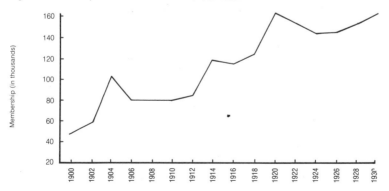

Figure 2. Comparison of membership of Missouri labor unions and the AFL, 1918–1929.

ganized labor made advances only where it had the economic power to force concessions from employers. Although membership increased mainly in industries that were already organized to some degree, the labor movement did make some important inroads into previously unorganized businesses in the period before the United States entered the war.

One of the most spectacular organizing efforts was the attempt to unionize the previously open-shop, urban transportation systems of the state. Vigorous efforts had been made to organize streetcar employees at the turn of the century, but these attempts ultimately failed.[13] The streetcar franchises operated on an open-shop basis; unions were neither recognized nor condoned. By 1916 most streetcar companies in the state had developed an effective strategy to undermine organizing attempts. Their first reaction to the existence of a streetcar employee's union was to recognize the union and sign a contract, thus preventing any disruption in service. The company then systematically began discharging union leaders and violating contract provisions. These actions forced the union to issue a strike call. By this time the company was prepared for the strike and was able not only to crush the union but also to use the strike as the pretext for withdrawing union recognition and reestablishing the open shop.

Nevertheless, the state labor movement in 1916 decided once again to initiate a statewide campaign to organize streetcar operators. The State Federation made a test case of the organization of a union in

13. The attempt to organize the streetcar workers in Saint Louis in 1900 resulted in an extremely bitter and violent strike that made a deep impression upon both the leaders and citizens of the city. See William Reedy, *The Story of the Strike,* and Jack D. Muraskin, "Missouri Politics during the Progressive Era, 1896–1916," pp. 85–88.

Springfield. It was a logical choice for several reasons: Springfield was the home of Federation President Reuben Wood; its labor movement was militant and well organized; the city was governed by an administration that was friendly toward labor; and many of the city's residents felt little loyalty to the absentee owners of the Springfield Traction Company.[14]

The Springfield streetcar strike evolved into one of the state's most bitter labor disputes, and it provides a vivid illustration of labor's militancy in the period preceding American entry into World War I. It also reflects the determined resistance of employers to union organization and the extent to which they would go to avoid collective bargaining.

When the employees of the Springfield Traction Company organized, the tested formula was followed; the company recognized the union and negotiated a contract. Immediately, the company began the systematic discharge of union leaders. When the secretary of the union was discharged, the union declared they would strike until union personnel were reemployed.[15]

The traction company next secured a temporary injunction restraining its employees from striking. Later, however, a judge of the Southern District of the federal district court for the Western District of Missouri ruled that he would not issue a permanent injunction since the company's action had created the conflict. Thus, the streetcar company temporarily lost one of its most formidable antistrike weapons, and the union had at least a chance for success. The streetcar motormen and conductors went on strike on October 5, 1916. Because they wanted to maintain public support, they immediately organized a system of "jitney" buses to provide rides for those persons who were normally dependent upon the streetcars for transportation. The buses, of course, also provided at least limited employment for the striking workers.[16] Citizens of Springfield generally respected the union's boycott, and the streetcars carried few passengers.

Shortly after the strike began, the traction company imported a group of Chicago strikebreakers. Their arrival precipitated a violent clash between the union members and the imported workers. The violence gave the company another chance to secure an injunction. This time the company approached a different judge, Arba S. Van Valkenburgh, of the federal court for the Western District of Missouri, who was reputed among labor circles to be an "injunction judge." Van Valkenburgh issued a sweeping restraining order prohibiting the officers and members of the local streetcar union, the

14. MSFL, *Proceedings, 1917,* pp. 13–23.
15. *Ibid. The Springfield Leader,* October 3, 1916.
16. *The Springfield Leader,* October 4, 1916. MSFL, *Proceedings, 1917,* pp. 18–23.

national officers of the Amalgamated Association of Street, Electric Railway and Motor Coach Employees of America, President Wood of the State Federation, and President Walter Ford of the Springfield Trades and Labor Assembly, from aiding the strikers or prolonging the strike. The prolabor position of local officials was reflected by the inclusion of restrictions of the actions of the mayor and various other city officials in the provisions of the injunction.[17]

When the injunction failed to break the strike, the traction company instituted a damage suit against the Springfield Trades and Labor Assembly for $150,000 and another against Mayor Gideon and other Springfield officials for $200,000. The filing of the damage suit was a tactical error that allowed union leaders to constantly remind Springfield citizens that an outside-owned corporation was attempting to intimidate their local, elected officials.[18]

Community opinion vacillated between sympathy for the strikers and unhappiness over the inconvenience and the reign of violence that accompanied the strike. Because the local press and business groups were openly hostile to the strikers, union leaders began publication of a daily, general circulation newspaper in an attempt to tell their side of the story and appeal for public support. Immediately, the Retail Merchants Association, one of the traction company's most important allies in Springfield, instituted an informal advertising boycott against the newspaper. But the union had other weapons at hand. When a delegation from the Women's Trades Union Label League visited Springfield merchants and threatened to open their own cooperatives, the boycott ended, and the labor newspaper received its share of newspaper advertising.[19]

Another employer group, the Jobbers and Manufacturers' Association, organized a Law and Order League that offered to furnish city officials with one thousand armed men to protect private property in Springfield. Citizens of Springfield were invited to attend an organizational meeting to elect officers. The election was postponed, however, when a thousand union members responded to the invitation; public meetings of the Law and Order League of Springfield were discontinued after the incident.[20]

As a final resort, the employer groups instituted a recall campaign to remove Mayor Gideon from office. Prior to the election in May,

17. The trial record of O. E. Jennings, the only union leader to be imprisoned as a result of the strike, contains much information concerning the strike and the violence that attended it as well as an indication of local sentiment and the attitude of local officials. See Francis M. Wilson, Papers. *The Springfield Leader,* October 24, November 1, 2, 5, 1916; May 8, 10, 1917. MSFL, *Proceedings, 1917,* pp. 18–23.
18. MSFL, *Proceedings, 1917,* pp. 18–23.
19. *Ibid. The Springfield Laborer,* January 25, 27, 28, 1917.
20. MSFL, *Proceedings, 1917,* pp. 18–23.

1917, organized labor had conducted a vigorous campaign in support of the Mayor, and Gideon had won an impressive victory, supported chiefly by the working-class wards on the city's north side. The recall effort obtained most of its support from the wards of middle-class businessmen on the south side.[21]

After the failure of the recall effort, the company's cause waned. Their position further deteriorated after two imported strikebreakers were tried and convicted for kidnapping and murdering a Springfield child. The strike was settled on the union's terms. On June 15, 1917, after a strike of 252 days, the traction company agreed to recognize and bargain with the union, to rehire all old employees, and to preserve their seniority. The settlement also included a wage increase. Labor's victory in Springfield was an important one. It demonstrated organized labor's determination to unionize the streetcar employees. Not only did labor prove it could win, but it also showed that resistance to organization could be prohibitively expensive.[22]

A few weeks after the Springfield settlement, the Kansas City streetcar operators organized and went on strike seeking recognition of their union. Although it was much shorter, the Kansas City strike followed the Springfield pattern. The company first recognized the union, but then precipitated a strike by discharging union personnel. Jitney service was inaugurated, and public opinion swung to the strikers when the railway company imported strikebreakers. One peculiarity of the Kansas City strike remained to plague labor leaders for some time, however. Forty-three Kansas City policemen were discharged for refusing to ride on streetcars to protect strikebreakers. After winning the strike, labor leaders turned their attention to getting these policemen reinstated. At that time Missouri law provided that the governor appoint police commissioners in Kansas City and Saint Louis. Organized labor pinned its hopes for having the policemen reinstated on convincing Gov. Frederick Gardner to remove the police commissioner who had ordered the dismissals. Labor leaders, however, received little solace from Gardner and began contemplating a general strike if the policemen were not rehired. The Kansas City Police Board removed much of the tension, however, by announcing its intention to reinstate the men whenever vacancies occurred. After the successes in Springfield and Kansas City, streetcar employees quickly formed unions in the other major cities of Missouri.[23]

21. *Ibid.*, pp. 73, 74. *The Springfield Laborer*, April 7–17, 1917. *St. Louis Labor*, May 26, 1917. *The Springfield Leader*, May 13, 16, 1917.

22. *The Springfield Leader*, June 7, 9, 15, 1917. *Railway Federationist*, June 25, 1917. *The Springfield Laborer*, June 15, 1917.

23. MSFL, *Proceedings, 1917*, pp. 78, 79, 178; *1918*, p. 47. *St. Louis Labor*, September 22, 1917.

As unionization moved into the transit industry, organizational activity also quickened in another open-shop bastion, the Missouri meatpacking industry. Missouri labor's most significant achievement during the war period was expansion into these two industries.

The Labor Movement After American Intervention

After the United States entered World War I, the attitude of Missouri labor leaders toward the international situation changed dramatically. While retaining some skepticism, they rationalized their support of the war in the moralistic and idealist terms that had been articulated by Woodrow Wilson. Although they were now ready to join the crusade to make the world safe for democracy, Missouri labor wanted it clearly understood that "a world made safe for democracy is synonymous with a world made safe for the laborer."[24] This attitude was clearly reflected in a resolution adopted by delegates at the 1917 convention of the State Federation that met after the American declaration of war. The delegates declared they would

> resist any and all attempts of Big Business, using this war as a pretext, to break down the benefits Organized Labor has accrued during the years, renewing our allegiance to the flag of our country by proclaiming the God-given fact that only human life is sacred, and that money and property rights are secondary thereto, our human sacrifice in this war being made solely that liberty for all mankind may be preserved forever to the future.[25]

When a system of military conscription was adopted in spite of organized labor's objections, the State Federation quickly responded with a proposal that wealth also be conscripted "to perish along with the lad who carries the flag of our country to victory; that the profits of those interested in war materials or necessities of life at the present abnormal demand be taken by our Government to pay the bill of death."[26]

Missouri labor supported the war effort in various ways. Reuben Wood became chairman of the Missouri Division of Labor for the sale of War Savings Certificates, and labor leaders at the local level joined in the campaign to sell war bonds. Missouri labor organizations also formed local chapters of the Alliance for Labor and Democracy, a Gompers-inspired labor organization that was designed to undermine the influence of pacifists and antiwar elements among labor. The only local body that declined to organize a branch of the Alliance as soon as the movement was initiated was the Saint Louis

24. J. L. Wines to Gompers, November 6, 1917, AFL, Papers, Series 117A, File 11A.

25. *Ibid.*

26. J. T. Smith to Gompers, April 22, 1917; Wines to Gompers, November 6, 1917, *ibid.*

Central Trades. By October, 1917, it finally endorsed a chapter begun in Saint Louis by the Building Trades Council.[27]

Even though labor leaders supported the American war effort, the deeply felt hostility towards war and militarism they had expressed earlier made them suspicious and defensive. The democratic rhetoric that had been adopted to justify United States involvement in the war, however, allowed these labor leaders not only to support the war, which most of their constituents apparently advocated in less qualified terms, but also to warrant a militant defense of trade unionism and the prerogatives of the working class during the war. To lose democracy at home would deny the justification for fighting for it abroad. This rationale greatly influenced labor's behavior during the war.

Organized labor received representation on several local, state, and federal boards and agencies created to facilitate the mobilization of men and machinery. Missouri labor was well represented on the District Exemption Boards that administered the conscription law.[28] Because of their concern with the equitable distribution of such resources as coal and oil, state labor leaders also served on the state advisory board of the Fuel Administration. They were less satisfied, however, with their representation on the Missouri State Council for Defense, an organization that was designed to coordinate the state's war effort. Labor's influence there was limited to only one out of the thirty delegates on the Council. Quickly becoming disillusioned with the Council's policies, the labor representative, Reuben Wood, threatened to resign.[29] Meanwhile, he explained the situation to the delegates at the State Federation convention in the autumn of 1917 and asked for guidance. The delegates passed a resolution urging Wood to remain, but they asked for additional labor representatives on the Council and demanded equal representation on all subsidiary committees concerned with the problems of labor mobilization.[30] The

27. MSFL, *Proceedings, 1918,* pp. 49–51. Forsythe, "St. Louis Central Trades," pp. 137, 138, 139. P. J. Morrin to Gompers, September 13, 1917, AFL, Papers, Series 117A, File 11A. Frank L. Grubbs, Jr., *The Struggle for Labor Loyalty: Gompers, the A. F. of L., and the Pacifists, 1917–1920,* pp. 39, 40, 41, 147, 148, *et passim.* Taft, *A. F. of L. in the Time of Gompers,* pp. 358–59. See also John C. Crighton, *Missouri and the World War, 1914–1917: A Study in Public Opinion,* pp. 82, 126, 127.

28. Gompers to R. T. Wood, June 27, 1917, Gompers, Letterbooks.

29. MSFL, *Proceedings, 1918,* p. 51; *1917,* p. 80. Wines to Gompers, August 6, 1917, AFL, Papers, Series 117A, File 11A.

30. MSFL, *Proceedings, 1917,* p. 80. *The Saint Joseph Union,* November 16, December 7, 1917. An example of Wood's disillusionment with the council occurred when he charged that Swift and Company in Saint Joseph was treating its workers unfairly. After considerable agitation on Wood's part, the State Council for Defense did appoint an investigator. Its choice for an investigator, however, was J. C. Barkley, manager of the Saint Joseph Stock Yards, which was owned by Swift and Company.

labor movement, however, never obtained the influence on these state boards to which it felt entitled.

Organized labor had several legitimate grievances during the war, but in few cases did the elaborate local, state, and federal machinery that had been designed to cope with such complaints operate effectively in Missouri. Even if one governmental agency made a decision that was favorable to organized labor, often it was either countermanded by another or ignored with impunity. Moreover, local and state governments and federal administrators were not always in agreement with stated national policy. They often failed to administer established policy enthusiastically and sometimes simply overlooked or even subverted it.[31]

One problem that plagued labor leaders throughout the war period was the introduction of women into industry. Various businesses organized industrial training schools for women on the grounds that they were necessary to conserve manpower for the war effort. Labor leaders believed that instead of a patriotic sacrifice, these industrial schools were a subterfuge for lowering prevailing wage scales. Men were being discharged and women hired in their places at much lower wages. That female workers were extensively used could not be doubted, as seen in a letter written by Jackson Johnson, president of the Saint Louis Chamber of Commerce, to Felix Frankfurter, chairman of the War Labor Policies Board. Johnson described a great demand for female labor in Saint Louis:

> We are manufacturing here the following principal items requiring a large proportion of female labor:
> Bandoleers; leggings; uniforms; shoes;
> o.d. materials; knapsacks; pharmaceuticals;
> Chemicals (requiring packing in bottles);
> tentage and equipment.
> We are also using an increasing proportion of female labor on our automatics, and other machines, and the young ladies have been doing exceptionally good work operating grinders on small steel specialities.
> We would like to formulate an organization here that would have the official sanction of the Government, and that could cooperate in this district with the plans you are now so admirably working out, to the end of bringing together in one place both the needs of our manufacturers and the available supply of female labor.[32]

31. Gary M Fink, "The Evolution of Social and Political Attitudes in the Missouri Labor Movement, 1900–1940," pp. 137, 138. Other examples will be presented later in this chapter.

32. Jackson Johnson to Felix Frankfurter, June 20, 1918, War Labor Policies Board, Papers, Record Group No. 4.

While the War Labor Policies Board apparently took no action on Johnson's proposal, his letter suggests that labor's concern over the introduction of female labor was justifiable.

Union officials had no objections to the introduction of female workers if they received pay equal to that a man would receive for equal work, but most employers refused to follow this policy, a stance that led labor leaders to conclude that businesses employed female labor for the purpose of lowering wages. If women were hired to conserve manpower, employers should have had no objection to paying the prevailing wage regardless of sex. When Reuben Wood complained about the problem, the State Council for Defense refused to investigate the practice. The council also declined to issue a general policy statement on the matter. Labor leaders were only slightly more successful when they reported the situation to federal authorities.[33]

Even more objectionable to labor leaders was the failure of many Missouri businesses to carry out the general wage-and-hour provisions announced by the Department of Labor, and in the case of war contractors, the refusal to fulfill the wage-and-hour provisions stipulated in their contracts. Many war contractors would also not bargain collectively with union organizations; some openly discriminated against union members. Indeed, the vigorous open-shop campaign, usually associated with the American Plan of the 1920s, began in Missouri shortly after American intervention in Europe. The organization of streetcar workers and the unionization of the meatpacking industry had provoked the various antiunion employers' associations of the state into a frenzied and uncompromising drive against organized labor. Employer belligerence, matched by an intensified militancy in the labor movement, ultimately threatened to bring Missouri's two largest cities to an economic standstill.[34]

The Kansas City General Strike

The climax of industrial unrest in Kansas City came in the early spring of 1918 when conflicts between labor and management caused a general strike that halted most economic activity for six days. It was essentially a sympathy strike that resulted from the city's laundry workers' and drivers' attempts to organize. Kansas City laundry

33. J. L. Hyatt to Arthur Holder, July 9, 1917; Gompers to Wines, July 9, 1917; Wood to Gompers, September 20, 1917, AFL, Papers, Series 117A, File 11A. *The Saint Joseph Union,* September 7, December 7, 1917. *Missouri Red Book, 1917,* p. 207. MSFL, *Proceedings, 1917,* pp. 80, 214, 215; *1918,* p. 87. Gompers to Wines, July 17, 1918, Gompers, Letterbooks.

34. George Orris and J. W. Williams to Gompers, April 19, 1918; William Reith to Gompers, March 19, 1918; James Anderson to W. B. Wilson, March 5, 1918; Alice Mary Kimball to Gompers, March 17, 1917 (1918?), AFL, Papers, Series 117A, File 11A.

owners had formed a Laundry Owners' Association, one of the functions of which was to prevent unionization. The leader of the Laundry Owners' Association, F. W. Porter, was also an influential member of the Kansas City Employers' Association. When the laundry workers' union failed to gain recognition, it went on strike in mid-February. The Employers' Association quickly responded by recruiting strikebreakers and a special strike police force that was accredited by the Kansas City Police Department. The arrival of the strikebreakers and special police soon led to skirmishes between striking workers and agents of the employers. The leadership of the Laundry Owners' Association steadfastly refused to meet with labor leaders or to accept any type of mediation or arbitration.[35]

The Industrial Relations Committee of the Jackson County Women's Committee and the Kansas City Council of National Defense conducted an investigation of the controversy and found that the average wage received by laundry workers varied from $4.50 to $6.00 per week and that working conditions were deplorable. Their report included the following description of the Fern Laundry, one of the largest in the city:

> horses were stabled in the basement, and the stench of the stable, mingled with steam, escaping gas, and bad air, permeated the half-lighted workrooms. Floors were wet, filth was everywhere, and toilets were in wretched shape. There were no restrooms and girl employes were eating lunch in vile and badly-ventilated workrooms. The building is a firetrap, and was condemned several years ago by city health authorities. No improvements have since been made. Probably no workers in the country labor under more unfavorable conditions than employes of this laundry.[36]

In an effort to weaken the union, the laundry owners offered to increase wages to $9 a week, but the striking workers refused. Organized labor in Kansas City viewed the situation as the initial campaign in a general offensive against organized labor by the Employers' Association. On March 4, the Board of Business Agents, an unofficial organization that wielded great influence in the Kansas City labor movement, called a general meeting of Kansas City labor organizations. A general strike was called for March 25 unless a satisfactory settlement could be reached.[37]

35. G. W. Addison to Wilson, March 16, 1918; Anderson to Wilson, March 5, 1918, *ibid.*

36. Addison to Wilson, March 16, 1918, *ibid.*

37. *Ibid.* Government mediator, Patrick Gill, apparently agreed with this assumption. He noted, "From what I can learn there is a certain element here which chooses to ignore the Department of Labor and fight out the issue of unionism. Kansas City has been chosen as the battleground." *The Kansas City Star,* March 29, 1918. Anderson to Wilson, March 5, 1918;

When the deadline arrived, the Board of Business Agents postponed the strike for forty-eight hours, hoping that a Kansas City minister would be accepted by the laundry owners as an arbitrator. The
Laundry Owners' Association, however, resolutely refused to arbitrate, and on March 27 the strike call was issued and respected by
most Kansas City trade unionists. The brewery workers immediately
closed Kansas City breweries. Construction work came to a halt as
the building trades unionists walked off their jobs. Unions of hotel
and restaurant employees, cooks, barbers, motion picture operators,
stage employees, and bakers also joined the strike. During the second
day of the dispute, the newly organized streetcar employees struck,
leaving the city without urban transportation. By the second day of
the strike, at least twenty-five thousand union laborers were on strike,
and although labor leaders requested that all workers in war-related
industries remain on the job, several factories working on government
contracts closed.[38]

Shortly after the strike call was issued, the National Guard began
patrolling the streets of Kansas City with bayonet-mounted rifles.
The Home Guard also mobilized, and all saloons closed in anticipation of serious rioting and violence. On March 30, W. D. Mahon, international president of the Amalgamated Association of Street and
Electric Railway Employees, arrived in Kansas City and immediately
began to force the Board of Business Agents into a more conciliatory
attitude by threatening to put his men back to work. At the same
time, Federal Mediator Patrick Gill organized a group of influential
Kansas City businessmen to bring pressure upon the Employers' Association and the Laundry Owners' Association to compromise. The
principal issues were the recognition of the laundry workers' union
and the restoration of contracts for those unions joining the sympathy
strike. The latter issue was especially important since the Employers'
Association, evidently hoping to make Kansas City an open-shop
area, argued that the strike voided all contracts and withdrew union
recognition.[39]

A compromise settlement proposed by Mayor George Edwards
was accepted as the basis for negotiations, although representatives
of the Employers' Association still refused to meet personally with
labor leaders. The final agreement did little for the laundry workers,

Addison to Wilson, March 16, 1918, AFL, Papers, Series 117A, File 11A.
The Labor Herald, March 22, 1918.

38. *The Labor Herald,* March 29, April 5, 1918. *The Kansas City Star,*
March 25, 26, 27, 1918. W. D. Mahon to Gompers, April 8, 1918, AFL,
Papers, Series 117A, File 11A. *St. Louis Labor,* April 6, 1918.

39. *The Labor Herald,* April 5, 1918. *St. Louis Labor,* April 6, 1918.
Mahon to Gompers, April 6, 8, 1918, AFL, Papers, Series 117A, File 11A.
The Kansas City Star, March 28, 31, April 1, 1918; March 26, 1918.

but it did restore union contracts. The Laundry Owners' Association agreed to settle on the following terms:

> We . . . agree to pay our female employes a minimum wage of $9 per week, and all employes receiving $9 or more per week an increase of $1 per week, excepting the salary and commission drivers.
> The above wage scale became effective February 19, 1918. We agree to reinstate all former employes, without discrimination, in their old positions, as vacancies occur, and provided those applying have not been guilty of engaging in violence or the destruction of our property.
> We further agree that we will give our old employes the preference under the above conditions.[40]

When employers compromised on the final issue, the wearing of union buttons, the strike ended. A few labor leaders, who admitted that the laundry workers had gained little, favored continuing the strike to gain recognition for the laundry workers' union. Their efforts failed when Mahon refused to cooperate. His threat to sign a separate agreement brought the strike to an end. The settlement almost blew up, however. Employers immediately violated the agreement by refusing to employ laborers wearing union buttons. The strike began again until the employers relented after a few hours of persuasion.[41] The unfortunate laundry workers, who had no effective organization to enforce their agreement, fared poorly. Two weeks after the strike, the editor of the *Labor Herald* reported that "the verbal promises made by the employers are not being lived up to . . . A walkout occurred at the Globe-Woodland Laundry when the girls, who had been promised a minimum of $9.00 per week found upon opening their pay envelope that the amount enclosed did not reach that figure. No girls were taken back at their old places and only a few of those who originally went out on strike are working in the local laundries."[42]

Sporadic strike activity continued in Kansas City through the summer and fall of 1918 but did not reach a serious crisis again until December. Shortly before Christmas, the streetcar employees went on strike demanding a wage increase. Their contracts had expired in September, and when the union and the Kansas City Railway

40. Bruce Forrester to George H. Edwards, n.d.; Adjustment Committee to Edwards, April 2, 1918, AFL, Papers, Series 117A, File 11A.
41. Mahon to Gompers, April 8, 1918, *ibid*.
42. *The Labor Herald*, April 19, 1918. The Kansas City general strike was the largest reported in the first two quarters of 1918. It was not, however, the only general strike that occurred during the war. There were also general sympathy strikes in Springfield (Illinois), Waco (Texas), and Billings (Montana). The Seattle General Strike occurred after the armistice. See the United States Department of Labor, Bureau of Labor Statistics, *Monthly Labor Review;* Alexander M. Bing, *War-Time Strikes and Their Adjustment*, p. 30.

Company failed to reach an agreement, the dispute was submitted to the War Labor Board for arbitration. The board recommended a wage increase to be financed by a small increase in fares.[43]

The Railway Company immediately increased fares from five to six cents, but it delayed increasing wages. By December the president of the Railway Company, P. J. Kealy, announced that the company could not afford to increase wages in the foreseeable future. Frank O'Shea, vice-president of the Amalgamated Association of Street and Electric Railway Employees of America, declared that he had discussed the situation with members of the War Labor Board and was told that the workers should insist that the company put the award into effect. He said that former President William Howard Taft had told him that "any corporation that exists by its own confession on the money that should go into wages of its employees isn't deserving of a place in any community." The streetcar employees voted to strike on December 11 and demanded the award that had been determined by the War Labor Board. While the union offered to accept Taft as a compulsory arbitrator, the company announced its intention to operate on the open-shop basis.[44]

The Kansas City Railway Company attempted to keep the cars running despite the strike, and for some unexplained reason, cars were operated by United States Army personnel for the first few days.[45] As a means of resolving the dispute, the Missouri Public Service Commission authorized the Railway Company to raise fares two cents, but the Kansas City Employers' Association, Kansas City Mayor Cowgill, and President Kealy of the Railway Company all opposed the fare increase, arguing that it would be detrimental to the city. Characteristic of his strong support for the company throughout the dispute, the Mayor refused to consider any fare increase and generally acceded to the wishes of the company concerning all aspects of the strike. Despite the generally peaceful nature of the strike, for example, he complied with the Employers' Association's request that the National Guard be called to ride the streetcars and protect company property.[46]

The union asked the War Labor Board to review the case and

43. *The Kansas City Times,* December 11, 1918.

44. *Ibid.,* December 12, 1918.

45. Gompers to Mahon, December 17, 1918, AFL, Papers, Series 117A, File 11A. There is no indication of where these soldiers came from or who authorized their use, but organized labor in Missouri experienced a great deal of discrimination and hostility from the United States Army during the war. See, for examples, Louis B. Wehle to Gompers, July 24, 1917; John T. Smith to Gompers, July 31, 1917; Williams to Gompers, April 6, 1917; Gompers to M. Cassidy, April 24, 1919, AFL, Papers, Series 117A, File 11A.

46. *The Kansas City Times,* December 12, 19, 28, 30, 1918; January 6, 1919.

arbitrate the dispute, but union leaders learned this action could not be taken during a strike. Consequently, the union voted to return to work under prestrike conditions, but the railway company locked out the strikers, and it soon became apparent that the War Labor Board did not have the power to enforce its award.[47]

The strike dragged on for several weeks, but a combination of forces, including the Missouri National Guard, the Kansas City municipal administration, and the Employers' Association, were too formidable for the union; the strike was lost and the union crushed. Kansas City labor leaders once again contemplated a general sympathy strike but in this instance decided against it. Once more it was the Employers' Association that had spearheaded the drive against union labor. Federal Conciliator James H. Dahn concluded that the strike could have been settled very quickly if the Employers' Association had not been intransigent. A few months after the strike ended, the Kansas City Railway Company took advantage of the authorization of the Missouri Public Service Commission and raised fares two cents without a corresponding increase in wages, much to the chagrin of Mayor Cowgill, who declared that he had been doublecrossed by the railway company.[48]

Labor Discontent in Saint Louis

In many respects industrial unrest was even more widespread in Saint Louis than in Kansas City. At one time during the war, between thirty thousand and fifty thousand workers were on strike.[49] During the first quarter of 1918, Saint Louis ranked second only to New York City in number of strikes. For the remainder of the year, Saint Louis ranked fourth in the number of strikes behind New York, Chicago, and Philadelphia. Wage increases and union recognition constituted the major issues in these disputes; employers, like those in Kansas City, were determined to stop union organization.[50]

47. Gompers to Mahon, December 20, 1918; Mahon to Gompers, December 21, 1918; Gompers to Mahon, December 21, 1918; Basil Manly to Gompers, December 23, 1918, AFL, Papers, Series 117A, File 11A. Gompers to C. B. Nelson, December 24, 1918, Gompers, Letterbooks. Lorwin, *The American Federation of Labor,* pp. 159–66. United States Department of Labor, *Report of the Secretary of the National War Labor Board,* pp. 11, 12.

48. *The Labor Herald,* December 28, 1918; August 8, 1919. *The Kansas City Times,* December 23, 1918.

49. Accurate statistics concerning the number of workers who took part in the strikes in Saint Louis were not located. Labor leaders estimated that thirty thousand union workers were on strike at one time, but not all strikers were union members, and it is difficult to estimate how many workers were laid off in associated industries because of the strikes. MSFL, *Proceedings, 1918,* p. 54.

50. United States Department of Labor, Bureau of Labor Statistics, *Monthly Labor Review,* pp. 207, 807, 808, 1842, 1843.

Problems at the Wagner Electric Company illustrated many of the issues involved in Saint Louis labor unrest, as well as the government's role in these skirmishes. Wagner Electric was an especially important wartime enterprise, holding several government contracts for the production of munitions. Company President Waldo A. Layman, a close associate of James Van Cleave, former president of the National Association of Manufacturers, strongly advocated the open shop and opposed any form of union organization.[51]

Contracts between the Wagner Electric Company and the War Department contained the usual clauses pertaining to the eight-hour day and the prevailing wage standard. Workers in the plant, however, claimed that the company ignored these contract obligations and worked its employees nine and ten hours a day without remuneration for overtime. They charged that wages were far below the union scale. In some instances women worked for fourteen to twenty cents an hour while the union scale for the same work was sixty cents.[52]

On March 6, 1918, thirty-five hundred employees of the Wagner Electric Company walked off their jobs, asking that the company fulfill its contract commitments with regard to hours and wages and demanding union recognition and collective bargaining.[53] Within a week after the outbreak of the strike, the War Department dispatched Maj. William C. Rogers to Saint Louis to assist Department of Labor Mediator Oscar C. Nelson in adjusting the problem. At a special meeting of the strikers, Major Rogers pledged that the Federal Government would ensure a just settlement of the controversy if the employees would first return to work. Rogers promised to notify

> Wm. A. Layman to cease his hostile attitude toward Union Labor and insist that he treat with his employes, and he would also instruct him to meet committees of employes and adjust differences that may exist or arise. Major Rogers also said warning would be given the firm to abstain from any discriminations against employes for holding membership in a union, and that if within thirty days a settlement was not reached he (Major Rogers) would personally take up the matter and see to it that the agreement be strictly lived up to and carried out; he would also adjust the wages, hours of labor and working conditions.[54]

Upon Rogers's assurances, the strikers returned to work. Nevertheless, it soon became obvious that Rogers was either unable or unwill-

51. David Kreyling to Gompers, September 19, 1917, AFL, Papers, Series 117A, File 11A. MSFL, *Proceedings, 1918,* p. 53. *St. Louis Star,* March 6, 1918. *St. Louis Labor,* March 16, 1918.

52. *St. Louis Labor,* March 16, 1918. MSFL, *Proceedings, 1918,* pp. 53, 54. *St. Louis Star,* March 7, 1918.

53. *St. Louis Labor,* March 16, 1918.

54. MSFL, *Proceedings, 1918,* p. 55.

ing to fulfill his pledges, and when the workers returned to their jobs, they discovered that the strike leaders and active unionists were not reemployed.[55] Everyone who was accepted for employment was required to sign a loyalty pledge containing the two following paragraphs:

> I further pledge myself to continue to be loyal in all respects to the Company; to do nothing in word or deed detrimental to the interests of the Company; and to acquaint you [Layman] promptly and personally with any information of a character hostile either to the United States Government or to the Company which may come into my possession.
>
> To this end, I hereby make application for enrollment as a member of the Volunteer Internal Reserve Guard of the Wagner Electric Manufacturing Company, and if accepted, hereby pledge myself to protect its property and interests to the best of my ability on all occasions.[56]

Although the War Department ordered the Wagner Electric Company to discontinue the practice of forcing employees to sign a loyalty pledge, other grievances remained.

The issues involved in this dispute typified the conflicts between labor and management that were growing increasingly serious in Saint Louis during the spring and summer of 1918.[57] Major Rogers, the War Department mediator, attempted to construct a general guideline defining the rights and privileges of both labor and management during the war. After several conferences with representatives of labor and employers, Rogers proposed a program of adjustment that quickly gained the endorsement of Saint Louis businessmen. He recommended that neither employers nor employees be discriminated against regarding union organization, and that neither labor nor management make any further attempt to change the *status quo* regarding labor organization. Changes of wages, hours, and conditions of labor should be secured as they had been in the past; workers who had not bargained collectively before the war would not be permitted to change their bargaining status during the war.[58] Rogers concluded

55. *St. Louis Labor,* May 4, 1918.
56. MSFL, *Proceedings, 1918,* pp. 56, 57, (The loyalty pledge is printed in full in the *Proceedings.*)
57. *Ibid.,* p. 57. Orris and Williams to Gompers, April 19, 1918, AFL, Papers, Series 117A, File 11A.
58. MSFL, *Proceedings, 1918,* p. 58. Rogers's justification for this provision revolved around a controversial statement Gompers was alleged to have made as a member of the Council of National Defense. Gompers's statement "advising that neither employers nor employees shall endeavor to take advantage of the country's necessities to change existing standards" was the subject

with a statement to the effect that acceptance of his proposal would be positive evidence of loyalty to the United States Government in its time of national crisis.[59]

Predictably, labor leaders rejected the proposal and offered an alternative method of ending strike activity in Saint Louis. They urged employers to recognize union organization where it existed and to bargain collectively with their employees. If satisfactory settlements could not be reached by this method, the dispute should be referred for mediation to the particular government agency it affected. If an agreement still could not be reached, a compulsory arbitration committee should be appointed that would consist of one representative each from labor and management and a third member who would be chosen by the other two. Labor leaders deeply resented the inference that they would be considered disloyal if they did not accept a proposal that would be detrimental to their interests.[60]

Labor leaders believed that their rejection of Rogers's proposal, in light of employers' acceptance of it, would alienate public support of the labor movement, so they immediately wrote President Wilson and Cabinet officials requesting that the National War Labor Board be convened in Saint Louis to investigate the causes of industrial unrest and then to mediate and arbitrate the differences between workers and their employers. When this proved impossible, a committee representing labor leaders from the Saint Louis Central Trades and Labor Union and the State Federation of Labor went to Washington to meet with pertinent government officials regarding industrial conditions in Saint Louis. After meetings with various agents of the War and Labor departments, several conditions creating industrial unrest in Saint Louis were adjusted. As a result of the conference, it was agreed that unions would be permitted to organize in previously open-shop establishments that held government contracts. The eight-hour day was recommended, and government officials pledged their assistance in carrying out these agreements. Furthermore, Major Rogers was relieved of any further responsibility for conditions in Saint Louis. Rogers had adopted an antagonistic attitude toward organized labor and had aligned himself with Saint Louis employers;

---

of considerable criticism by labor leaders in Missouri and throughout the nation. Gompers later argued that the statement was intended to mean "no lowering of present standards," and that it was not intended to preclude strikes during the war or to prevent organization and collective bargaining. Taft, *A. F. of L. in the Time of Gompers,* pp. 346, 347. Cassidy to Jeremiah T. Hurley, May 13, 1917; Gompers to Hurley, May 24, 1917, AFL, Papers, Series 117A, File 11A.

59. MSFL, *Proceedings, 1918,* p. 58.
60. *Ibid.,* pp. 60–62.

it probably came as no surprise to labor leaders when a few months later he accepted a position as vice-president of the Employers' Association.[61]

In July, 1918, the War Labor Board assumed jurisdiction of the remaining industrial disputes in Saint Louis; disputes involving several businesses that for years had led union opposition. The Board summoned twenty-three representatives of organized labor and eighteen employers. Labor leaders responded to the summons, but the employers sent lawyers who argued that the War Labor Board had no jurisdiction in the controversies. They likewise refused to allow examination of any of their records or account books. Nevertheless, the War Labor Board did assume jurisdiction and proceeded to hear testimony regarding industrial problems in Saint Louis.[62]

By late summer the strike situation in Saint Louis had become a major concern of government agencies responsible for war production and industrial relations. Felix Frankfurter of the War Labor Policies Board wrote Frederick N. Judson, a Saint Louis lawyer and alternate for William Howard Taft on the War Labor Board, that the "St. Louis industrial situation [is] exceedingly depressing to us and . . . calls for the promptest possible judgment." Frankfurter worried about the adjustment of wage rates in Saint Louis regarding the general policy of wage standardization advocated by the War Labor Policies Board. He asked Judson to use his influence with Saint Louis employers to "make them realize that while St. Louis is a large city, it is only part of the United States, and the guiding test of action must be not in St. Louis but the war."[63]

Nevertheless, the War Labor Board failed to arrive at any agreement regarding industrial relations in Saint Louis, and the industrial unrest continued in the city through the armistice and postwar periods. Moreover, it is unlikely that the industrial problems in Saint Louis would have been solved even if the War Labor Board had arrived at a decision. The board rarely used the legal authority available to it, but instead relied heavily upon "moral suasion" and public

61. Joseph E. Woracek to Gompers, April 15, 1918, AFL, Papers, Series 117A, File 11A. *St. Louis Star,* April 5, 1918. *St. Louis Labor,* April 13, 1918; April 26, 1919. *Missouri Red Book, 1918–1919,* pp. 878, 879. MSFL, *Proceedings, 1918,* pp. 63, 64.

62. These disputes involved several of organized labor's most bitter antagonists in Saint Louis, including the Wagner Electric Company, Koken Barbers' Supply Company, Rice-Stix Dry Goods Company, and the Kroger Grocery and Meat Company. These companies had long been considered "unfair" by Saint Louis Central Trades and Labor Union. MSFL, *Proceedings, 1918,* pp. 29, 46, 51, 66, 67. *Missouri Red Book, 1918–1919,* p. 879.

63. Frankfurther to Judson, August 2, 1918, War Labor Policies Board, Papers.

opinion for the enforcement of its awards. Saint Louis employers, such as Waldo Layman, had already proven themselves immune to such pressures, and their cavalier treatment of the War Labor Board provided little assurance that they would have obeyed its decisions.[64]

64. *St. Louis Labor,* November 2, 1918. United States Department of Labor, *Report of the Secretary of the National War Labor Board,* pp. 11, 12.

Chapter V

THE LABOR LOBBY
IN THE POSTWAR ERA

THROUGHOUT the war period, Missouri labor leaders worried about problems of readjustment after the war, and even before the November Armistice, the state labor movement began formulating a program of reconstruction. The proposal, written by William Kindorf, Socialist delegate from the Saint Louis Cigar Makers International Union, Local No. 44 and approved by the Saint Louis Central Trades and Labor Union, was adopted in September, 1918, at the Missouri State Federation Convention. It called for a compulsory and universal eight-hour day applicable to all public and private industries. Closely related was a minimum wage law that provided equal pay to both sexes and a wage scale high enough to "guarantee to the workers such necessaries and comforts as will assure them a decent American standard of living and with due allowance for such contingencies as sickness and old age." Foreseeing the possibility of an unemployment problem after the war, the program called for federal subsidies to local and state governments enabling them to provide productive work for all unemployed citizens. One of the important uses to which these subsidies were to be put was a system of urban renewal that would entail the demolition of old and unsanitary buildings and the construction of public housing for the working class.[1]

After the armistice was signed and peace negotiations had begun, the labor movement pragmatically expanded and amplified its postwar reconstruction proposals. In addition to the traditional demands for common ownership of public utilities they promoted the nationalization of the nation's railroads and coal mines. The State Federation expanded on its previous support of public housing to advocate low interest, government-guaranteed loans to promote private housing for the working classes. The labor movement also reiterated its support of a system of old-age pensions by pointing out that in countries like Great Britain, France, and Germany, such social reforms had been valuable.[2]

The labor movement, however, soon found that its hopes for a

1. *St. Louis Labor,* August 31, 1918. MSFL, *Proceedings, 1918,* pp. 121, 122.
2. *Ibid., 1921,* pp. 110, 111; *1918,* pp. 156, 157, 170.

comprehensive reconstruction program would be frustrated in the postwar era by the same hostility and intransigence in the political realm that it was already encountering on the economic front. Labor's only legislative accomplishments during the war and postwar period were the defeating of measures that the labor movement opposed. Besides the usual resistance to change, other circumstances frustrated labor's ambitions in the state legislature. During the years following the war, the legislative assemblies often were controlled by one party and the administration by the other, or the Senate was controlled by one party and the House by its opposition. This situation further distracted the state legislature, which did not function very efficiently even under ideal conditions, and labor legislation often suffered. Meanwhile, the labor movement had serious internal conflicts that compromised the effectiveness of the labor lobby. Finally, organized labor's increased militancy, which had both an economic and political expression, seriously subordinated labor's lobbying activities to other, more urgent concerns.

A bill requiring the city of Saint Joseph to establish two shifts for fire fighters was the only proposal originated by the labor movement that became law during the 1919 session of the General Assembly. A scaffold bill requiring more stringent safety requirements in the building trades passed in the House but did not get on the Senate calendar. A similar fate befell an eight-hour law for women and a miner's bathhouse bill, which was passed by the House by a vote of 114 to 3. Labor successfully opposed bills to establish a state constabulary, to abolish the state primary law, and to require compulsory arbitration of all labor disputes of employees of common carriers. Labor's greatest efforts during the session, however, were devoted to the passage of a workmen's compensation law.[3]

During the 1917 session of the General Assembly, a compensation bill had passed in the House but died in the Senate. Differences of opinion occurred within the labor movement concerning the provisions of the 1917 law, so a special conference was held in October, 1918, to consider amendments that would make the bill acceptable to all labor organizations. At the same time, the State Federation employed as its chief legal counselor, Alroy S. Phillips, a former state senator and one of the state's leading authorities on workmen's compensation.[4]

Workmen's compensation was a major issue in determining the organizational structure of the 1919 General Assembly, and the legislative committee expressed satisfaction with the appointments that

3. *Ibid., 1920,* pp. 91–95.
4. Ruth W. Towne, "The Movement for Workmen's Compensation Legislation in Missouri, 1910–1925," pp. 1–8. *The Labor Herald,* January 10, 1919. MSFL, *Proceedings, 1920,* pp. 24, 25.

were made by the Republican House. The Speaker and a majority of the members of the workmen's compensation committee endorsed the proposed labor bill. Labor was not so fortunate in the structuring of the Democratic-controlled Senate, where the president pro-tem sponsored the employers' version of the compensation bill.[5]

The House accepted the labor bill without crippling amendments and passed it by a vote of 105 to 12. Prior to this action by the House, the Senate Committee on Workmen's Compensation failed to hold hearings on a companion bill that was introduced in the Senate. Although a majority of the Senate committee assured the labor representatives that the House bill would be reported favorably, the labor lobbyists became suspicious of the committee's continued dilatory tactics. Earlier in the session, both houses had adopted a joint rule stipulating that after April 18 any bill passed by one body in the legislature would not be considered by the other. Labor representatives feared that the Senate committee might be pursuing the tactics used in 1917 of not reporting a bill until the end of the session and then substituting an unacceptable version.[6]

As the committee continued to delay its report, President Wood of the State Federation began to doubt the sincerity of Sen. Conway Elder of Saint Louis, who had promised to support the labor bill. A union delegation from Elder's district met with him and urged him to vote for the House bill. He assured the delegates of his continued support of the labor bill. A week later, on April 16, two days before the deadline for passing new legislation, the Senate committee considered the House bill and rejected it by a vote of four to three. Elder voted with the majority. A substitute bill that had been written by the Employers' Association was then reported, and an attempt on the floor of the Senate to overrule the committee's recommendation to reject labor's bill was defeated by five votes.[7]

By noon of the 17th, the legislative committee, after carefully studying the employers' bill, decided to support it despite lower compensation payments and the substitution of private insurance for state insurance.[8] The legislative committee seemed to be heeding the counsel of AFL President Gompers who had written Wood:

> See to it during this session you get the principle established and do not allow technical controversies of legal hair-splitters to

5. *Ibid.,* p. 85. Towne, "Movement for Workmen's Compensation," p. 67.

6. MSFL, *Proceedings, 1920,* p. 85. *St. Louis Post-Dispatch,* February 24, 1919.

7. *St. Louis Post-Dispatch,* April 17, 1919. MSFL, *Proceedings, 1920,* p. 86.

8. Gompers to R. T. Wood, January 4, 1917, Gompers, Letterbooks. MSFL, *Proceedings, 1920,* p. 86.

deflect you from your course this time. Bear in mind that no initial legislation of that kind in any State or in any country was ever perfect to commence with. Neither will you at first succeed in obtaining the enactment of a perfect measure. But after you obtain legislation establishing the justice of the principle that industry should bear the burden of industrial accidents and that the State should administer the law you will soon find from experience what provisions of the law are weak and what should be repealed or what should be added.[9]

The opponents of workmen's compensation assumed their tactics would kill that bill for the session, so the labor lobby's opportunistic action took them completely by surprise. Sen. W. W. Green, for example, as a member of the Senate compensation committee, supported the substitute bill but, as chairman of the calendar committee, refused to schedule the bill on the calendar. His committee then passed a resolution requiring a two-thirds vote before a measure could be added to the calendar. Only after the presiding officer of the Senate threatened to discharge the calendar committee was the bill listed on the Senate calendar. The bill then passed in the Senate and in the House.[10]

The State Federation's support of the substitute bill once again split the labor movement. The Kansas City and Saint Louis central labor unions, led by the building trades, opposed any compensation measure that did not provide for state insurance. They also argued that the low rate of compensation discriminated against the better-paid workers in the building trades. Dissident labor leaders soon began circulating petitions at union meetings that called for having the law referred to a vote of the general electorate.[11]

In an attempt to unite the labor movement before the November elections, Wood met with representatives of Associated Industries, an employers' association representing numerous manufacturers in Missouri, to reach an agreement for improving the compensation law. Associated Industries also opposed the unsatisfactory and often expensive legal procedures that were necessary before injury claims could be settled. As a result of the conference, the two organizations signed a contract stipulating that both parties cooperate to amend

9. Gompers to Wood, January 4, 1917, Gompers, Letterbooks.

10. *St. Louis Post-Dispatch,* April 17, 19, 1919. MSFL, *Proceedings, 1920,* pp. 88, 89.

11. *The Labor Herald,* August 15, 1919. *St. Louis Post-Dispatch,* April 23, 29, 1919. *The Missouri Mule,* August 16, 1919. Minutes of Local Union No. 6, Brewers and Maltsters, Saint Louis, July 13, 1919. To subject a measure to a referendum election, petitions containing the signatures of 5 per cent of the legal voters in two-thirds of the congressional districts had to be filed within sixty days of the end of the session of the General Assembly.

the 1919 law at the following legislative session. There were nineteen suggested amendments, the net effect of which provided for competitive state insurance and raised compensation rates by one-third. The agreement further stipulated that if the law were defeated in the 1920 elections, the proposed amendments would be written into a new law to be introduced jointly during the Fifty-first General Assembly.[12]

The agreement not only caused division among the employers but also failed to heal the breach in the ranks of labor. Incensed over the contract agreement, the Kansas City employers broke with Associated Industries and formed their own organization, the Kansas City Employers' Association. Charles M. Miller, representative of the association, angrily declared that "Associated Industries was tied by the State Federation of Labor both hands and feet. I have not heard it claimed by the sponsors of the contracts for the Associated Industries that anything was derived or benefit obtained from these contracts 'except an act at any price.'" He argued that the contracts would "place on the employer of Missouri the highest workmen's compensation act now in force in any of the other states." Although the amendments eliminated all their objections to the legislation except compulsory state insurance, the agreement still failed to satisfy metropolitan labor leaders. When a motion to endorse the agreement was made at an October meeting of the State Federation's local nonpartisan campaign committees, representatives from Saint Louis and Kansas City refused to discuss workmen's compensation and walked out of the meeting.[13]

The law failed in the general election by 30,000 votes out of more than 700,000 cast. Although the Saint Louis vote was close, the majority voted in favor of the proposition, and Kansas City voters approved the measure three to one. The law was defeated, however, because of opposition in the rural areas, where many farmers believed they would be responsible for supporting, for life, any farm laborers they hired who were injured on the job.[14]

A resolution passed by the Kansas City Central Labor Union reveals the bitterness of the intraunion fight. The resolution "condemned and denounced" the editor of the oldest and most respected labor newspaper in Kansas City, Thomas H. West of the *Labor Herald,* for his support of the workmen's compensation law. Mean-

12. MSFL, *Proceedings, 1920,* p. 29; *1921,* pp. 77–81. *The Labor Herald,* October 22, 1920.
13. "Remarks by Charles M. Miller," December 7, 1920, Arthur M. Hyde, Papers. Ernest Sweeney to Hyde, January 5, 1921; Hyde to Sweeney, January 13, 1921; Bruce Forrester to Hyde, December 28, 1920, Arthur M. Hyde, Papers. MSFL, *Proceedings, 1921,* pp. 77, 78.
14. *The Labor Herald,* November 19, 1920. *Official Manual, 1921–1922,* pp. 476, 477.

while, the editor of the *Missouri Mule,* a new labor paper sponsored by the Kansas City Central Labor Union, accused West of being anti-labor and darkly hinted that he was involved in advertising frauds, as well as being guilty of illegally soliciting funds in the name of labor. West recognized the irony of being "denounced and condemned" for supporting the policies of the AFL and the State Federation of Labor, of which the Kansas City Central was a subordinate affiliate.[15]

Another reflection of the split within labor's membership was the fact that four compensation bills were introduced in the 1921 session of the General Assembly; the highest benefits were proposed by the Kansas City Central Labor Union and the lowest by the Kansas City Employers' Association. The Saint Louis Central Trades introduced the third bill corresponding closely to the original labor proposal of 1919 and quite similar to the fourth bill—the compromise proposal agreed to by the State Federation and Associated Industries. The bill sponsored by the Saint Louis group had compulsory state insurance, whereas the compromise bill provided for competitive state insurance. The Saint Louis unions agreed to support the compromise bill if compulsory state insurance were added, but Wood, unable to convince the representatives of Associated Industries to accept the change, felt honorbound to support the compromise bill as it stood.[16]

The compromise bill became the focal point of debate over compensation legislation, with most of the opposition coming from Kansas City labor and employers. Frank Peterson and Charles Nelson of the Kansas City labor movement told legislators that the compromise bill "cooked up by the insurance companies and the employers' association and swallowed by Rube Wood, is objectionable to our membership." They charged that Wood had sold out to the employers and that "labor had rejected his leadership." Conversely, the Kansas City Employers' Association argued that the compromise bill was unacceptable because its benefits were higher than those of neighboring states and it contained a provision for socialistic, competitive state insurance.[17]

15. Wilford R. Sears, "The Kansas City Building Trades and Trade Unionism," pp. 95–101. Thomas H. West to Gompers, November 22, 1920, Gompers, Letterbooks. *The Missouri Mule,* October 4, November 20, 1920. C. B. Nelson to Gompers, December 1, 1920, Gompers, Letterbooks. *The Labor Herald,* November 20, 1920.

16. MSFL, *Proceedings, 1921,* pp. 98, 99. *St. Louis Post-Dispatch,* February 24, 1921. Wood did not try very hard to convince the representatives of the employers to accept the labor-sponsored bill. He felt that if the discussions were reopened, labor risked losing what it had gained from the agreement. See Wood to Phillips, December 30, 1920, Alroy S. Phillips, Papers.

17. *The Missouri Mule,* January 15, 28, February 19, 1921. *St. Louis Post-Dispatch,* January 7, 1921.

The denunciation of Wood and the State Federation's legislative committee became so bitter that several state legislators questioned the State Federation's authority to speak for labor. Wood complained that "even our friends in the House and Senate seemed to begin to think that we were insincere." The embattled legislative committee was so afraid of being misquoted that it found it necessary to hire a court stenographer to record its testimony before various committees.[18]

In this atmosphere of division and distrust, two other bills that labor vehemently opposed made progress through the General Assembly. One, the McCullough–Bennett bill, outlawed strikes and provided for the establishment of an industrial court with authority to arbitrate all labor disputes. Sponsored by the Manufacturers' Association and modeled after the Kansas Industrial Court, the bill received a favorable committee report and had gone through the second reading. The second bill, introduced in the House by W. L. Vandeventer, gave justices of the peace the powers of a grand jury and forbade subpoenaed witnesses to reveal that they had testified, under penalty of a heavy fine and a maximum three-month jail sentence. The bill was obviously designed primarily for use against strikes.[19]

In an effort to stop this legislation and to promote unity within the labor movement, the legislative committee attended a February meeting of the Saint Louis Central Trades and Labor Union, explained the seriousness of the situation, and successfully promoted a motion to encourage union secretaries to write their representatives in the House and Senate to urge them to protest the passage of adverse legislation and to reaffirm the legislative committee's authority to speak for organized labor. The unity move succeeded. As letters poured into Jefferson City from Saint Louis and throughout the state, the legislative committee's influence grew steadily until the end of the session. The McCullough–Bennett bill lost by a substantial majority on its third reading, and the Vandeventer bill died in the House. Meanwhile, the compromise workmen's compensation bill passed along with a child labor law, although the intent of the latter was severely damaged by amendments. Here labor's momentum ended. A scaffold bill, a bathhouse bill for miners, and an eight-hour law for women all failed in the Senate.[20]

Missouri labor's temporary show of unity ended when the legislative session adjourned. Divisions over workmen's compensation continued and dominated the annual convention of the State Federation

18. MSFL, *Proceedings, 1921,* p. 111.
19. *Ibid.*
20. *Ibid.,* pp. 87–89, 112, 113. Harriet Robertson to Hyde, April 13, 1921, Arthur M. Hyde, Papers.

meeting in the spring of 1921. Wood described the disastrous effects of the split in his annual report:

> I take this opportunity of informing the delegates to this conven-
> tion, in my humble opinion, the State Federation of Labor can
> ill afford to continue waging such a bitter fight at each succeeding
> session of the Legislature. Considering the time devoted by the
> officers of the Federation, in addition to the contributions received
> from the affiliated Unions, no less than $50,000 has been spent
> in the last nine years by the organized workers for the enactment
> of an adequate workmen's compensation law. Nearly all of our
> other important legislation presented to the legislature affecting
> one trade or another, had to be sacrificed, owing to the fact that
> the Legislative Committee could not find time, aside from its duties
> in the bitter battle for a compensation law that has been waged
> in each session of the Legislature, to devote the proper energy to
> any other legislation, always realizing that a Workmen's Compen-
> sation law was of far greater importance than the enactment of
> any other measure.
> The dissension caused in our ranks by this fight has had a most
> demoralizing effect on the progress of the Labor Movement of this
> State. We cannot continue this indefinitely, lest we want to see
> our movement disrupted and destroyed.[21]

Convention debate centered around a resolution that would endorse the compromise compensation law. Perhaps the most vocal
champion of the compromise was David Frampton, organizer for the
United Mine Workers. His international union had sent him to Missouri to support the law. "Our organization has spent thousands of
dollars for the propaganda for and the passage of such a law, and
having gained the first decisive victory along these lines we are not
inclined to permit the opponents to bring about the defeat by means
of the referendum. Papers pretending to represent union labor, like
the sheet called 'Missouri Mule,' have openly and willfully misrepre-
sented our movement and are, in my opinion, a disgrace to the Labor
Movement."[22]

The resolution was accepted by a substantial majority. By a
smaller margin, the *Missouri Mule* was censured. With delegate
voting majorities firmly in hand, the convention officers went on to
chastise any affiliated organization or member of the State Federation
that deliberately opposed the policies of the Federation as outlined
in convention sessions. Such behavior would subject the perpetrator
to suspension from the Federation unless the action had the approval
of national or international unions. Nevertheless, Frank Peterson of

21. Wood to Phillips, May 31, 1921, Alroy S. Phillips, Papers. MSFL, *Proceedings, 1921,* p. 87.
22. *Ibid.,* pp. 139, 140.

the Kansas City Building Trades Council, still defiant, warned the delegates, "you may resolute as long as you please in this convention, we are going to bring this law to a referendum vote."[23]

The dissidents carried the conflict all the way to the national convention of the AFL in July, but they lost there also. Opposed only by Charles Nelson of the Kansas City Central Labor Union, a resolution passed endorsing the Missouri compensation law and urging its enactment. AFL Vice-President William Green, considered the organization's authority on such legislation, expressed his astonishment "that any delegate to the convention should have the hardihood to arise in his place and defend the abrogation of such a law."[24]

Nonetheless, the Kansas City Central Labor Union refused to be silenced, and along with the Kansas City Employers' Association and lawyers who profited from personal-injury suits, successfully led a petition campaign for a referendum on the workmen's compensation bill. The Building Trades Council of Saint Louis and the Saint Louis Central Trades and Labor Union both supported the 1921 bill and urged their members not to sign referendum petitions. In the referendum held during the 1922 elections, Missouri voters again rejected the workmen's compensation law.[25]

In 1923, the State Federation failed to get another workmen's compensation bill enacted. Realizing that unity on the issue must first be achieved within labor's ranks, the officers of the State Federation called a conference of all affiliated central labor districts and councils of the metal and building trades' unions to draft a workmen's compensation bill that would be satisfactory to all Missouri labor organizations. The conference produced an extremely liberal law that included all the provisions advocated by organized labor. Even the abrasive Kansas City labor leaders found it impossible to oppose the measure. The conferees agreed to put the proposal on the ballot by initiative petition and levied a special State Federation assessment of ten cents per member to finance the effort. A large portion of this money was used for the circulation of petitions in rural areas and in Kansas City's Fifth District where opposition was previously the strongest. Despite the unity conference, Kansas City labor remained a problem. Officials of the Kansas City Central Labor Union and the Building Trades Council, who had opposed previous bills because the terms were not liberal enough, made no effort to circulate the initiative petitions. This inactivity reaffirmed the assumption of many state labor leaders that Kansas City labor officials simply op-

23. *Ibid.,* pp. 139, 140, 142, 143, 148, 149.

24. *Ibid., 1922,* p. 94. *The Labor Herald,* July 1, 1921.

25. MSFL, *Proceedings, 1921,* p. 85. Towne, "Movement for Workmen's Compensation," pp. 147–52. *The Labor Herald,* May 13, 1921. *St. Louis Labor,* May 14, 1921. *Official Manual, 1923–1924,* pp. 281, 282.

posed any compensation measure.[26] Nevertheless, the State Federation succeeded in getting the proposal on the ballot, but it was defeated in the general election of 1924 by a margin of three to one. Wood could not resist an "I told you so" after the election:

> The experience we received in the campaign in our efforts to secure the enactment of a workmen's compensation law through the initiative, with provisions so much higher than any of the 42 states that have such legislation on their statutes, as to place it in the category of a radical law in the minds of the great majority of the voters of the state, should be a lesson to the members of the Federation.
>
> There is as much lack of sense and good judgement in trying to put through a law of that kind as there is in a newly organized union, when negotiating their first wage agreement to attempt to secure a much higher rate of wages than is received by an old established organization in the same line of occupation.[27]

In the 1925 session of the General Assembly, the legislative committee of the State Federation changed its tactics. Instead of introducing a bill of its own, the committee waited until the employers initiated a proposal and then proposed amendments to it to create a satisfactory law. The tactic succeeded, and the House and Senate together accepted a sufficient number of amendments to make the bill satisfactory to the labor lobby.[28]

Even though the compensation bill was passed by the legislature, it still faced a great deal of opposition. In contrast to earlier efforts, however, the 1925 bill was endorsed by such varied organizations as the Missouri Bankers' Association, Missouri Farmers' Association, Associated Industries, Industrial Employers of Missouri, Missouri Farm Bureau Federation, Missouri Press Association, Missouri Retail Merchants Association, and Norman Thomas's League for Industrial Democracy, which matched all money raised from union sources for the referendum campaign.[29]

Thus encouraged, organized labor conducted a vigorous campaign for an affirmative vote in the general election. Help also came from outside. AFL President William Green wrote newspaper articles, delivered speeches, made radio broadcasts in Saint Louis and Kansas

26. *The Labor Herald,* August 24, 31, 1923; March 27, September 28, 1924. MSFL, *Proceedings, 1926,* pp. 13, 14. Phillips to John B. Andrews, Alroy S. Phillips, Papers. Charles Sumner to Gompers, December 6, 1920; W. E. Bryan to Gompers, December 4, 1920, Gompers, Letterbooks.

27. MSFL, *Proceedings, 1926,* pp. 12, 13. *Official Manual, 1925–1926,* pp. 421, 422.

28. MSFL, *Proceedings, 1926,* pp. 47–49. Phillips to Wood, December 13, 1924, Alroy S. Phillips, Papers.

29. Norman Thomas to Phillips, July 9, 1926; Phillips to Thomas, July 13, 1926, Alroy S. Phillips, Papers. *The Labor Herald,* October 15, 1926.

City, and attempted to persuade obstinate Kansas City labor leaders to support the law. An AFL-produced motion picture was shown that depicted the advantages of workmen's compensation. At the same time the State Federation sent speakers into every county, and union locals distributed literature urging support of the bill. As a result of this zealous campaigning, voters finally approved the workmen's compensation law in the 1926 general election by an overwhelming margin. Thomas West of the *Labor Herald,* ran the simple but explicatory headline, "AT LAST."[30]

The struggle, however, had been expensive. For more than a decade, workmen's compensation consumed the major energies of labor lobbyists in Missouri, and in the process, numerous other bills of interest to labor received secondary priority. Practical labor leaders believed the espousal of more controversial reforms to be idealistic until a workmen's compensation bill was passed. Moreover, besides seriously dividing the labor movement, the campaign cost the financially insecure State Federation more than $100,000.

Was workmen's compensation worth all of the time, energy, and money expended? Nearly a decade later, after several frustrated attempts to strengthen the law, President Wood told State Federation convention delegates that if the law was not soon strengthened, the labor movement should introduce legislation to repeal it. Thus, the law apparently had not worked as labor leaders had hoped or expected. Nevertheless, a study of the campaign for a workmen's compensation system in Missouri fails to support the argument that business interests had deceived labor into accepting a reform program through which injury claims would be limited and workers would be forced to contribute to industrial accident insurance funds. Indeed, while considerable support for a workmen's compensation system existed among business groups, organized labor clearly assumed the leadership in the campaign for a workmen's compensation system. Highly skilled, well-organized workers, of course, needed such legislation much less than poor, unskilled workers; and the opposition that did exist within the labor movement consisted of strong unions that had been able to individually negotiate agreements with employers covering industrial accidents and business agents profiting from the referral of damage-suit cases to law offices. The poor, ignorant, and unskilled worker could least afford a lengthy court action and was most likely to be unaware of the legal procedures involved. Moreover, the opposition to workmen's compensation in the General

30. Green to F. J. Peterson, September 22, November 2, 1925, William Green, Letterbooks. *The Labor Herald,* January 8, February 5, 12, September 10, October 8, 15, 29, November 5, 1926. *St. Louis Labor,* July 24, October 30, 1926. *The Kansas City Star,* October 21, 1926. *Official Manual, 1927–1928,* pp. 292, 293.

Assembly was predominantly composed of the same legislators who consistently opposed other labor legislation. Meanwhile, compensation legislation received considerable support from rural legislators, who in other cases exhibited little inclination to further the legislative goals of the business community. In any case, labor leaders viewed the measure as a constructive social reform that would provide immediate succor to injured workers and their families.[31]

The labor lobby's experience with workmen's compensation legislation illustrated the great difficulty that reformers in Missouri encountered when they sought to enact substantial and meaningful reform legislation. On the other hand, labor was almost always successful in defeating measures it opposed. The labor lobby successfully led the opposition to the establishment of an industrial court for the compulsory arbitration of labor disputes and a state constabulary, which labor leaders felt would be used to coerce striking workers. The state primary law and the initiative and referendum procedures were successfully defended while the initiation of a state sales tax was defeated.

Thus for the state labor movement, the postwar era was, for the most part, a period of legislative *status quo*. Labor neither achieved very much nor lost anything. Nevertheless, industrial change continued and, if the state's working class did not progress too, it would fall behind. As a result of this legislative inertia in the state's General Assembly, many Missouri labor leaders began to question the state legislature's willingness or ability to deal effectively on the local level with the changing social and economic realities of twentieth-century America.

31. MSFL, *Proceedings, 1935*, p. 20. See James Weinstein, "Big Business and the Origins of Workmen's Compensation," pp. 156–74. Roy Lubove, "Workmen's Compensation and the Prerogatives of Voluntarism," pp. 254–79. Cf. Robert F. Wesser, "Conflicts and Compromise: The Workmen's Compensation Movement in New York, 1890s–1913," pp. 345–72. See *The Saint Joseph Union*, April 27, 1917. *Railway Federationist*, July 6, 1917. Minutes of Local Union No. 6, Brewers and Maltsters, Saint Louis, Missouri, February 9, April 13, 1919. *The Kansas City Star*, January 13, 1917.

Chapter VI

FRUSTRATION AND
THIRD-PARTY POLITICS

LABOR LEADERS carried on "business as usual" during the biennial sessions of the General Assembly, but labor's experiences during and immediately after the war fueled an increasingly militant and radical attitude. The inability to attain desired legislation and the failure of executive officials to administer existing labor laws vigorously were both seen as the product of labor's faulty political strategy. Exasperated with the seeming futility of nonpartisan political tactics, state labor leaders committed themselves to the search for a fundamentally new political strategy.

From the union leaders' viewpoint, the nonpartisan tactic had not only failed to unify labor for political purposes but also led to numerous conflicts within the movement. Both leaders and members seemed more inclined to continue older partisan loyalties than to make a realistic assessment of labor's friends and enemies without regard to party affiliation. A prominent Saint Louis labor leader clearly recognized this problem during a debate on political strategy at a State Federation of Labor convention. "We fools have never yet learned to vote together in one way. We talk one way in our meetings and conventions and then go out and vote another way."[1]

There were numerous instances of labor leaders, labor editors, and local union members allowing partisan political preferences to take precedence over their labor union affiliations, and traditional political practices contributed to conflicts within the labor movement in still other important ways. The compromises that were necessary to make the labor movement function realistically within the existing party system often caused acrimony. The long and divisive campaign for a workmen's compensation law illustrated the problem, so did organized labor's attempt to endorse a gubernatorial candidate in 1920. Arthur Hyde, candidate for the Republican gubernatorial nomination, appeared before a meeting of the Joint Conference of Non-partisan Political Committees of the State Federation of Labor and the legislative representatives of the four independent railroad brotherhoods in July, 1920. After responding satisfactorily to most of the committee's questions, he agreed to write the secretary of the State Federa-

1. *St. Louis Labor*, September 22, 1917.

94

tion reiterating his position on several points that were vital to labor. On July 22, the State Federation received a letter from Hyde endorsing the organization's legislative goals, collective bargaining, and the use of the strike as a legitimate means of redressing grievances. Hyde also declared his intention to appoint representatives from the unions to important posts that could affect the interests of labor. His only objectionable position was his frank, unequivocal support of prohibition.[2]

Upon receiving Hyde's statement, the executive committee of the State Federation endorsed his candidacy in the Republican primary, but this support was promptly denounced by the central labor unions of Saint Louis and Kansas City. The unions in the metropolitan areas were supporting Hyde's Republican opponent, E. E. E. McJimsey, a Springfield newspaper publisher, because they considered him a liberal on the prohibition question. McJimsey represented the conservative wing of the Republican party, whereas Hyde had been a "Bull Mooser" in 1912 and had supported the Progressive party until 1916. After his defeat in the primary, McJimsey exposed his own reactionary frame of mind by blaming his defeat on progressive Republicans and the "socialistic" *Kansas City Star*.[3]

The split within labor's ranks widened after the primary. In the general elections, the two metropolitan central unions supported the Democratic nominee, John M. Atkinson, while State Federation officials backed Hyde. The Democratic nominee had opposed workmen's compensation legislation; because of this transgression, the executive board of the State Federation, the railroad brotherhoods, and the United Mine Workers resolutely refused to support him. The Kansas City and Saint Louis unions selected their candidate solely on the basis of his stance on prohibition.[4]

In seeking an alternative to traditional and often fratricidal political tactics, labor leaders looked especially to the examples provided by the North Dakota Non-Partisan League and the British Labour Party. Many Missouri labor leaders believed that a political and economic alliance between the farmers and workers of the state would be invincible. Envisioning such an alliance, C. G. Brittingham, of the Brotherhood of Locomotive Engineers, told the delegates of the State Federation they could learn something from the farmers of North Dakota. "Brothers, this is one of the great issues which will interest the workers and the farmers 'after this war, and we might as well prepare for it. Without our own political organization, without

2. MSFL, *Proceedings, 1921,* pp. 64–66.

3. *Ibid.,* pp. 67–70. *The Missouri Mule,* May 22, July 31, 1920. James L. Lowe, "The Administration of Arthur M. Hyde, Governor of Missouri, 1921–1925," pp. 8–10, 13–22.

4. MSFL, *Proceedings, 1921,* pp. 72–74. *St. Louis Labor,* May 17, 1919.

our own political independence, we shall not be able to solve the great problems that will confront us after the war."[5]

Shortly after the war, the State Federation, in cooperation with the four independent railroad brotherhoods, launched a movement to create such an alliance. They held meetings of farmers and workers in cities and towns throughout the state, but few farmers attended. Still enjoying wartime prosperity, Missouri farmers did not seem particularly interested in a political farmer–labor alliance.[6]

Efforts to promote farmer–labor cooperation in economic affairs were somewhat more successful. The promoters hoped to see producer and consumer cooperatives organized in most of Missouri's larger cities. The Sedalia cooperative, one of the earliest, engaged "in a general mercantile business including buying and selling, manufacturing, storage, transportation, handling or dealing in agricultural, dairy and similar products and to promote cooperation with producers on the farm." Sedalia trade unionists had established the cooperative to counter antiunion activity of employers. When a local garment manufacturer locked out his unionized employees and refused to bargain collectively, the unions established a large producer cooperative to compete with him.[7] One of the more ambitious cooperative ventures began in Springfield when six thousand representatives of the Springfield trade unions and the Greene County Farmers' Association met and voted to establish a cooperative store with an initial capital of $100,000. The cooperative sold groceries, hardware, dry goods, shoes, women's ready-to-wear goods, fuel, and other consumer items. The Kansas City Cooperative Society was incorporated under Missouri law with capital of $50,000. Shortly after the Saint Louis Central Trades formally endorsed the cooperation principle, individual unions, trades, and the Socialists opened several cooperatives around the city. By the autumn of 1920, with numerous cooperative organizations around the state, the State Federation inaugurated a state convention of all cooperative associations and societies to promote intrastate cooperation among such organizations. For similar reasons, the State Federation actively participated in the Cooperative Interstate Convention held in Fort Scott, Kansas.[8]

Labor's interest and involvement in the cooperative movement was evidence of organized labor's growing class consciousness. In or-

5. *St. Louis Labor,* September 22, 1917.

6. *The Saint Joseph Union,* March 21, 28, 1919. *Railway Federationist,* February 8, 15, 1919.

7. *Railway Federationist,* February 1, 8, September 29, 1919.

8. Wilford R. Sears, "The Kansas City Building Trades and Trade Unionism," pp. 135, 136. *St. Louis Labor,* January 31, March 20, June 26, November 27, 1920; February 5, August 13, 1921. MSFL, *Proceedings, 1920,* pp. 96, 97.

ganizing cooperatives, the Rockdale principle was adopted—membership was restricted to members of the working class, and the number of shares an individual could buy was limited.[9] Nevertheless, despite the great vigor with which it was initially pursued, the cooperative movement was almost as ephemeral as the farmer–labor political alliance. Although little evidence remains to explain their failure, most of the cooperatives apparently went bankrupt during the 1921–1922 depression.

Toward a Third Party

Although they were interested in some form of independent political action, the state labor movement found no acceptable alternative to the usual nonpartisan tactics to pursue in the 1920 elections. The speeches and debates resounding throughout the convention hall of the State Federation meeting in the spring of that year, however, reflected the dissatisfied and pessimistic mood of the labor movement. President Wood, in his annual report, told the delegates that there were only two methods of remedying the deplorable condition of the nation:

One is a bloody revolution, which has for its purpose the complete elimination of the present capitalistic system. The other and sane way is to elect to the National Congress a sufficient number of men who will join with the small minority now in the Congress and Senate who will impeach two-thirds of the Supreme Court judges, curb the arbitrary law-making power which has been assumed by the Supreme Court, and who will actually legislate in the interest of the people instead of acting in the capacity of tools and lackeys of Big Business, as is being done by the majority of the members of the National Congress of today.[10]

After a vigorous debate on politics and the difficulty in gaining meaningful labor reforms, the convention delegates passed a resolution declaring that:

We can no longer trust to the two political parties now in control of the legislative and executive machinery of our country the protection of our rights or the maintenance of our liberties, upon their mere promise to serve us. They have proved recant to their trust; they have forfeited their right to the support of Organized Labor.[11]

In some Missouri cities, labor leaders acted more forcefully to obtain better representation. Springfield workers sponsored a labor ticket in the 1920 municipal elections, while in Kansas City, inde-

9. Sears, "Kansas City Building Trades," pp. 135, 136. *St. Louis Labor,* January 31, 1920. *Railway Federationist,* September 29, 1919.
10. MSFL, *Proceedings, 1920,* p. 43.
11. *Ibid.,* p. 160.

pendent labor tickets appeared in municipal elections of both 1918 and 1920. Although third-party movements were not introduced in other Missouri cities, workers took an active role in party primaries and attempted either to nominate union members for public office or to receive positive assurances that potential nominees would support labor measures. The Saint Louis Central Trades, for example, sent out questionnaires containing more than one hundred questions that candidates had to answer satisfactorily before receiving labor's endorsement.[12]

Employer Offensive

More pressing economic matters, however, somewhat mitigated labor's involvement in local politics. The employer offensive against trade unionism, which had been reinvigorated during World War I, picked up momentum during the early years of the 1920s. As trade associations pressed for the American Plan of industrial labor relations, labor responded with an "educational and propaganda" campaign of its own. In Saint Louis a Labor Education League, which had been organized after a lockout of union printers and fought the open shop campaign. Reflecting a "growing feeling of labor solidarity and class consciousness," mass meetings were held in each St. Louis ward.[13] Four thousand people attended a meeting in the tenth ward demonstrating their support for the locked-out printers. The demonstrators, already exhibiting a militant and radical mood, were further encouraged by the rhetoric of Saint Louis labor leaders. Swept up in the emotional atmosphere, State Federation President Reuben Wood defended the Russian Revolution. "I simply mention Russia," he declared:

> in order to show you that whenever the American workers get ready to take possession of their own Government they will be as much misrepresented, as much denounced and as much fought as have been the workers in Russia. The workers made the world, they feed the world, and the time will come when they will rule the world![14]

Organized labor in Kansas City faced a similar open-shop offensive, and, although the movement was less radical and militant than the Saint Louis group, it resolutely held its own. By the mid-1920s, the open-shop campaign began to lose much of its vigor. Efforts to destroy trade unionism failed in such important Missouri industries

12. *The Labor Herald,* March 8, 15, 22, 29, 1918; March 12, April 9, May 14, 19, 1920. *St. Louis Labor,* June 19, July 17, 1920.
13. *St. Louis Labor,* November 12, 1921.
14. *Ibid.,* October 1, 1921. See also *The Labor Herald,* August 18, 1922; *St. Louis Labor,* January 1, 1921.

as boots and shoes, printing, and building construction.[15] Although the employer offensive effectively checked the expansion of trade unionism in Missouri, it could not roll back earlier advances. By 1922 the labor movement had lost only 5 per cent of the membership it had gained during the war; the decrease was caused as much by the 1921–1922 depression as by the efforts of employer associations.[16]

The waning of the open-shop offensive did not free Missouri labor from problems, however. Indeed, 1922 became a hectic and decisive year for Missouri labor. Two events in that year, the Missouri Constitutional Convention and the strike of railroad shop craft employees, convinced labor leaders they had little to lose if they participated in independent labor politics. Meanwhile, the convening of the Conference for Progressive Political Action in Chicago held the promise of a national movement for a new party alliance.

The Missouri Constitutional Convention

The Missouri Constitutional Convention of 1922–1923 did much to discredit the major parties in the eyes of Missouri labor leaders. Labor had advocated the drafting of a new state constitution for some time, evidently hoping to write reforms into the constitution that they

15. Selig Perlman and Philip Taft, *History of Labor in the United States: Labor Movement, 1896–1932,* Vol. 4, p. 494. Sears, "Kansas City Building Trades," pp. 159–62. Herbert J. Vogt, "Boot and Shoe Industry of St. Louis: Origin, Growth and Causes of Its Development," p. 62. Gompers to Maurice Cassidy, August 11, 18, 1921, Gompers, Letterbooks.

16. The source for the membership figures was the *Missouri Red Book, 1919–1922,* and the *St. Louis Times,* December 31, 1924. Membership figures for the period 1925–1930 were not found, but judging from the membership figures of the State Federation of Labor, which were usually an accurate gauge of membership in the state labor movement, Missouri experienced a slight growth in membership during these years. The success of the Missouri labor movement, relative to the national labor movement, in consolidating the membership gains it had achieved during World War I and in successfully resisting the employers offensive can best be explained by examining the nature of organization during the war period. Most of the new members that Missouri labor added to its roles were working in industries that had already been organized to some degree; few unskilled workers in industries that utilized mass production had been organized in Missouri during the war. For membership figures of the State Federation of Labor, see Fred R. Graham, "A History of the Missouri State Federation of Labor," pp. 25, 26.

The depression appears to have been especially severe in Missouri. It was reported that sixty-nine thousand workers in Saint Louis were unemployed, and in the building trades, more than half of the workers were out of work. Although the situation was especially serious in Saint Louis, other Missouri cities also experienced serious unemployment. *St. Louis Labor,* September 17, 1921. Arthur M. Hyde to A. C. Lamb, September 29, 1921, Arthur M. Hyde, Papers.

had not been able to attain through lobbying the state legislature. Many labor leaders and organizations participated in the New Constitution Association of Missouri, which carried through the movement to call a constitutional convention. Labor wanted clauses in the new constitution dealing with such issues as old-age pensions, antiunion injunctions, the right to organize and choose representatives for collective bargaining, and authorization of the General Assembly to enact compulsory or elective social insurance laws.[17]

Even before the convention assembled, however, labor leaders realized they had much to fear and little to gain from the deliberations of the delegates. Indeed, the method of choosing the delegates and the type of delegates elected upset many Missourians. The call for the constitutional assembly stipulated that each party nominate fifteen delegates and that fifteen be selected on an independent basis. The Democratic and Republican state committees, however, held a conference and decided to offer coalition candidates as independent delegates; each party would name seven candidates, and the fifteenth delegate would be chosen from Saint Louis.[18]

Many Missourians considered the action of the two parties a breach of faith. Labor, with good reason, agreed; the coalition slate was almost entirely composed of corporation lawyers. The State Federation of Labor hastily formed an alliance with the State Farm Bureau and the Missouri Farmers' Association and fielded a slate of five candidates; the slate probably would have been elected if it had been placed in a more favorable position on the ballot. Since the Secretary of State had positioned the coalition ticket at the top of the ballot, however, it won. Labor's prospects seemed bleak. The only union delegate elected to the convention was Republican Joseph Hauser of Saint Louis, from the Twenty-ninth Senatorial District. Labor felt only minimal consolation when Governor Hyde appointed a second labor delegate, C. G. Brittingham of the Brotherhood of Locomotive Engineers, to succeed William Sacks of Saint Louis, who had resigned to run for the United States Senate.[19]

The convention was so reactionary that the labor delegates spent

17. MSFL, *Proceedings, 1916,* p. 57. Pamphlet of the New Constitution Association of Missouri, Edward Goltra, Papers. Gompers to C. G. Brittingham, July 12, 1922, Gompers, Letterbooks. Proceedings of the Missouri Constitutional Convention, 1922, 1923, *Journal and Debates,* Vol. I, 15th day, p. 2; 31st day, p. 3; 35th day, p. 6; Vol. II, 96th day, pp. 9ff, 63, 67, 97; 97th day, p. 14ff.

18. *Missouri State Journal,* December 17, 1921. MSFL, *Proceedings, 1922,* pp. 57–60.

19. MSFL, *Proceedings, 1922,* pp. 57–60; *1924,* p. 16. *St. Louis Post-Dispatch,* January 19, 1922. *St. Louis Labor,* January 14, 28, 1922. *The Labor Herald,* June 23, 1922. Brittingham died during the convention and was replaced by a delegate who did not represent the labor movement.

most of their time either defending such traditional labor and progressive gains as initiative, referendum, and the direct primary, or
preventing the enactment of such odious proposals as a state constabulary and an industrial court instead of promoting additional reforms. The new constitution was submitted to the voters at a special
election in February, 1924, in the form of twenty-one amendments.
The State Federation officially opposed several of the amendments
and endorsed none. Only five amendments were approved, and all
amendments opposed by labor were defeated.[20]

The Railway Strike

The national strike of the railroad shop craft unions shortly after
the convening of the Constitutional Convention further demonstrated
to many Missouri labor leaders that the established political parties
could not be trusted, regardless of preelection promises. The shop-
men went on strike in protest against a wage slash inspired by the
Railroad Labor Board. Railway managers vowed to break the strike
and reestablish the open shop.[21] Even before the strike began, railway
officials began to exhort Governor Hyde to call out the Missouri National Guard to protect railroad property and strikebreakers. A letter
to the Governor from C. E. Schaff, Receiver for the Missouri, Kansas, and Texas Railroad, was typical. "It will be our purpose," Schaff
wrote, "to call upon you at the proper time for sufficient peace officers to protect our property and to restrain strikers or strike sympathizers from interference with and assaults upon the loyal employees
who remain in our employ and the new men whom we expect to
employ." Obviously perturbed by the tone of the letter, Hyde responded tartly that he believed "the men will conduct their strike
lawfully and quietly as is already indicated by their conduct. The
duty of maintaining the peace lies in the first instance upon the local
officers, such as the police, sheriff, etc., I hope this will be sufficient.
It is not our intention to anticipate a situation which may never
arise."[22]

Hyde won immediate praise from the striking unions for his impar-
tial conduct. During his campaign for governor, Hyde had made a
strong appeal for the support of the labor movement, and had re-

20. MSFL, *Proceedings, 1924*, pp. 99, 100. Gompers to R. T. Wood, November 25, 1922, Gompers, Letterbooks. Proceedings of the Missouri Constitutional Convention, Vol. III, 108th day, pp. 42, 43; 109th day, pp. 9–18;
110th day, pp. 4–38; 113th day, pp. 28, 29; Vol. IV, 125th day, pp. 64,
65, 73, 78–91; 126th day, pp. 13–18, 38, 40; 127th day, pp. 18, 22–24. *St.
Louis Labor*, December 8, 1923; February 2, 1924. *Official Manual, 1925–1926*,
pp. 425–38.
21. Lewis Lorwin, *The American Federation of Labor: History, Policies
and Prospects*, pp. 205–10.
22. C. E. Schaff to Hyde, June 29, 1922; Hyde to Schaff, July 3, 1922,
Arthur M. Hyde, Papers.

warded it by promoting their programs in the first two years of his term. The relationship between Hyde and President Wood of the State Federation had been cordial. Wood praised the Governor for his efforts on behalf of workmen's compensation legislation in 1921, and both men cooperated in an attempt to frustrate the efforts of Missouri Democrats to require that legislation secured by the Republican administration be submitted to a referendum election.[23]

The railroad managers intensified their campaign, and, in addition, various employers' associations supported by chambers of commerce demanded that Hyde call out the National Guard. Under relentless pressure, Hyde wired the governors of Illinois, Ohio, and Indiana on July 7, 1922, asking whether they planned to use the National Guard; only the Illinois governor seemed inclined to do so. The following day, one week after the strike began, Hyde ordered the National Guard companies to assemble at their armories, and on the 17th he dispatched them into several communities.[24]

Because little serious violence occurred, Hyde had done what he said he would not do—anticipate the need for state action. The decision resulted in part because of complaints by the railroad companies that small towns such as Marshall, Moberly, Mexico, Chaffee, and New Franklin, which were controlled by organized labor or labor sympathizers, made no effort to protect nonunion workers. Some railroad executives threatened to stop mail delivery if Hyde did not give immediate assurances that those workers would be adequately protected. Besides exerting pressure on the state administration, the railroads also threatened to move their shops out of communities in which protection of strikebreakers was allegedly lacking, a move with serious economic implications for most small towns.[25]

Hyde's action predictably incensed Missouri labor leaders. Reuben Wood publicly called the Governor a liar. The Governor had promised to confer before calling out the National Guard, Wood claimed,

23. Missouri-Pacific Federated Shop Trades to Hyde, July 3, 1922; F. R. Lee to Hyde, July 17, 1922; Wood to Hyde, May 6, 1921; Hyde to Wood, May 9, 1921, *Ibid. The Labor Herald,* May 20, 1921.

24. Saint Joseph Chamber of Commerce to Hyde, July 6, 1922; Hyde to Anthony Ittness, July 11, 1922; Elmer Donnell to Hyde, July 11, 1922; Albert Davis to Hyde, July 11, 1922; Hyde to Len Small, July 7, 1922; Warren McCray to Hyde, July 7, 1922; Robert Harris to Hyde, July 7, 1922; George Sutton to Hyde, July 7, 1922; Hyde to Small, July 7, 1922; McCray to Hyde, July 7, 1922; Harris to Hyde, July 7, 1922; Sutton to Hyde, July 7, 1922, Arthur M. Hyde, Papers. Lowe, "Administration of Arthur M. Hyde," pp. 244, 245.

25. Folder 757 of the Arthur M. Hyde, Papers, contains a great deal of the correspondence between the Governor and these town officials as well as correspondence from railroad officials. J. E. Taussig to Hyde, July 9, 1922; Thomas S. Waddell to Gen. W. A. Raupp, July 10, 1922, Arthur M. Hyde, Papers.

but even as the Governor made this promise, he had previously signed an order mobilizing the Guard. Wood offered newspapermen the sworn statements of witnesses to these conversations. Warren Harding is "the greatest strike-breaker in history," said Wood, "[and] next to him in this capacity is Governor Arthur M. Hyde." Hyde, on the other hand, described Wood to a friend as a confirmed Socialist and an agitator hardly worthy of notice. Hyde increased his commitment to the railroads during the course of the strike by requesting them to pay two-thirds of the cost of the special legal officers hired to prosecute criminal acts in the strike areas. Because the Governor's budget was too small to meet the expense, the railroad executives agreed to assume the responsibility.[26]

The Governor accelerated the already rapid deterioration of relations with organized labor by endorsing President Harding's actions in the 1922 coal strike. Hyde vowed to take "immediate steps . . . to resume production in the mining industry and to protect and safeguard those engaged therein." As a result, Arch Helm, president of United Mine Workers, District No. 25, condemned the Governor for defending the "coal barons' point of view" and for his antagonism to any form of organized labor. Hyde further aggravated the miners by vetoing a bathhouse bill requiring mine owners to provide bathing and changing facilities at the coal fields, legislation he had promised to support in his election campaign.[27]

Many skeptical Missouri labor leaders always assumed that most Democratic and Republican politicians, while sincerely befriending organized labor, would invariably side with capital when circumstances forced a choice between the classes.[28] Hyde's actions during the railroad strike of 1922 appeared to document this assumption. The Governor grew increasingly hostile to organized labor after the outbreak of the strike. By August he wrote Governor Allen of Kansas "that the logic of events in the present unsettled condition of national affairs, particularly with reference to strikes, points the moral of your Industrial Court."[29] Hyde wanted any information that the Kansas governor might have concerning the court.

In the spring of 1923, the editor of *Industrial Progress,* a magazine dedicated to the open shop, asked Hyde for a statement on the

26. *Moberly Monitor-Index,* August 14, 1922. Miscellaneous clippings from *Chillicothe Constitution,* May 22, 1924, in Arthur M. Hyde, Papers. Hyde to Rev. E. Y. Keiter, August 21, 1922; Hyde to Luther Burns, March 23, 1923; Burns to Hyde, March 31, 1923, Arthur M. Hyde, Papers.
27. Arch Helm to Hyde, July 25, August 4, 1922; Hyde to Helm, July 25, 1922; Helm to Hyde, August 4, 1922, Arthur M. Hyde, Papers. Clipping from *Chillicothe Constitution,* May 22, 1924, in Arthur M. Hyde, Papers. MSFL, *Proceedings, 1921,* pp. 65, 66.
28. *St. Louis Labor,* June 24, 1922.
29. Hyde to Allen, August 14, 1922, Arthur M. Hyde, Papers.

"right of every free American to labor without any other's leave."[30]
Hyde responded with a statement virtually endorsing the open
shop. "Let us all understand what the law and liberty means," he
declared:

> A man has a right to quit work whenever for any reason the work
> is distasteful to him or his remuneration unsatisfactory. He has
> this right singly or collectively, whether he is called a striker or
> not.
> A man also has a right to work, whenever and wherever work and
> wages can be found which are satisfactory to him, regardless of
> whether he is called a strike-breaker or not.
> No man has any right to use threats, intimidation, or force to cause
> another man to quit his job. The right to work and the right to
> quit work are both indispensable to human liberty. Whoever de-
> nies, impairs or abridges either of these rights, does to that extent
> enslave his fellow-man, and does to that extent jeopardize his own
> liberty.[31]

By the end of his term, Hyde was completely hostile to labor. An
incident that occurred in the summer of 1924 provides an illustration.
Charles H. Moyer, president of the International Union of Mine, Mill
and Smelter Workers, wrote Hyde asking for an investigation of the
situation in Bonne Terre, Missouri, in which organizers of the AFL
and the mine, mill, and smelter's union were being harassed, intimi-
dated, and ordered to leave the area by local officials. Relying upon
information supplied by a secretary of the local chamber of commerce, Hyde replied that miners in the area did not want to join
unions, and union organizers used terrorism and intimidation to
coerce workers. The Governor, who called out the National Guard
in mere anticipation of damage to railroad property, in this instance
declared himself unable to prevent trouble if the organizers returned
to the area. An AFL general organizer, Ernest Flood, responded bitterly that if Hyde's reply represented his actual statement concerning
the facts in the incident, then the Governor was "a liar, a black
mailer, and a coward."[32]

The Conference for Progressive Political Action

Because of their own predilections and the series of unfavorable
events culminating in 1922, Missouri labor leaders exhibited an im-

30. Henry Lewis to Hyde, March 20, April 2, 1923, *ibid.*
31. Hyde to Lewis, April 7, 1923, *ibid.*
32. Charles H. Moyer to Hyde, July 7, 1924; Edwin Griffin to Hyde,
June 27, 1924; Hyde to Frank Morrison, July 3, 1924; Ernest Flood to
Hyde, July 25, 1924, *ibid.*

mediate interest in the Conference for Progressive Political Action (CPPA) meeting in Chicago in February, 1922. They responded quickly to the conference's call for the formation of state organizations to advance the demands for general progressive reforms, and a state CPPA, which brought together representatives of organized labor, farmers' associations, and the Socialist party, met in Sedalia on June 20, 1922. Although they assumed it was too late to organize a labor ticket for the 1922 elections, discussions concerning the eventual establishment of an independent party organization dominated the meeting. David Kreyling, the Saint Louis Central Trades official, in a speech reviewing the history of Missouri labor's political failures, argued in favor of the creation of labor's own political party. President Wood of the State Federation supported the logic of Kreyling's analysis. "For all of these many years, we have been making [a] laughing stock out of [ourselves] by our old political methods as officially advocated by the A. F. of L." The general mood of the delegates was revealed by their request that Arthur Henderson of the British Labour party be invited to the next conference. Henderson's "presence at such an American Labor and Reform Conference can only have a beneficial effect upon our movement in this country and will result in much good for the entire American working class."[33]

The Missouri branch of the national conference sent a large delegation to the Cleveland meeting of the CPPA in December, 1922. The position they would take at the Cleveland meeting was previewed by earlier actions of both the Saint Louis CPPA and the State Federation of Labor. At an October meeting, the Saint Louis organization resolved in favor of the immediate formation of a nationwide workers' and farmers' political party. In supporting the resolution, David Kreyling, while professing his loyalty to the AFL, opposed its "official opposition to an independent labor party movement." "What good can we accomplish, by electing a few friends of labor who have the capitalist yoke on their necks, no matter how good their intentions may be otherwise."[34] President Wood told the convention:

> It is fairly well established that the time-worn non-partisan political program of the AF of L has proven a dismal failure, in so far as any substantial results for permanent political advancement for the workers are concerned and I believe the Chicago Conference was a start in the right direction, that will lead ultimately to the formation of a political organization patterned something after the British Labor Party, in the very near future.[35]

33. *St. Louis Labor,* June 10, 24, 1922.
34. *Ibid.,* October 7, 1922.
35. MSFL, *Proceedings, 1922,* pp. 72, 73.

These heady words were later endorsed by the State Federation convention. At the Cleveland meeting, Missouri delegates joined those from the Wisconsin Federation of Labor, the Minnesota Farmer–Labor party and the Socialist party, in demanding the immediate formation of a labor party. But the proposal was defeated 64 to 52.[36]

Regardless of the CPPA action, Saint Louis labor already had made moves toward the formation of an independent labor party. At a meeting of Saint Louis labor organizations that was held shortly after the Sedalia conference, a commitment was made to form a labor party after the 1922 elections. David Kreyling became temporary chairman. In early January, the Saint Louis CPPA formally initiated the American Labor party and nominated a slate of candidates for the municipal elections in April. Ward organizations and a city central committee were formed, and a trade union Socialist, William Brandt, became a full-time, salaried manager of the Labor party campaign. The party platform called for a system of proportional representation in the board of aldermen, an extensive program of municipal ownership, and a "fundamental reform" in the management of the city hospital and other city institutions. In addition, the party endorsed traditional reforms demanded by organized labor.[37]

Despite a vigorous campaign, the labor ticket made a poor showing in the municipal elections, attracting only 7 per cent of the city's voters. Disappointed but not disheartened, Saint Louis labor leaders decided to hold a delegate convention, establish a permanent party organization, and elect regular officers.[38]

Early in 1924, the third session of the national CPPA convened in Saint Louis. This time it endorsed the formation of an independent ticket, and a national nominating convention was called in Cleveland for July 4, 1924. During the Saint Louis meeting, Reuben Wood was added to the twenty-member National Committee. At the Cleveland convention, which nominated the La Follette–Wheeler ticket, Wood served on the critically important credentials committee.[39]

At a meeting held in Saint Louis on July 15, 1924, to launch the third-party movement in Missouri, Wood was chosen state chairman. On July 26, the Liberal party of Missouri came into being. The new party issued an extensive party platform including provisions for state

36. *St. Louis Labor,* December 23, 1922. *The Labor Herald,* December 29, 1922. Nathan Fine, *Labor and Farmer Parties in the United States, 1828–1928,* pp. 403, 404. The best available account of the Progressive movement is Kenneth C. MacKay, *The Progressive Movement of 1924.*

37. *St. Louis Labor,* July 22, 1922; January 13, February 3, 24, 1923.

38. *Ibid.,* April 14, May 12, 1923.

39. *Ibid.,* February 16, 1924. Fine, *Labor and Farmer Parties,* pp. 405–8. *The Labor Herald,* July 18, 1924. The key importance of the credentials committee is discussed in MacKay, *Progressive Movement,* pp. 110–12.

aid to public education, a system of public works for the unemployed, the establishment of an up-to-date cooperative marketing system, and assurance of the right of collective bargaining. The Liberals also endorsed the more traditional labor reforms, such as convict labor regulation, workmen's compensation, and anti-injunction measures, and commended La Follette's denunciation of the Ku Klux Klan.[40]

The leaders of the Liberal party devoted most of their initial energy and resources to the task of acquiring the one thousand signatures required from each congressional district to get electors for the La Follette-Wheeler presidential ticket on the state ballot. With this task completed, and the party on the official ballot for the November elections, labor and party leaders started raising a $100,000 campaign fund to finance a vigorous campaign for the Progressive ticket.[41]

Despite limited resources, Liberal party leaders conducted an active campaign, but the presidential effort proved a dismal failure in Missouri. Although La Follette received 16.5 per cent of the national vote, he had only eighty-four thousand votes or about 6 per cent of the total votes cast in Missouri in the presidential election. Two thirds of the La Follette vote cast in Missouri went to the Socialist party, which he also headed, instead of to the Liberal party. The third-party effort in Missouri failed for a number of reasons. Concentrating on the presidential race, the Liberals did not field a complete slate of candidates for state offices. The Socialist party, which did offer a full slate of candidates, greatly outpolled the Liberals. Their source of support was also reduced when the Saint Louis Building Trades Council and the Brotherhood of Railroad Trainmen endorsed the Democratic candidates for both the state and national offices. In Kansas City, where unionists still smarted from their conflicts with state labor leaders over the workmen's compensation, there was no active support for the third-party campaign. The election returns also indicate that, compared to other midwestern states, the La Follette ticket got almost no support from the rural areas of Missouri. The overwhelming problem, however, was the Missouri trade unionists' unwillingness to follow the direction of their leaders. In short, Missouri labor leaders failed to inspire the rank-and-file unionists with their own strong convictions regarding the necessity of a new political strategy.[42]

40. *St. Louis Labor,* August 2, September 20, 1924.

41. *Ibid.,* August 2, 1924. MSFL, *Proceedings, 1926,* pp. 18, 19.

42. MSFL, *Proceedings, 1926,* pp. 18, 19, 45. *Official Manual, 1925–1926,* pp. 193, 194. Goltra to Joseph T. Davis, October 16, 1924; Goltra to W. N. Doak, October 7, 1924; F. J. McNamara, *et al.,* to Gompers, August 7, 1924; Edward Goltra, Papers. Maurice Cassidy to *St. Louis Star,* October 30, 1924, Alroy S. Phillips, Papers.

Nonetheless, Missouri labor's involvement in independent labor politics was neither precipitant nor capricious. Its leaders debated the proposition for more than two decades, and the march of events following the United States' involvement in World War I made their final decision almost inevitable. Involvement in third-party politics, however, failed to resolve Missouri labor's dilemma regarding political strategy. Indeed, independent labor politics proved even more disastrous than the nonpartisan tactic.

Part Three

TESTING
THE
DEMOCRATIC ALLIANCE

After third-party politics failed as a vehicle for establishing the influence of the working class in government, the Missouri labor movement pursued an entirely different strategy by forming an alliance with the Democratic party and integrating itself into the party organization. It was not an entirely planned or conscious decision but evolved naturally from labor's experiences during and after the war. The Missouri labor movement had long advocated government-sponsored social welfare reform, and the decade of the thirties provided an opportunity to test the validity of both its reform objectives and its new political alliance with the Democratic party. The decade was a period of change for Missouri labor. As the Federal Government took an increasingly active role in the conflicts between labor and management and itself became a major employer of labor, the relationship between government and labor was substantially altered. Change also occurred within the labor movement as conflicts over organizing strategy eventually divided labor, and in the process, exposed other alterations that had already occurred. Taken together, these changes served to reinforce the assumption previously held by many Missouri labor leaders that political action was vitally important to the labor movement. While generally pleased with the reforms introduced under the sponsorship of the Democratic party and Franklin D. Roosevelt, labor often expressed its disappointment with the administration of these measures, especially at the state and local level. Although the alliance with the Democrats on the national level was advantageous, it was not as productive in local politics. Despite some unhappiness, however, Missouri labor extended its commitment to the Democratic party during the decade, and labor leaders assumed increasingly important roles in the state party organization.

Chapter VII

ALLIANCE WITH
THE DEMOCRATS

THE Progressive movement of the early 1920s and the national election of 1924 marked a major watershed in the political behavior of the organized labor movement in Missouri. Many of the state's most influential and respected labor leaders had long assumed that, if an independent labor party ticket were endorsed and supported by the national labor movement and if it were represented by an attractive, well-known candidate, a third party would provide organized labor with a viable alternative to their nonpartisan role in the established two-party system. The La Follette movement appeared to satisfy all of these prerequisites, so the meager Liberal–Socialist vote in Missouri shocked those labor leaders who regarded the independent political movement as a panacea for all of labor's political frustrations.

While admitting that the results of the election were not what had been anticipated, Reuben Wood expressed the thoughts of many labor leaders when he rather bravely argued that the effort had been worthwhile. "I think the conservative will agree that it was apparent we did not get a fair count in many instances, but in the face of this situation the count of 84,000 votes in Missouri and the showing throughout the country was very good."[1]

Unwilling to become the victims of their own euphemism, however, Missouri labor leaders accepted the conclusion that they could not deliver a labor vote outside of the established party system and hastily retreated to the traditional nonpartisan tactic. Indeed, Wood argued that Missouri labor never doubted that policy. The endorsement of the La Follette–Wheeler ticket resulted from the actions of the established parties themselves and did not reflect any fundamental change in labor's basic political strategy. "We should feel gratified," he concluded, "when we peruse the non-partisan political declaration of the A. F. of L., which was unanimously adopted at the Atlantic City Convention (October 5–16, 1925)."[2]

In reality, the nonpartisan policy seemed little more attractive than it had been before the La Follette campaign, and Missouri labor lead-

1. MSFL, *Proceedings, 1926*, p. 19.
2. *Ibid.*, pp. 19, 20.

ers were still highly amenable to any alternative strategy that held the promise of more effectively exerting labor's potential political influence. Such an alternative evolved between the years 1925 and 1932, but it was more a pragmatic response to the exigencies of the day than a consciously or rationally conceived political strategy. During the course of these years, the labor movement, in everything but rhetoric, abandoned its old nonpartisan posture and in its place adopted a very partisan alliance with the Democratic party. Indeed, since independent third-party politics had been discredited, there was no alternative to cooperation with the Democrats. The Republican party, on both the state and national levels, became increasingly conservative and hostile to the labor movement. Nevertheless, as labor relied increasingly on the Democratic party to promote its policies, it became essentially a pressure group within the party organization and relinquished a measure of its previous independence.

In the earlier years of the century, when the Republican party contained a strong and vigorous progressive faction, organized labor had a meaningful alternative to the Democrats. By bolting in 1912, Theodore Roosevelt and his progressive followers forfeited control of the party to its conservative faction, which consolidated its control and exhibited little sensitivity to the needs and objectives of organized labor.[3]

Certainly the Republican administrations of Warren G. Harding and Calvin Coolidge did little to endear themselves to the labor movement. Harding's statements and policies during the railroad and mining strikes of the early twenties quickly incurred the enmity of the labor movement, and Coolidge, who had established his antiunion position even before he entered the White House by breaking the Boston police strike, nurtured his reputation as a businessman's president. Labor leaders were just as deeply disturbed by the actions of the Republican-controlled national Congress, which passed legislation strongly opposed by organized labor and refused to consider any of those measures that labor considered vital. In short, by the 1920s labor could see little attraction in a Republican party that was controlled by big business interests and was dedicated to serving the selfish needs and desires of the business community.[4]

The Republican party of Missouri went through a similar evolution. The first two Republicans to reside in the Executive Mansion since Reconstruction, Herbert S. Hadley and Arthur M. Hyde, both identified themselves as progressive, but Republican progressivism

3. The problems and conflicts within the Republican party are discussed by George H. Mayer, *The Republican Party, 1854–1966.*
4. For a somewhat different view, see Robert H. Zieger, *Republicans and Labor, 1919–1929.*

lost much of its influence during the twenties. By the end of the decade the party in Missouri had become essentially a party of businessmen. To some extent this change within the party was paralleled by the evolving attitudinal commitments of the Hyde administration. At the beginning of his term, Governor Hyde vigorously courted labor leaders. He ended it with a business–conservative view of the labor movement that prepared him ideologically for entry into Herbert Hoover's Cabinet.[5]

Some Missouri Republicans regretted the change within the party. George Dugan, an influential outstate Republican editor, predicted eventual Democratic control in Missouri if the Republican party continued to drive away the labor vote. Dugan offered several illustrations to support his contention. Elective and appointed Republican officials at the local level were "poisoning the railroad vote, the miners vote, and all organized labor" against the party. Prophetically, he suggested that such behavior would "Give the city 'Ward Boss' a club to drive off the [labor] vote if it is not stopped at once."[6] Another progressive Republican, Alroy Phillips, criticized the quality of Republican officeholders and condemned their role in undermining social legislation:

> I am very much disgusted with the whole Outfit . . . As a Republican I am ashamed of them. It is regretable [sic] that the Republican Party has not been able to develop and put in office more men of real ability, with a high sense of duty and the courage to perform it. To be clear, I mean I am tired of seeing clerks in office and would enjoy the occasional sight of a big man holding office to serve the people and not himself.[7]

Only in the Missouri General Assembly did the Republican party maintain any degree of rapport with labor leaders. During the twenties, Republicans in the state Senate established a somewhat more favorable labor voting record than the Democrats, while in the House both parties supported labor at comparable levels. The significance of the Republican party's actions in the state legislature, however, was qualified. Little party discipline or party voting existed in the General Assembly, and both parties consistently failed to fulfill campaign promises to the labor movement. During this period, moreover, labor leaders became increasingly disillusioned with the state legislature's willingness to enact meaningful reforms and exhibited a growing inclination to look to the national Congress for desired

5. See William T. Miller, "The Progressive Movement in Missouri"; Lloyd E. Worner, Jr., "The Public Career of Herbert Spencer Hadley"; James L. Lowe, "The Administration of Arthur M. Hyde, Governor of Missouri; 1921–1925," especially pp. 240, 241, 249.

6. George Dugan to Walter Dickey, n.d., Arthur M. Hyde, Papers.

7. Phillips to Sam Baker, July 25, 1925, Alroy S. Phillips, Papers.

legislation. Finally, as the party in power during the twenties, the Republicans bore the responsibility for the actions of its national and state administrations. A survey of organized labor's response to the ten governors who served in Missouri during the first four decades of the twentieth century indicates that labor leaders placed the three Republican governors of the 1920s at the very bottom of the list (Table 1).[8]

Table 1. Labor's View of Missouri Governors (1900–1940)

Good
Joseph Folk, Democrat, 1905–1909
Herbert Hadley, Republican, 1909–1913
Lloyd Stark, Democrat, 1937–1941

Satisfactory
Frederick Gardner, Democrat, 1917–1921
Guy Park, Democrat, 1933–1937

Fair
Alexander Dockery, Democrat, 1901–1905
Elliott Major, Democrat, 1913–1917

Poor
Arthur Hyde, Republican, 1921–1925
Sam Baker, Republican, 1925–1929
Henry Caulfield, Republican, 1929–1933

Arthur Hyde did little to ingratiate labor to the Republican party during his term of office, and the two Republican administrations that followed further alienated the labor movement. The handling of Missouri's convict lease system by Republican administrations illustrated the problem. Long opposed by labor, the system was regulated by a law passed in 1917 that provided for ending the practice of leasing prisoners to private contractors and establishing a state-use system instead. But the 1917 act never became fully effective. Although the Hyde administration ended the leasing of convicts, it failed to implement the state-use system. Convict-made commodities still sold on the open market in competition with the goods produced by free labor.[9]

What meager progress the Hyde administration made was lost by his Republican successor, Sam Baker, who assumed the governorship in 1925. Baker courted the labor vote during his campaign, often

8. This is a subjective evaluation based upon organized labor's relationship with and response to the various Missouri governors.
9. Fred R. Graham, "A History of the Missouri State Federation of Labor," pp. 68, 69.

waving a union card to demonstrate sympathy with organized labor. As governor, however, he made no effort to enforce the convict labor law. In addition, in August, 1926, he allowed the state prison board to enter into a contract with the Western Coal and Mining Company to lease convicts for use in its coal mines near Lexington. One hundred forty union miners lost their jobs to 150 convicts. President Wood of the State Federation protested to the Governor and the prison board without success. Shortly thereafter, Wood, Arch Helm, and David Frampton of the United Mine Workers, and Judge John P. Leahy addressed a large protest meeting held at Lexington. Leahy had been engaged to sue both the state prison board for violations of the law regulating the employment of convict labor and the Western Coal and Mining Company for breaching its contract with the United Mine Workers. After much publicity and threatened legal action, the Governor in September instructed the prison board to withdraw the prisoners from the mines in Lexington. Frustrated and bitter, President Wood concluded that the prison leasing system "could not possibly exist except with the quiet encouragement and sanction of the State Administration . . . no Governor of Missouri has had the temerity or courage to even make a resemblance of effort to carry out the purposes and intent of the law."[10]

Republican governors alienated the labor movement in other ways. Governor Baker vetoed a bill ardently promoted by labor that defined safety standards for the construction industry; labor had been lobbying for a more effective "scaffold law" since 1913. Labor also opposed Baker's proposal to levy a 10 per cent amusement tax on theatres, athletic events, tobacco, cigars, and cigarettes. The tax was regressive, labor argued, and would be born primarily by the working class. Baker's successor, Gov. Henry Caulfield, strongly advocated a state constabulary, which the labor movement believed was designed for use during labor disputes.[11]

As Missouri Republicans antagonized labor, a significant faction of the Democratic party began to attract various elements of the urban working class. During the 1920s the Missouri Democratic party made major inroads into the Republican party's voting strength in the state's major urban areas by capturing a significant share of the black vote and strengthening its appeal among laboring elements and ethnic groups.[12]

10. MSFL, *Proceedings, 1927,* pp. 72, 73; *1928,* pp. 68, 69.

11. *Ibid., 1926,* pp. 42, 43, 50, 100–104; *1929,* pp. 9, 10. "Report of the Legislative Committee," pp. 14–21. *St. Louis Labor,* May 4, 1929.

12. Franklin D. Mitchell, *Embattled Democracy: Missouri Democratic Politics, 1919–1932,* Chaps. 5–8. Unfortunately, this otherwise excellent study of the Democratic party in Missouri during the twenties does not deal with the role of the labor movement in Missouri Democratic politics.

Democrats appealed for working-class support by catering to the interests of labor leaders. Democrats, of course, had always wanted labor votes, but many Democratic candidates assumed that soliciting the labor vote too specifically would alienate businessmen, farmers, and other special-interest groups.[13] Among many Missouri Democrats, especially in rural districts, this assumption seemed less valid during the decade of the twenties than it had previously. The farmers' hostility toward big business, so vividly exhibited during the Populist movement, reemerged during the 1920s as the agricultural prosperity of World War I dissolved into an economic depression that racked rural America for nearly two decades. Many spokesmen for the rural areas believed that problems in agriculture resulted from the excessive economic power of big business. Moreover, as the Republican party increasingly became identified as the businessman's party, the Democrats reinvigorated their quest for votes among all nonbusiness elements of the population.

At the same time that Democrats sought nonaligned voters, increasing political activism made organized labor a highly visible interest group with a large membership. Furthermore, those people concerned about the growing imbalance of economic power began to accept the concept of a community of interests between producers on the farm and urban workers. Perhaps this line of reasoning was nowhere more obviously manifested than in a speech delivered in Saint Charles by Missouri's respected and influential congressman from the Ninth District, Clarence Cannon.

> I hold no brief for organized labor. I have not always agreed with its policies, but I prefer it infinitely to organized and predatory capital. The fight between the two can never be a fair fight. Capital is fighting for profits. Labor is fighting for bread. To the one it means merely a few more shares of stock, a few more trips to Europe, another ocean-going yacht. To the other it means food and clothing and shelter and medicine, school for the children and a contribution for the church and the opportunity to rear his family in that comfort and decency which is the right of every industrious citizen . . .
>
> The strike is never the choice of labor. One is thoughtless indeed who imagines that labor wants to strike. No more sad and unwelcome news can come to the home than that a strike has been ordered. Capitol [*sic*] has all the advantage. He merely closes his shop and sits in comfort to wait, while labor with family existence dependant upon him fights back the wolf from the door. Fighting our battles as well as his own. For organized labor never yet fought

13. Mitchell to Frederick Gardner, February 26, July 13, 1916, Ewing Y. Mitchell, Papers. Phillips to Mark McGruder, February 25, 1920; McGruder to Phillips, February 27, 1920, Alroy S. Phillips, Papers.

a battle that the humblest unorganized toiler did not share in the fruits of his victory. And Labor organizations never yet made a sacrifice but what it was made for the unorganized toiler as well as for itself.

The farmer especially has much at stake with labor in its battle against capital. For labor and not capital is the principal consumer of agricultural products. The laboring man is the farmer's principal customer, and if labor receives a living wage he is able to pay the farmer a living price for his food. And if labor is ground down to a starvation wage the farmer must accept a starvation price for his [products].[14]

Another politician who recognized a mutuality of farmer and laborer interests and expressed hostility to big business was Ralph F. Lozier from the essentially rural Second Congressional District. When Lozier attempted to capture the House seat of longtime Democratic incumbent William Rucker in 1916, he virtually conceded the labor vote to Rucker, who had established a favorable record on issues concerning labor in Congress and relied for support upon his church connections and professional contacts made while serving as president of the Missouri Bar Association. Lozier campaigned vigorously as an uncompromising prohibitionist and did not survive the primary.[15]

Challenging Rucker for the same seat six years later, Lozier changed his campaign strategy and directed his appeal almost exclusively to the farm and labor vote. As if to prove the sincerity of his conversion, he sought advice early in the campaign from Frank Walsh, a Kansas City lawyer with a national reputation as a reformer and champion of organized labor. "Taking an aggressive stand in opposition to the reported concerted movement of 'Big Business' to put organized labor out of commission,"[16] Lozier developed an extensive labor platform containing the following plank:

> Statutory recognition and encouragement of labor's right of collective bargaining and the right to organize and to speak and act by and through its representatives; and the enactment of such legislation as will improve labor conditions and enable labor to receive its fair and just proportion of the wealth it creates.[17]

Immediately endorsing Lozier's candidacy, Walsh called his platform "the real Magna Charta of Labor." In a letter obviously meant for publication, Walsh praised Lozier's character and honesty and assured labor leaders that "Ralph Lozier is a man whom, if elected,

14. "Excerpt from Speech delivered on Labor Day, St. Charles, September 4, 1922," Clarence A. Cannon, Papers.
15. Lozier to W. B. Wilson, April 25, 1916; Lozier to Robert E. Lozier, April 25, 1916, Ralph F. Lozier, Papers.
16. Lozier to Walsh, May 10, 1922, *ibid.*
17. Lozier to N. H. Porter, July 21, 1922, *ibid.*

will stand squarely and honestly behind every pre-election declaration and promise."[18]

Lozier reproduced thousands of copies of Walsh's letter for distribution to members of organized labor. Meanwhile, he began attacking his opponent's labor record. In all his years in Congress, Rucker's activity on behalf of labor has consisted of merely "voting right," Lozier charged. "He cannot point to a single Bill he ever initiated or had part in making which would tend to remove in any way any of the burdens now resting upon the shoulders of labor. He cannot point to a single speech in the halls of Congress in behalf of the laboring man." Lozier promised to actively initiate and aggressively fight for legislation "necessary to promote the general welfare of the public [and] protect labor in the enjoyment of its right [to] maintain and improve the standards of life and conditions of employment."[19]

During the campaign Lozier held several meetings with labor organizations and tried to contact by mail every union member in the Second District. He also set up a system whereby selected individuals in each union would be responsible for getting all the members to the polls on primary day. With this superb organization, Lozier easily won the Democratic nomination, crediting his victory to the "aggressive support that I received from the Union Labor organizations." He assured labor leaders of his indebtedness "to the laboring men in the Second Congressional District for my nomination," and promised to "actively and aggressively strive to secure the enactment of such legislation as is necessary to . . . protect labor in enjoyment of its rights."[20]

During the general election campaign, Lozier relied heavily on the labor vote. Although he refused to endorse the La Follette candidacy because of his loyalty to the Democratic party. Lozier expressed sympathy for La Follette's cause and actively cooperated with labor's Organization for Progressive Political Action. In the flush of victory after the general election, Lozier wrote Frank Walsh of his "very great obligations to the laboring men of the District, nearly all of whom supported me both in the Primary and general elections."[21]

18. Walsh to J. J. Porter, June 3, 1922, *ibid.*
19. Lozier to R. R. Kelley, July 28, 1922; Lozier to N. H. Porter, July 21, 1922, *ibid.*
20. Lozier to William Scanlon, June 27, 1922; Lozier to Will Hinton, July 3, 1922; Lozier to W. E. Van Treese, July 3, 1922; Lozier to Ralph Porter, July 3, 1922; Lozier to Frank R. Lee, July 5, 1922; Lozier to L. E. Shelton, July 17, 1922; Lozier to Hinton, July 18, 1922; Lozier to Reuben T. Wood, August 4, 1922; Lozier to Lee, August 2, 1922, *ibid.*
21. Wood to Lozier, September 20, 1922; Lozier to the Executive Committee, Missouri State Organization for Progressive Political Action, October 25, 1922; Lozier to Walsh, November 27, 1922, *ibid.*

Once in office Lozier carried out his campaign pledges by responding to requests from labor leaders and usually supporting legislation they advocated.[22] Organized labor was pleased with Lozier's performance and supported him until his defeat in the Democratic primaries of 1934. Labor's political romance with Lozier, while somewhat unusual, mirrored a trend among Missouri's Democratic congressmen, particularly rural congressmen with few labor organizations in their districts, who established surprisingly favorable labor records in Congress and received labor endorsements during primary and general election campaigns.[23]

During the 1920s organized labor's endorsement of Democratic candidates became a more common factor in Missouri politics. In 1920 the labor movement supported Democrats in slightly less than half of all contests for state office, the Missouri Supreme Court, and the United States Congress. Between 1928 and 1932, organized labor's commitment to the Democratic party grew at an accelerated pace, with the result that by 1932 organized labor endorsed Democrats for all such offices (Figure 3).[24] The deepening depression of the early thirties contributed to this trend toward the Democratic party, but its importance should not be overemphasized. Other circumstances affected labor's political decisions as well. Prohibition remained a vital issue to the labor movement. The growing sentiment against the experiment within Democratic party ranks, bringing the nomination of Al Smith in 1928, certainly affected the party in Missouri where Democrats who previously supported prohibition began to waver. By 1932 many were ready to abandon the experiment in social control.[25] As this and other issues developed that united labor

22. Lozier to National Legislation and Information Bureau, July 21, 1923; Lozier to J. M. Creed, February 27, 1923; Lozier to E. W. Jenkins, March 29, 1924; Lozier to F. R. Lee, *et al.,* March 14, 1924; J. H. Englen, *et al.* to Lozier, May 21, 1924; Lozier to District 25, UMW, May 27, 1924; Lozier to W. B. Ellis, April 8, 1924; David Gramling to Lozier, November 26, 1931; March 15, April 16, 27, September 24, 1932, *Ibid.* Perhaps the only area in which Lozier's political program differed from that of organized labor was his affirmative position on prohibition.

23. Lozier to R. R. Lee, October 30, 1924, Ralph F. Lozier, Papers. MSFL, *Proceedings, 1926,* p. 22. *St. Louis Labor,* October 30, 1926; July 21, November 3, 1928. *The Labor Herald,* November 4, 1932. Lozier's defeat in 1934 was due in part to the reorganization of congressional districts, which forced him to run against another incumbent congressman.

24. MSFL, *Proceedings, 1921,* pp. 24, 25, 72–74; *1926,* pp. 25–27. *St. Louis Labor,* November 3, 1928. *The Labor Herald,* November 4, 1932.

25. Two examples are Charles M. Hay and Ralph F. Lozier, both influential Missouri Democrats. See "Radio Speech of A. J. Pickett, General Chairman, Brotherhood of Railway Clerks," Charles M. Hay, Papers. Lozier to Roy Fulton, August 22, 1932; Lozier to A. C. Good, July 20, 1932; Ralph F. Lozier, Papers. See also, Mitchell, *Embattled Democracy,* pp. 133, 139, 140, 142, 147–56 *passim.*

and the Democrats ideologically, a number of influential Missouri
Democrats began redoubling their efforts to forge a potential alliance.
In doing so, they became increasingly cognizant of labor's sensibilities
and aware of the need of many labor leaders for recognition. Perhaps
the activities of Kansas City political boss, Thomas J. "Boss" Pendergast, best illustrated this development within the Democratic party.
During the Republican twenties, Pendergast developed a smooth-
running, efficient Democratic political organization in Kansas City
and Jackson County, which enhanced his power and influence in the

Figure 3. Percentage of Democratic candidates endorsed by Missouri
labor unions, 1920–1932.

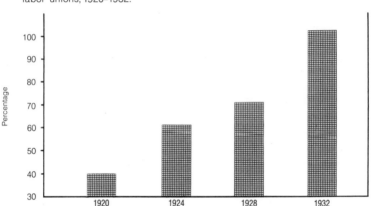

state's Democratic party organization. In an effort during the early
thirties to extend his influence throughout the state, Pendergast made
a major effort to forge an alliance with Missouri labor leaders.[26]

Actually, Boss Pendergast began making conciliatory moves
shortly after Kansas City labor organized the third-party ticket in
the municipal elections of 1918. Eager to attract labor's support for
his slate in 1920, Pendergast tapped John T. Smith, the most prominent official in the Kansas City Central Labor Union, for the office
of comptroller. At the time Smith served as secretary–organizer of
the union, the only full-time, salaried position in the central body. He
had previously held a similar office in the Missouri State Federation
of Labor. All organization candidates were elected, and Smith eventually became an official in the Pendergast organization while maintaining his association with the labor movement. Upon the death of
the Kansas City labor leader, Tom Pendergast and other influential

26. Pendergast's efforts to expand his influence are described in Lyle W.
Dorsett, *The Pendergast Machine,* pp. 147–51. Dorsett does not discuss Pendergast's relationship with the labor movement, but he does provide an excellent
study of the Kansas City boss's progression from a ward healer to a Democratic leader with state and national prominence.

leaders of the Kansas City organization served as honorary pallbearers.[27]

Pendergast also attracted the support of labor, by publishing articles in his newspaper, the *Missouri Democrat,* endorsing its proposals. The editors of the paper made a special point to describe the friendly relationship between the labor movement and Democratic candidates and officeholders, and to criticize Republicans in the state government for their alleged antiunion activities. Meanwhile, Pendergast personally exhibited an increasing sensitivity to union labor. When labor leaders complained in 1928 that the contractor for one of his cement plants used nonunion labor, the job was immediately unionized. Two years later Pendergast "welcomed" unionization of the teamsters, chauffeurs, and helpers employed by his Ready Mixed Concrete Company.[28]

Pendergast pleased labor leaders most, however, by endorsing Reuben T. Wood's candidacy for Congress. A combination of circumstances gave Pendergast unusual power over the Missouri congressional delegation. After the 1930 census, the number of Missouri representatives to Congress was reduced by three. By 1932, the legislature had still failed to adopt a reapportionment plan to accommodate the decrease, so all congressional candidates were forced to run at large. Because of Pendergast's control over the large bloc of votes in Kansas City and Jackson County, he gained considerable sway over the state Democratic organization, including great influence over the naming of Democratic candidates for Congress. Congressional hopefuls almost swarmed into Kansas City seeking the Boss's endorsement. Before the filing deadline in 1932, fifty-six Democratic aspirants vied for Missouri's thirteen congressional seats. Ultimately, Pendergast endorsed twenty-two candidates, including organized labor's Reuben Wood of Springfield and Mary Ryder of Saint Louis, the only woman contender. It soon became clear, however, that while the Boss had endorsed several aspirants, he would actively support only a few. One of the few, Reuben Wood, was elected. The fate of organized labor's second candidate in the congressional sweepstakes, Mary Ryder, vividly demonstrated Pendergast's political importance. Mrs. Ryder, running without Pendergast's active support, received more votes than Wood in Saint Louis and ran even in the outstate areas. Wood's ninety thousand votes in Jackson County won

27. *The Labor Herald,* March 12, 1920; October 10, 1930. *The Kansas City Journal,* March 11, 1920. *Kansas City Star,* March 10, 1920. *Missouri Democrat,* March 5, 1926.

28. *Missouri Democrat,* October 30, 1925; August 27, September 3, 1926; January 29, July 22, 1932. *The Labor Herald,* February 3, 1928; February 22, 1929; March 13, 1931.

him the nomination while Mrs. Ryder received only twenty-six thousand and finished twenty-first.[29]

Pendergast's growing influence in the labor movement was further evidenced by David Gramling, chairman of the Missouri Division of the Brotherhood of Locomotive Engineers. Second District Congressman Ralph Lozier, wondering whether he would have organized labor's support in the 1932 primary elections because of his position on prohibition, wrote Gramling asking for his evaluation of the situation. Although Gramling was personally opposed to the Kansas City organization, he admitted Pendergast's endorsement of Lozier's candidacy assured him of labor's support. Gramling told Lozier that "the boys" had some reservations about voting for Lozier until he received the Pendergast endorsement, then they had "quickly fallen into line."[30]

In addition to endorsing labor candidates, by early 1932 Pendergast had forged a firm alliance with at least three influential unions in Missouri, the Brotherhood of Railroad Trainmen, the Missouri State Federation of Labor, and the Kansas City Central Labor Union. His endorsement of the unpopular candidate, Charles Howell, for the United States Senate in 1932 tested the strength of that alliance, and it held firm.[31]

In the Democratic primary Howell faced two opponents, Charles Hay and Bennett "Champ" Clark. Of the three, Hay had the best labor record and had received labor's endorsement for the same office four years earlier. Hay continued in statements and speeches to endorse the objectives of the labor movement and agreed to support a six-hour day, if necessary, to solve the unemployment problem.[32] Shortly after filing, Hay received the endorsement of the chief executives of the sixteen standard railroad brotherhoods. The railroad unions, vigorously supporting his candidacy, sent a special representative into Missouri to work for Hay among railroad workers. A few days before the primary, they flooded the state with copies of a national weekly newspaper, *Labor,* published by the railroad brotherhoods and sent to each local union member. It was a special Missouri edition dedicated to Hay's candidacy.[33]

29. Dorsett, *Pendergast,* p. 150. *Kansas City Journal-Post,* July 26, 1932. *Official Manual, 1933–1934,* pp. 412–23.
30. Gramling to Lozier, September 24, 1932, Ralph F. Lozier, Papers.
31. Dorsett, *Pendergast,* p. 151.
32. "Labor Day Address of Charles M. Hay, delivered at Moberly, Missouri, Monday Afternoon, September 7th, 1931," Charles M. Hay, Papers. Before Hay prepared this speech, he communicated with both Senators Wagner and La Follette to ask for advice and available materials pertaining to the labor and employment situation. Hay to Wagner, July 14, 1931; Hay to La Follette, July 15, 1931, Charles M. Hay, Papers.
33. Edward Keating to Hay, March 19, 26, 1932, *ibid.*

As in some earlier elections, however, organized labor split over candidates for the Senate in 1932. Despite Hay's favorable labor record and his endorsement by the railroad brotherhoods, the State Federation of Labor, the Kansas City Central Labor Union, and Missouri railway trainmen endorsed Charles Howell. The national leadership of the Brotherhood of Railroad Trainmen was distressed over the endorsement. These Missouri unions chose Howell ostensibly because Hay was a prohibitionist.[34] The prohibition issue, although important to organized labor, had not been significant prior to the 1932 primaries and after the primaries did not interfere with labor's endorsements of Democrats in the 1932 general elections.[35] The question of refusing endorsement to dry candidates with favorable voting records on issues concerning labor reform was certainly troublesome, and President Wood of the State Federation admitted it would be "suicide" not to endorse such men. Actually, Hay's stand on prohibition was a mild one. Although he expressed reservations regarding the Democratic plank on prohibition, Hay was willing to compromise, stating that if elected he would vote to submit a proposition to the states for the repeal of the Eighteenth Amendment. Furthermore, Bennett Clark was the "dripping wet" in the contest but received no labor backing, while Howell had equivocated on the issue until the party platform was written. In the confusion, Bennett Clark, the candidate least acceptable to the labor movement, swept to a primary victory.[36]

The gubernatorial campaign of 1932 provided further evidence of organized labor's growing commitment to the Democratic party and also of the increasing influence Tom Pendergast exerted in the labor movement. Eager to extend his influence beyond Kansas City, Pendergast became extremely interested in controlling the governorship. Realizing the need for a candidate with considerable outstate support, Pendergast chose the unsuccessful Democratic nominee of 1928, Francis Wilson, who had run a strong race in the face of a Republican landslide. In 1928 Wilson had demonstrated considerable support in the rural areas of the state, a factor that made him less

34. *The Labor Herald,* March 11, July 15, 1932. Hay to George M. Harrison, June 3, 1932, Charles M. Hay, Papers. *St. Louis Post-Dispatch,* June 3, 1932.

35. The State Federation, for example, endorsed such dry congressmen as Lozier, Romjue, Milligan, and Cannon in 1932. *The Labor Herald,* November 4, 1932.

36. William Scanlon to Wilson, February 16, 1932, Francis M. Wilson, Papers. Hay to Keating, August 16, 1932; "Radio Speech of A. J. Pickett, July 30, 1932," Charles M. Hay, Papers. Mitchell, *Embattled Democracy,* pp. 268, 269.

dependent upon the Kansas City machine and Boss Pendergast. The Kansas City politico, however, was more interested in supporting a winner than losing the race with a weak, dependent crony. Because Pendergast's primary interest was patronage, he had every reason to expect that a successful and grateful Wilson would honor Kansas City's requests.[37]

Wilson's candidacy created serious problems for organized labor that had roots in certain bitterness aroused in the 1928 campaign. Wilson's record for promoting labor's causes was, at best, mixed. On the one hand, his favorable record as a state senator and as United States Attorney for the Western District of Missouri made him a difficult candidate to pass over. Among his accomplishments was the successful defense of the constitutionality of the Adamson Eight Hour Law. During the 1928 campaign, the Brotherhood of Railroad Trainmen endorsed him and took an active role in his campaign. However, most other Missouri labor organizations were less enthusiastic about Wilson. Two organizations that were especially indifferent were the Kansas City Central Labor Union, which went on record only "as having no objections to his candidacy," and the Joint Labor Legislative Committee, which endorsed him only casually.[38]

Labor leaders in 1928 felt uneasy about Wilson for a number of reasons. As a United States Attorney, he had vigorously prosecuted union leaders for violations of a federal injunction in the Springfield streetcar strike, and he sent one prominent Missouri labor leader, O. E. Jennings, to jail.[39] Wilson's position as Receiver for the Street Railway Company in Kansas City was another mark against him because of the long history of conflict between the company and organized labor, and the maintenance of a company union on the streetcar system under Wilson's receivership still rankled Kansas City labor.[40] Finally, Wilson's chief ally in the labor movement, the Brotherhood of Railroad Trainmen, had a strained relationship with other members of the Missouri Joint Labor Legislative Committee; and during the primary campaign, the committee had expelled

37. Dorsett, *Pendergast*, pp. 93, 94.

38. H. H. Washburn to Wilson, July 5, 1925; W. A. Wheeling to Wilson, December 16, 1927, Francis M. Wilson, Papers. *The Labor Herald*, June 22, 1928.

39. See the trial record of O. E. Jennings, Francis M. Wilson, Papers. Jennings and Reuben Wood were close personal friends, which probably prompted Wilson's fears that the influential leader of the State Federation of Labor was not friendly toward his candidacy. Wilson to E. W. Jenkins, April 4, 1926, Francis M. Wilson, Papers.

40. *The Kansas City Times*, August 14, 1922.

E. W. Jenkins, Wilson's most active supporter in the labor movement, for undermining committee policies.[41]

Nevertheless, Wilson won the primary and also the support of the Joint Labor Legislative Committee in the general elections, but his Republican opponent, Henry S. Caulfield, also received a labor endorsement because of his satisfactory record while serving as congressman from the Eleventh District.[42] During the campaign, Wilson's role as Receiver of the Kansas City Street Railway Company came back to haunt him when Max Dyer and C. B. Nelson, officials of the Kansas City Central Labor Union, issued a circular entitled, "How Francis Wilson Treated Union Labor Before He Was a Candidate for Governor." The authors of the circular reported that Wilson, as a joint receiver, had signed the following notice posted in the company's car barns:

UNION MEN have been approaching street car employees with a view of organizing a new union. Any men seen talking or associating with Labor Union Officials at home or on duty, or seen loitering around Labor Temple, 14th and Woodland, will be immediately dismissed from the service of the company.[43]

When approached by a committee from the Central Labor Union on the matter of organizing the streetcar workers, the joint receivers, including Wilson, reportedly "could see no necessity of recognizing or allowing their men to join the Amalgamated Association of Street and Electric Railway Employees," because the workers had their own organization.[44]

Four days before the election, the Republican State Central Committee distributed the Kansas City circular to labor centers throughout the state. Wilson was upset by the incident and made a radio broadcast challenging the circular's validity and defending his conduct as Receiver for the Street Railway Company. Although Wilson claimed that the circular harmed him in a close gubernatorial contest,

41. Wheeling to Wilson, May 15, 1928, Francis M. Wilson, Papers. The conflict between the Brotherhood of Railroad Trainmen and other Missouri labor organizations started in 1924 when the railway trainmen supported the Democratic ticket rather than endorsing the La Follette–Wheeler candidacy. Labor leaders were convinced that the representatives of the trainmen had tried to capitalize on their loyalty to the Democratic party during the 1925 session of the General Assembly to the detriment of the regular labor lobby. MSFL, *Proceedings, 1926,* p. 45.

42. *St. Louis Labor,* November 3, 1928.

43. "How Francis Wilson Treated Union Labor Before He Was a Candidate for Governor," n.d., Francis M. Wilson, Papers.

44. *Ibid.*

the trend toward Republicanism in 1928 probably would have been more than he could withstand.[45]

The evolving political loyalties of organized labor, as well as Pendergast's growing influence, were clearly revealed when Wilson again declared his candidacy for the same office four years later. Forgetting former grudges, labor quickly and nearly unanimously backed the Pendergast candidate in the primaries. Breaking a longstanding policy, the State Federation endorsed Wilson before the official filing deadline.[46] Meanwhile, Max Dyer signed an affidavit repudiating the circular he drafted four years earlier. He had been misinformed, Dyer stated, and had since investigated Wilson's labor record and found him to be a consistent friend of organized labor. During the campaign, labor leaders actively worked for Wilson's nomination and election, organizing Wilson for Governor Clubs, stumping the state, arranging meetings, and distributing literature in his behalf. In the primary, however, they had to expend considerable time and energy repudiating the circular of 1928, which had been reissued by Wilson's Democratic opponent.[47]

Wilson won the Democratic primary easily but died shortly before the November elections. The Democratic State Central Committee chose as his successor, Guy B. Park, a Pendergast candidate, although better-known Democrats were available. Organized labor immediately endorsed the Pendergast candidate. Curiously, Park's Republican opponent, E. H. Winter, received labor's endorsement four years earlier when he ran for lieutenant governor because of a "splendid labor record as Speaker of the House in the 54th General Assembly."[48] Winter apparently had done nothing in the meantime to offend labor, except, perhaps, to be a Republican.

Evidence of the growing alliance between labor and the Democratic party manifested itself throughout the state. While Pendergast cultivated labor leaders in western Missouri, two influential Saint

45. Wilson to Scanlon, June 13, 1932; Wilson to Ben E. Hulse, January 18, 1932, *ibid. Official Manual, 1929–1930*, pp. 237, 238.

46. Wilson to Wood, January 22, 1932, Francis M. Wilson, Papers. The State Federation's early endorsement suggests that Pendergast, who was extremely anxious for the state to have a Democratic governor, had already agreed to endorse Wood.

47. Hulse to Wilson, January 12, 1932; pamphlet, "Francis M. Wilson and Labor Unions," n.d.; Wilson to Hulse, January 18, 1932; Al Munsey to C. A. Leedy, Jr., June 24, 1932; Edgar C. Nelson to J. B. Hooper, May 25, 1932; Wilson to Scanlon, June 13, 1932; Wilson to Ellis, June 20, 1932; Lamb to Leedy, July 7, 1932; J. E. Boggs to Nelson, July 27, 1932; Garrard T. Sherman to James H. Hull, October 31, 1932, Francis M. Wilson, Papers.

48. *The Labor Herald,* October 28, November 4, 1932. *St. Louis Labor,* November 3, 1928.

Louis politicians, Mayor Bernard Dickmann and Congressman Richard Igoe, quietly built political fences in the eastern part of the state. The Saint Louis politicians integrated labor leaders into the city's Democratic party organization, and willingly intervened in labor's behalf with both state and national governmental agencies and elected officials. On the state level as well, labor leaders and union members assumed positions in the Democratic party organization, serving in delegations to state and national nominating conventions, and receiving appointments to labor oriented boards and agencies on both the local and state levels. Many union political clubs that once included the word *nonpartisan* in their titles, now substituted *Democratic*.

While labor's expanding influence in the Democratic party was advantageous, it did forfeit some of the cherished independence of action that had characterized it in the days of nonpartisanship.

As the Democratic party took labor-endorsed candidates into the fold, labor sometimes had to accept party leaders not always to its liking. Two such men were State Sens. Michael Casey of Kansas City and Michael Kinney of Saint Louis. Both men, through seniority, had become powerful figures in the state Senate. In the past, their use of that power often had deeply offended organized labor, especially their opposition to workmen's compensation, old-age pensions, the direct primary, and other important social reforms. Despite labor's repeated denouncements, Senators Casey and Kinney were firmly entrenched and respected leaders in the Democratic party organizations of their respective districts. Labor leaders apparently found it expedient to endorse rather than oppose them, thus eliminating the risk of offending local Democratic organizations.[49]

But the important trend was the move toward Democratic–labor accommodation. By 1932, the labor movement in Missouri already acted as an element of what later would be termed the *Roosevelt Coalition*. Labor had rejected both nonpartisanship and an independent labor party. Influenced by local and national political developments, it moved into an alliance with the Democratic party. The Democratic electoral sweep of state and national offices in 1932 would soon provide labor leaders the opportunity to assess the effectiveness of their new political alliance.

49. *The Labor Herald,* November 4, 1932. *Missouri Democrat,* April 8, 1927. MSFL, *Proceedings, 1928,* pp. 37, 81, 82; *1930,* pp. 15, 16. Gramling to Lozier, September 24, 1932, Ralph F. Lozier, Papers.

Chapter VIII

DEPRESSION DECADE

As most of American society, the attention and concern of Missouri's organized labor movement during the 1930s centered on the Great Depression and the recovery and reform efforts associated with it. While changes in the 1930s significantly altered the nature of the labor movement and its position in American society, the New Deal acted less as an initiator of change than as an accelerator of changes already underway. In broad terms, the depression decade witnessed the culmination of several social and political trends that had been established much earlier by the state labor movement.

The coming of the depression, signaled by the stock market crash in late October, 1929, quickly made its impression on the Missouri labor force. Unemployment, which had been growing during the twenties, mounted sharply during the early thirties. By 1930 the average rate of unemployment was 15.9 per cent of the work force. A year later it reached 27 per cent; in 1932, 38.1 per cent. Unemployment peaked in 1933 at 38.6 per cent and then slowly declined through the remainder of the decade. Between 1929 and 1933, the value of manufactures produced in the Saint Louis industrial area decreased 56 per cent, a decline slightly greater than the national average. Almost 52,000 plant employees were jobless by 1933, and wages fell 53 per cent, from a total payroll of $198,008,000 to $92,396,000. The state suffered a 50 per cent decline in retail sales and a 59 per cent reduction in wholesale sales.[1]

The construction industry in Missouri was most severely depressed. In the peak unemployment year of 1933, 77 per cent of the building trades' workers were without jobs. Following the building trades, unemployment was most severe among metalliferous miners (67 per cent), steam railroad workers (43 per cent), and general manufacturing employees (40 per cent).[2]

Labor leaders seemed less surprised with the severity of the depression than most Missourians. They had expressed concern about weaknesses in the economy long before the stock market crash and

1. Joseph M. Klamon, *et al.*, *A Survey of the Labor Market in Missouri in Relation to Unemployment Compensation*, pp. 79, 80. David D. March, *A History of Missouri*, Vol. 2, p. 1355.
2. Klamon, *Survey of the Labor Market*, pp. 79, 80.

had warned that growing unemployment and industrial surpluses would lead the nation into economic disaster. Labor leaders determined three related causes for this economic maladjustment: the overwhelming power of the business sector of the economy; the introduction of labor-saving machinery that increased the amount produced per laborer but was not accompanied by associated reductions in prices or adjustments in wages; and, resulting from these conditions, a highly unequal distribution of wealth. Labor leaders rejected the notion that industrial surpluses that occurred because of these conditions could be dumped on the foreign market and instead insisted that the American economy depended upon an internal market. The only way to deal with surplus production was to increase buying power by putting more money into the pockets of the average consumer.[3]

As labor leaders contemplated the problems of the depression and attempted to suggest a program for recovery, they concluded that government must assume greater responsibility for the stability of the economic system and the security of the individual. Actually, labor began promoting reform in the 1920s as a result of unfavorable economic developments antedating the depression. These proposals included a legislated maximum five-day week as a means of distributing employment to more workers and a six-hour day without reductions in pay as an additional attempt to increase employment and buying power. To alleviate the harshness of unemployment, labor favored the establishment of a state unemployment insurance fund to provide workers with adequate compensation during periods of unemployment.[4] Primarily the product of industrial change during the decade of the twenties, these reform proposals complemented older social welfare objectives such as old-age pensions, maximum hour and minimum wage laws for women, child labor reform, health and sickness insurance, and relief funds for the unemployed.[5]

The Transition of Federalism

In their efforts to achieve reform, however, labor leaders gradually adopted an essentially different strategy than the one followed before the depression. Continually frustrated on the state level, labor leaders increasingly began to look to the Federal Government to implement major reform legislation. Although this interest in federal solutions

3. MSFL, *Proceedings, 1928,* pp. 63–65; *1929,* pp. 5–7; *1930,* pp. 5, 6.
4. *The Labor Herald,* June 5, 1931. MSFL, *Proceedings, 1928,* p. 45; *1929,* pp. 55, 62. *The Progressive Press,* January 2, 1931.
5. See Chap. 3.

to state problems intensified with the social reforms enacted under the New Deal, the trend had begun long before Franklin Roosevelt's inauguration.

Disillusionment with the state legislature's capacity to reform had been growing steadily. The long, arduous, and expensive campaign for an unsatisfactory workmen's compensation system and the frustrating efforts to reform the convict labor system aggravated labor's disenchantment with the General Assembly. Meanwhile, during the late twenties and early thirties, federal action on two reforms long sought by Missouri labor encouraged labor leaders to look more to the national government.

Missouri labor leaders believed they had finally found the solution to the problem of convict labor when Missouri Sen. Harry Hawes and Congressman Cooper of Ohio jointly introduced a bill in 1928 to regulate the transportation of convict-made goods in interstate commerce. The bill prohibited the transportation of convict-made articles into any state that employed the state-use system. Because Missouri could become the dumping ground for these products from nearby states if it continued the practice of using convict labor, labor leaders assumed that federal action would force the state legislature to respond. Consequently, labor representatives actively cooperated with Senator Hawes in his successful efforts to push the bill through Congress by testifying before House and Senate committees and lobbying congressmen from Missouri. After the passage of the bill, President Wood of the State Federation told convention delegates that the labor movement had entered the campaign for federal legislation because of the impossibility of gaining any meaningful reform on the state level.[6]

Another issue that focused the attention of Missouri labor leaders on Washington was the regulation and reform of the issuance of injunctions during labor disputes. During many sessions of the General Assembly, the labor injunction was on the "preferred list" of reform legislation desired by the State Federation. Enactment of such legislation seemed remote in the twenties, however, and labor leaders relegated it to the position of desired-but-unattainable legislation. Missouri labor's active interest in the measure was renewed by a federal anti-injunction measure sponsored by Sens. Henrik Shipstead and George Norris, and by Congressman Fiorello La Guardia. Missouri labor representatives followed the same procedures they had used to promote convict labor reform. They lobbied the state's congres-

6. *St. Louis Labor,* January 28, February 18, May 26, 1928. *The Labor Herald,* May 29, 1931. Harry B. Hawes to Francis Wilson, February 13, 1928, Francis M. Wilson, Papers. MSFL, *Proceedings, 1928,* pp. 26, 27, 68–73; *1929,* pp. 12, 13.

sional delegation, and a number of the state's labor leaders went to the nation's capital to work for a positive vote.[7]

The labor movement's disenchantment with the state legislature increased as the Federal Government began responding vigorously to the problems created by the Great Depression, in stark contrast to the near paralysis of state government. Even in the early days of the depression under Hoover, a variety of public works and relief measures were introduced in Congress by such senators as Robert La Follette, Burton Wheeler, and Edward Costigan. Labor strongly endorsed these efforts and also supported the thirty-hour week bill introduced by Sen. Hugo Black.[8] When Franklin D. Roosevelt assumed office and inaugurated emergency relief and recovery programs similar to those advocated by Missouri labor, a trend that was already well established progressed even further.

Missouri labor leaders enthusiastically endorsed the relief, reform, and recovery measures of the New Deal. They had first advocated many such measures during the Progressive Era; they had included them in their post-World War I reconstruction program; they had been proposed in Missouri's 1921–1922 Constitutional Convention and were included in the Liberal party platform that supported the La Follette–Wheeler ticket in 1924. Thus in broad terms the New Deal fulfilled the somewhat eclectic program of social and labor reform previously adopted by the labor movement.

Of the three types of legislation enacted during the thirties, reform measures were the least controversial among trade unionists. Labor had long advocated programs for old-age security, unemployment insurance, minimum wage and maximum hour laws, a national employment service, child labor reform, promotion of public and private housing, and the right of an individual to join a union and bargain collectively. New Deal relief and recovery programs, although equally desirable, created more controversy. Labor leaders strongly approved of the principles upon which these programs were founded, but the actual practices once in operation sometimes produced unexpected and unfortunate results that tempered labor's enthusiasm for them. Moreover, the administrators, especially on the state and local level, did not always fulfill the ideals of the proponents of the measures. The National Recovery Administration provides one example.

Although originally supporting Hugo Black's thirty-hour a week bill as the most desirable recovery proposal,[9] Missouri labor leaders accepted the NRA as an acceptable substitute. They especially ap-

7. *The Labor Herald,* June 6, 1930. Lozier to David Gramling, March 15, 1932, Ralph F. Lozier, Papers.

8. *The Labor Herald,* May 30, 1930; June 3, 1932. *The Progressive Press,* December 19, 1930. MSFL, *Proceedings, 1933,* pp. 9, 41.

9. MSFL, *Proceedings, 1933,* pp. 9, 41.

proved of Section 7a, which guaranteed the right of collective bargaining and provided for industrial codes, which would set minimum wages and maximum hours and abolish child labor. Nevertheless, labor leaders soon became disillusioned because of the lax enforcement of the labor provisions of NRA codes. Shortly after the NRA was created, Reuben T. Wood, congressman and president of the State Federation of Labor, toured the state urging members of labor unions to take advantage of the provisions of the act to organize the unorganized. "This is the greatest opportunity which has ever presented itself," he told labor leaders, "for President Roosevelt is with you. Some employers are opposed to the act and for that reason there must be no delay in bringing the unorganized into the fold. The time to act is NOW."[10] As an organizing campaign got underway in Missouri, labor leaders found that many employers simply ignored the collective bargaining provisions with impunity or organized company unions, thus subverting the principle of the measure. Labor leaders also discovered that many employers who displayed the Blue Eagle, the symbol of code acceptance, violated the wage-and-hour provisions of the codes. Particularly galling were the prison labor contractors, labor's old nemeses, who "patriotically" displayed the Blue Eagle on their products.[11]

Administration of New Deal relief and public works programs was even more controversial than the enforcement of NRA codes. Since the turn of the century, organized labor in Missouri had advocated programs of public works to relieve distress during periods of unemployment; and during the depression, labor leaders joined other organizations in Missouri to sponsor and campaign for a $10 million bond issue for the rehabilitation of the state's eleemosynary institutions. After its passage, they lobbied federal officials for complementary federal relief and public works authorizations. Similarly, labor in Kansas City, Saint Louis, and other Missouri cities supported bond issues designed to raise funds for public works construction.[12] Thus, it was not the principle of the public works program to which

10. *The Labor Herald,* July 28, 1933.
11. MSFL, *Proceedings, 1934,* pp. 51, 52. Martin Wagner to Hopkins, April 24, 1935; Meyer Perlstein to Edward J. Roche, August 20, 1935; W. D. Hamly to Hopkins, May 9, 1935, Works Progress Administration, Papers, Record Group No. 69. George S. Darner to Green, March 15, 1935, AFL, Papers, Series 117A, File 7. William Brandt to Park, February 15, 1935; Theresa Singleton to Park, January 10, 1935; George Voigt to John J. Cochran, October 24, 1933, Guy B. Park, Papers.
12. Frank Reiser to Park, April 4, 1934; G. Cash to Park, May 6, 1934; Reuben Wood to Park, May 2, 1934; "Organized Labor Bond Committee for City, State and Board of Education Bond Issues," April 19, 1934; Wood to Park, June 8, 1934, Guy B. Park, Papers. P. J. Morrin to Green, May 24, 1934; G. W. Hines to Green, April 6, May 24, 1934, AFL, Papers, Series 117A, File 9.

labor leaders objected, but its administration. Unlike federal authorities, Missouri labor leaders refused to draw distinctions between public works and work relief. They assumed government had a responsibility to provide work for persons unable to find employment and saw no justification for applying different wage standards to public and private jobs involving similar types of work.

The New Deal program that best fit Missouri labor's concept of work relief was the Public Works Administration. PWA projects required a relatively large skilled labor force, especially from the well organized but, to a large extent, unemployed building trades' workers. A "prevailing wage" provision also was adopted, which stipulated that workers on public projects would receive the same wage scale as those privately employed. Nevertheless, PWA had severe limitations. Appropriations were limited, and Administrator Harold Ickes moved at a glacial pace in starting new projects. PWA never became a large employer of Missouri's jobless.[13]

After PWA, Missouri labor leaders were most enthusiastic about the relief provisions of the Civilian Works Administration. The CWA took half its workers from the relief rolls and the remainder from among people without jobs who were not subjected to the humiliation of a "means" test. CWA paid prevailing minimum wages and provided some employment for skilled workers. Although it was a federally sponsored and administered relief program, CWA depended upon local and state officials to administer the program; and shortly after the program began, complaints reached Washington offices about the failure of Missouri CWA administrators to enforce the minimum wage scale and other provisions of the program. After a period of intense acrimony, these problems were largely resolved by the actions of federal officials, and by the spring of 1934, the CWA program was working smoothly in Missouri. Consequently, labor leaders were disappointed when Roosevelt ordered Harry Hopkins, the federal administrator, to phase the program out as quickly as possible. With four million CWA workers fired during the spring of 1934, the relief burden again reverted to the Federal Emergency Relief Administration, an agency that administered the relief program Missouri labor considered least satisfactory. While CWA workers were paid an average of $15.04 a week, FERA paid only $6.50. Moreover, a means test was required to be placed on the FERA rolls.[14]

13. Frank J. Murphy to Green, March 10, 22, April 16, 1934; M. G. Severinghous to William C. Roberts, April 7, 14, 1934; J. L. Rogers to Green, May 27, 1934; Severinghous to Robert Wagner, April 14, 1934, AFL, Papers, Series 117A, File 9. William Anderson, et al. to Franklin Roosevelt, January 11, 1935, WPA, Papers.

14. Gary M Fink, "The Evolution of Social and Political Attitudes in the Missouri Labor Movement, 1900–1940," pp. 237–41. William E. Leuchtenburg, *Franklin D. Roosevelt and the New Deal,* p. 123.

Labor leaders were heartened when in January, 1935, the President asked Congress to appropriate $5 billion for a new program of emergency public employment, but cooled to the proposal upon learning it constituted merely a more sophisticated version of FERA relief. The new program established a "security wage" higher than the FERA dole but less than prevailing wage rates. Only those who had submitted to the means test and registered for public relief were eligible.

Although several New Deal agencies shared the appropriation, the most important and controversial was a new division, the Works Progress Administration, set up under the direction of Harry Hopkins. Labor leaders soon expressed three major grievances regarding the concept and operation of WPA. First, WPA was essentially a program for unskilled, common labor. When labor officials requested that 10 per cent of the WPA jobs be reserved for skilled workers, as had been the case with CWA, they were told that WPA intended to provide work only for the destitute on relief.[15]

Labor's second grievance involved the "security wage." Labor officials complained that WPA projects usually required the use of some skilled labor, and that paying a security wage in these cases counteracted the effort the labor movement had expended to establish the wage scales. The actual effect of the WPA security wage upon the wage scales established by organized labor was difficult to determine, and WPA officials never made a concerted effort to find out. They argued that the burden of proof rested with complaining unions, and labor leaders found it almost impossible to find an employer willing to admit that he was influenced by the WPA wage scale. Moreover, labor leaders argued that WPA did much work ordinarily performed by union contractors, in some cases monopolizing building materials and preventing the expansion of construction projects by private contractors and, in turn, inhibiting the hiring of laborers.[16]

Labor's third major complaint involved the WPA's eligibility requirements for employment. It employed only the destitute who would otherwise depend on relief. Labor leaders opposed this policy because their unions spent hundreds of thousands of dollars to ac-

15. Leuchtenburg, *Franklin D. Roosevelt,* pp. 124, 125. Searle F. Charles, *Minister of Relief: Harry Hopkins and the Depression,* pp. 145, 146. William Anderson, *et al.* to Roosevelt, January 11, 1935, WPA, Papers.

16. James Mullane to Roosevelt, September 17, 1935; Millard Morgan to Hopkins, October 12, 1935; John Church to Hopkins, January 24, 1936; Max Dyer to James Farley, February 24, 1935; Church to John J. Cochran, March 20, 1936; M. J. McDonough to Nels Anderson, September 30, 1936; Daniel O. Collins to David K. Niles, April 27, 1937; John O'Connor to Niles, June 27, 1938; J. R. Anderson to Frances Perkins, April 30, 1935; Church to Cochran, March 20, 1936, WPA, Papers.

commodate the needs of their members without state and federal relief by sharing available work and taxing employed union workers
for the benefit of the unemployed. Now they faced discrimination
on WPA work because of these accomplishments. These inherent
problems with the WPA concept of work relief were compounded,
in the eyes of Missouri labor leaders, by the inflexible and unsympa-
thetic administration of the program by state and local officials.[17]

Regardless of their disappointment with the limited character and
insensitive administration of New Deal programs, however, labor
leaders found them vastly superior to any methods applied by the
state government. Resistance to change completely frustrated the
efforts of reformers to enact a "little New Deal" in Missouri.[18] Because they were primarily concerned with a balanced budget and the
retrenchment of state expenditures, Missouri legislators and administrators of both parties failed to respond with adequate programs to
solve the problems created by an industrial society generally or the
depression in particular. For example, legislators continued to regard
unemployment and relief as local concerns. Federal Relief Administrator Hopkins twice threatened to cut off all federal relief payments in Missouri before the state legislature appropriated matching
funds.[19]

Although labor leaders saw some of their legislative objectives
achieved in the 1930s, they too often had to measure success, as in
the 1920s, in terms of hostile legislation defeated. When the legislative session of 1933 ended, for example, the State Federation's
legislative committee reported exasperatedly, "We have never held
a General Assembly in the State of Missouri where the possibility
for the loss of many good laws was so pronounced as was this past
session." The situation two years later remained unchanged. "It is
the opinion of many who have watched many sessions of the Assembly that this session will go down in history as the one which had
to assimilate the hardest drive ever made against the General Assembly by the special interests." Even as late as 1939, labor's report
remained gloomy. "While we were not successful in having many of
our bills enacted into laws, your committee feels gratified in the
thought that no particular legislation was passed that might be harm-
ful to the successful operation of our Organization."[20]

17. Fink, "Evolution of Social and Political Attitudes," pp. 245–49.
18. The Missouri state legislature was not unique in its resistance to change
during the thirties. James T. Patterson found such a reaction to the problems
of the thirties to be the rule rather than the exception. See Patterson, "The
New Deal and the States," and Patterson, *The New Deal and the States:
Federalism in Transition.*
19. March, *History of Missouri,* pp. 1358, 1370–72.
20. MSFL, *Proceedings, 1933,* p. 78; *1935,* p. 129; *1939,* p. 117.

The program labor offered these do-nothing legislatures of the 1930s included a broad range of labor, economic, and social reforms. Although most of these legislative efforts failed, a few major reforms were enacted, partly out of fear of losing Missouri's share of federal matching funds.

The labor lobby advocated several laws directly related to the activities of organized labor. One was a state law similar to the Norris–La Guardia Act that would restrict the injunction powers of state courts. They endorsed legislation prohibiting the importation of strikebreakers and curbing the activities of private detective and employment agencies. Labor also wanted state legislation paralleling the labor provisions of the NIRA and later the National Labor Relations Act. A "little Wagner Act" was introduced to cover employees in businesses not involved in interstate commerce, and the creation of a state labor relations board was proposed to serve the same function as the National Labor Relations Board. None of these bills passed or even gained serious consideration, despite labor's vigorous efforts.[21]

A similar fate awaited organized labor's efforts to inaugurate the state-use system for the disposal of goods produced by convict labor. Despite labor's optimism, the enactment of the Hawes–Cooper Act, which restricted the interstate transportation of convict-made goods into any state adopting the state-use system, had little effect on Missouri legislators. In the end, the influence of prison labor contractors prevailed. Even with the support of many concerned businessmen, labor found its efforts to reform the state's contract labor system as frustrating in the thirties as it had previously.[22]

Although its activities were primarily defensive, organized labor also exhibited an interest in the regulation and, in some cases, municipal ownership of public utilities. Labor lobbyists opposed attempts by public utility companies to abolish the Missouri Public Service Commission and replace it with a new agency. These businesses resented the commission because it had earlier objected to a projected merger of utility companies in Saint Louis. Besides reorganiz-

21. *Ibid., 1933,* pp. 64, 65; *1935,* pp. 73, 93; *1937,* pp. 92, 93; *1939,* p. 73. *St. Louis Labor Tribune,* March 2, 1940.
22. MSFL, *Proceedings, 1933,* pp. 74, 75; *1935,* pp. 97–101. Ben F. McDonald to Park, February 22, 1935; George Patterson to Park, January 12, 1933; J. B. Bush to Park, March 21, 1935; Thomas N. Dysart to Park, March 26, 1935, Guy B. Park, Papers. The labor lobby did come within one vote of success in 1935, but the opposition of rural legislators, representatives of the printing trades, and Governor Park ultimately doomed the measure. Representatives of rural Missouri opposed the bill, because they believed it would increase the price of binder twine then produced by convict labor. Printers opposed the law in the fear that the state penitentiary would be contracted for the state's printing.

ing the Public Service Commission, utility interests also wanted to repeal and revise all laws governing public service corporations. The proposed revision, according to labor, would seriously weaken existing regulatory legislation as well as repeal much judicial precedent. There was considerable hostility toward the measure throughout the state, not only from labor but also from newspapers and from many officials of the State Democratic Central Committee. Although the General Assembly approved it, it was vetoed by the Governor.[23]

Organized labor also expressed its interest in municipal ownership in a more positive way. During a special session of the state legislature in 1934, the labor lobby vigorously supported a proposal by Governor Park to exempt revenue bonds from the limit of indebtedness for Missouri that had been set in the constitution. Under this provision, Missouri cities would have been permitted to raise funds to purchase or establish public utilities. When the state legislature defeated the bill, Reuben Wood asked Governor Park to lead an effort to put the measure on the ballot by initiative petition and promised labor's active support, but the Governor declined.[24]

As in the 1920s, labor still fought for the enactment of child and women labor legislation but with little more success. Throughout the thirties the State Federation of Labor attempted to persuade the state legislature to ratify the child labor amendment to the United States Constitution. The Joint Labor Legislative Committee asked Governor Park to lead the fight for the amendment in the state legislature in 1933, but Park, explaining that the measure would endanger his legislative program, asked the labor representatives not to pursue the amendment that year; in return, he promised to support the measure in 1935. Labor leaders agreed and made the amendment a preferred measure when questioning candidates for election to the state legislature in 1934. Nevertheless, when outlining his legislative goals to a joint session of the state legislature a year later, Park ignored the child labor amendment and never vigorously supported it. It failed in the General Assembly during the thirties as it had during the twenties. The labor lobby encountered similar resistance to maximum hour and minimum wage laws for women.[25]

23. MSFL, *Proceedings, 1933,* pp. 75–78. H. H. Washburn to Park, March 28, 1933; Gramling to Park, April 25, 1933; George T. Lackey to Park, J. W. Miller to Park, April 4, 1933, Guy B. Park, Papers. *The Labor Herald,* June 2, 1933. *Messages and Proclamations of the Governors of the State of Missouri,* Vol. XIII, pp. 402, 403.

24. MSFL, *Proceedings, 1934,* pp. 97–100; Wood to Park, January 19, 1934, Guy B. Park, Papers.

25. Bernard F. Dickmann to Park, October 24, 1933; John Bernard to Park, October 24, 1933; R. E. Moon to Park, January 9, 1935, Guy B. Park, Papers, MSFL, *Proceedings, 1934,* pp. 59, 68; *1935,* pp. 69, 70; *1937,*

Stimulated by federal action, the General Assembly did make some advances in the area of social insurance, including improvement of the workmen's compensation law, old-age pensions, and passage of unemployment insurance. The workmen's compensation system legislated in 1926 soon revealed major flaws undermining its effectiveness. Private insurance companies adopted the practice of appealing even the smallest personal injury claim through the courts. Because litigants often could not afford the costly procedure of defending their awards, decisions in favor of the insurance companies were rendered by default, and through this procedure, insurance companies established a number of judicial precedents materially weakening the law. When its effort to correct this abuse was frustrated in the General Assembly, the State Federation, in 1930, sponsored an amendment to the law through initiative petition establishing compulsory state insurance, but the measure failed by a large margin. By 1935, still with no change in the law, President Wood of the State Federation vowed that if the provisions were not soon strengthened, the labor movement would introduce legislation to repeal the law. Nevertheless, several sessions of the General Assembly elapsed before it was improved.[26]

Attempts to enact old-age pension legislation met with somewhat more success. During the 1927 session of the General Assembly, a labor-supported old-age pension bill was defeated in the House by only six votes. Continuous labor agitation for the issue resulted in the first substantial victory in 1931 when the state legislature passed and submitted to the electorate an enabling act amending the Missouri Constitution to permit the General Assembly to enact an old-age pension law. In the 1932 general elections, Missouri voters approved it by a large margin, and the following year the General Assembly enacted an old-age pension bill but failed to appropriate money to carry out its provisions until two years later. The pension remained inadequate, however, until 1937 when the program was realistically financed with the addition of federal matching funds.[27]

Although labor leaders fought for the law, they remained unhappy

---

pp. 85, 90, 91. *The Labor Herald,* June 2, 1933; February 12, 1937. *Messages and Proclamations of the Governors of the State of Missouri,* Vol. XIII, pp. 341–66.

26. MSFL, *Proceedings, 1933,* pp. 65–67; *1935,* pp. 17–20; *1937,* pp. 117, 118. Gramling to Phillips, January 22, March 7, 1935; Phillips to Wood, July 22, 1938, Alroy S. Phillips, Papers. *St. Louis Post-Dispatch,* April 18, 1930. *Official Manual, 1931–1932,* pp. 269, 270.

27. *St. Louis Labor,* November 19, 1927. *The Progressive Press,* January 2, 23, 1931. *The Labor Herald,* June 6, 1930; June 5, October 16, 1931; May 27, June 3, 1932. *Official Manual, 1933–1934,* pp. 396, 397. MSFL, *Proceedings, 1927,* p. 105; *1930,* p. 84; *1933,* pp. 46, 47; *1934,* p. 66; *1935,* p. 20.

with it, because they preferred that the minimum age to collect the pension be sixty years instead of the seventy years required by the existing law. Eventually a sixty-five year age minimum was adopted to conform to federal standards. Labor also objected to the tendency to interpret and administer the law as an assistance or relief measure.[28]

Organized labor likewise was somewhat successful in its efforts to secure an unemployment compensation law. Legislation was finally passed in 1937, but only after Missouri lost nearly $5 million in federal matching funds because of its failure to act earlier. Because they realized that the law would be passed in 1937, labor leaders attempted to obtain as liberal a law as possible. Even so, the measure was not entirely satisfactory, although the labor lobby did successfully eliminate two of the bill's odious features that were strongly supported by business interests. The most objectionable section contained a 1 per cent employee assessment to help finance the plan. Labor also disliked the employer reserve fund feature and favored instead a pooled fund. Under the employers' reserve plan, each employer paid into an individual fund from which compensation was drawn until that reserve was exhausted. Under the pool arrangement, all payroll tax money went into one fund, which provided compensation for all eligible unemployed persons who had contributed until the entire fund was depleted.[29]

Despite these modifications, the law still contained several features organized labor wanted to change, including a reduction in the legal waiting period before benefits could be collected, increases in maximum weekly benefits, and a lengthening of the time period that benefit payments could be received. Although Gov. Lloyd C. Stark supported these revisions, state legislators exhibited more interest in reducing benefits than raising them, and nothing was accomplished.[30]

Trade unionists and other Missourians paid a high price for these limited social reforms—a sales tax. Efforts to initiate a sales tax failed throughout the twenties, but in 1934 a ½ per cent tax was approved to finance unemployment relief. A year later it was raised to 1 per cent and was also used to provide revenue for the old-age pension system and public school allotments. When revenue still proved inadequate, the tax was increased to 2 per cent in 1937.[31]

The labor movement had actually opposed the introduction of a general sales tax since 1922, advocating instead a progressive income

28. MSFL, *Proceedings, 1936*, p. 12; *1937*, pp. 110, 111. March, *History of Missouri*, pp. 1380, 1381.

29. MSFL, *Proceedings, 1937*, pp. 107–9, 117.

30. *Ibid*, pp. 107–9. For an analysis of the law, see "Missouri Unemployment Compensation Law," n.d., AFL, Papers, Series 117A, File 8D.

31. March, *History of Missouri*, p. 1380.

tax and high inheritance and estate taxes. Because the labor lobby recognized the need for additional revenue to finance the state's relief needs and old-age pensions, however, it did not actively oppose the enactment of the sales tax in 1934. It did attempt to modify the law to make it more equitable and successfully led the opposition to an amendment making the tax applicable to all wages and salaries in excess of fifty dollars a month. Labor failed in its efforts to exempt food, fuel, clothing, and other necessities of life from the provisions of the law.[32]

The failure of the Democratic-controlled state government to make more progress in the enactment of labor, economic, and social reforms inevitably led to some disillusionment with politics. The Missouri Joint Labor Legislative Committee felt disillusioned, frustrated, even betrayed, and said so to a Senate Judiciary Committee in 1935 as it was considering anti-injunction legislation.

> We have made repeated attempts to get favorable consideration for this legislation by your Committee and we have failed. We are advising you frankly that this bill is considered as our MEASURING STICK for this session and there is still time for the passage of the bill, if you will turn it loose with a favorable report.

> As we advised your Committee, the State and National platforms of the Democratic Party for 1928 and 1930 PROMISED LABOR THIS ANTI-INJUNCTION REFORM, and due to the faith of Missouri labor in Franklin D. Roosevelt and his program, approximately 265,000 Missouri labor votes followed his party in the last election, confident that we would receive the benefits of his program of social justice. Now we find ourselves PLEADING FOR A CRUMB, even though we believe WE SHOULD HAVE A PLACE AT THE TABLE, and, our pleas for those things we were promised fall upon deaf ears . . .[33]

After an equally disappointing session of the General Assembly two years later, the attorney for the State Federation of Labor, Cliff Langsdale, complained about the seemingly perverse conduct of the state legislature.

> The liberals and labor organizations carried this state last fall by more than a half million majority. The Associated Industries of Missouri and the Liberty League had nothing to do with it, yet they come down here and get what they want from the legislature we elected. We have some weeding out to do in the next primary . . . We must Democratize the Democrats of Missouri.[34]

32. *The Labor Herald,* March 3, April 14, May 26, September 15, 1922; March 12, 1926. MSFL, *Proceedings, 1934,* pp. 94–97; *1935,* pp. 124–27. James W. Miller to Stark, January 18, 1938, Lloyd C. Stark, Papers.
33. MSFL, *Proceedings, 1935,* p. 93.
34. *The Labor Herald,* May 28, 1937.

Yet as Langsdale's speech reveals, the unhappy trade unionists had no intention of breaking with the party.

Continuity and Change Within the Labor Movement

During the decade of the thirties, great changes occurred in the Missouri labor movement, many of them resulting from forces and conditions over which the labor movement had little control, particularly the Great Depression and the New Deal. Internal influences peculiar to the labor movement itself also altered its behavior. Internal and external forces were highly interrelated, and changes within the labor movement, in part, resulted from modifications in the external setting in which it operated.

One significant external factor precipitating significant internal change resulted from Missouri's evolving industrial development. Although significant changes occurred in the state's economy between 1919 and 1933, there was not a great deal of heavy industry in the state. The vast majority of goods manufactured and processed were nondurable, consumer products: the boot and shoe industry, which employed the largest number of workers, was by far the most important in both periods. During these years, the production of bread and bakery products moved from seventh place to second, and women's clothing, not in the top twenty in 1919, moved into fourth place in 1933. Two of Missouri's oldest industries, liquor and tobacco products, ranked in the top twenty in 1919 but dropped from the list in 1933. In terms of the value of manufacturers, wholesale meat packing ranked first, followed by boots and shoes, flour and grain-milling products, bread and bakery products, and printing and publishing. The latter two had replaced automobiles (which fell from the list in 1933) and foundry and machine-shop products, both of which ranked in the first five in 1919.[35]

Although the changes in Missouri's industrial composition were not extensive, they significantly affected the state labor movement. Older unions that had been so influential in the early years of the labor movement, such as the cigarmakers, the mineworkers, and the brewery workers, were being drastically weakened because technological innovation provided mechanical substitutes for many aspects of their work. Consequently, their membership, prestige, and influence were declining precipitantly. The cigarmakers' unions, although they still claimed in their membership a number of the state's major labor leaders, almost ceased to exist by 1933. For the mineworkers, the decline in the demand for coal, internal dissension, and the inferior quality of Missouri coal seriously weakened the union. In 1914 UMW locals had almost ten thousand members, but by 1933

35. Klamon, *Survey of the Labor Market,* pp. 11–14.

they could count less than two thousand. Prohibition was the primary cause of the decline of the brewery workers' unions. Although the UMW and brewery unions recovered in the thirties, they never regained the prominent position once held in the state labor movement.[36]

Significant in terms of numbers, the change was even more important to the labor movement's ideology. These unions traditionally assumed a position on the left wing of the labor movement, and as they lost influence, that of the more conservative, business unionism-oriented building trades grew. The growing influence of the building trades' unions was fed by a variety of circumstances including the declining strength of the Socialist party in the labor movement, the resolution of the imbroglio over workmen's compensation legislation, and the depressed state of the building trades' industry that led many building trades' union leaders to reassess their somewhat isolated position in the state labor movement.

Changes within the labor movement became most obvious in the State Federation of Labor. In the early years, the State Federation was influenced by a coalition of metropolitan left-wing unions and outstate railroad and mineworkers' unions. By the mid-thirties, most of the railroad brotherhoods, whose active involvement in the affairs of the state labor movement had steadily declined, dropped from the membership rolls, a factor which, along with the decline of the UMW, pushed the State Federation into a closer alliance with the building trades' unions. When allied with the teamsters' unions, the building trades could control the State Federation, and they exercised that control whenever necessary.[37]

Another significant change that was taking place within the state labor movement was the gradual emergence of a new generation of labor leaders, rising first at the local union level and then eventually reaching into the higher levels of organization. The ranks of the older generation were depleted by death, retirement, and promotion to positions in the national unions.[38] Unlike the earlier generation of union

36. By 1933 only three cigarmakers' locals were affiliated with the State Federation of Labor; four UMW locals and five brewery workers' unions were represented. MSFL, *Proceedings, 1933,* pp. 18–23.

37. *Ibid.* The power of this alliance was especially evident in the debates and votes on industrial unionism, see MSFL, *Proceedings, 1936,* pp. 73, 74, 91, 92.

38. A survey of the executive officers, vice-presidents, and executive board members of the State Federation of Labor and the equivalent leaders of the various city central unions and building trades councils reflects these changes in trade union leadership. The major exceptions were Reuben Wood, who remained the nominal head of the State Federation and an old Socialist, William Brandt, who replaced David Kreyling as the leader of the Saint Louis Central Trades and Labor Union.

leaders, many of whom had been schooled in such diverse social movements as the Knights of Labor, Populism and Socialism, single-tax agitation and Bellamy clubs, the new leaders were rooted in the labor movement itself; they lacked the scope and breadth of vision of their predecessors.

Compared to their predecessors, the new labor leaders appeared much less idealistic, more practical, and even cynical. They seemed to have less dedication to reforms that were beneficial to the entire working class. Indeed, judging from the eagerness with which they sought patronage appointments, many seem to have viewed the labor movement as a vehicle for personal advancement.[39] Nevertheless, since they associated their own success with that of their union, they were also men who analyzed labor policy in terms of its possible effect upon their organization.

This new group of labor leaders had to cope with one of the most serious internal conflicts facing organized labor, its division into rival AFL and CIO factions. Without strong commitments for or against the principle of industrial organization, most Missouri labor leaders showed little hostility to the CIO and had great difficulty accepting the official description of the CIO as a dual union movement. Missouri labor leaders always exhibited more interest in conciliating differences and reunifying the labor movement than in humiliating and punishing recalcitrant unions. As organizational men, they did not find industrial unionism as much a threat to the effectiveness of their organizations as they did the division of the labor movement.[40]

As the rift in organized labor widened, AFL and CIO unions in Missouri still found compromise possible in most situations. They usually honored each other's strikes, cooperated in efforts to influence local officials and government agencies, and worked together politically in the campaigns of 1936 and 1940.[41] AFL union leaders in Missouri deeply resented instructions from AFL headquarters ordering AFL-affiliated unions to disassociate themselves from Labor's Non-Partisan League in 1938, because it allegedly had become an arm of the CIO.[42]

The conflicts arising from the division of the labor movement were primarily economic and jurisdictional. On the other hand, a mutual

39. See Chap. 9.
40. For an expanded discussion of Missouri labor's response to the division of the labor movement, see Gary M Fink, "Unwanted Conflict: Missouri Labor and the CIO," pp. 432–47.
41. For example, *The Hannibal Labor Press,* October 14, 1938; William Brandt to Stark, September 20, 1940, Lloyd C. Stark, Papers; *St. Louis Labor Tribune,* October 15, 1937; March 17, 1938; June 15, 1940.
42. For examples of protests to this decision, see AFL, Papers, Series 117A, File 11C.

allegiance to the Democratic party and a broad range of agreement on policy issues bound them together. CIO unions supported AFL-affiliated union members in campaigns for public office, and AFL leaders reciprocated. At times this accommodation brought both groups into conflict with the national leadership of their respective union affiliations.[43]

Despite the unhappiness of Missouri union leaders over the division of the labor movement, it ultimately produced positive advantages. The successes of the CIO pushed the older craft unions into new and more extensive organizing drives of their own; once-sacred jurisdictional boundaries were becoming less sacrosanct as the AFL pushed industrial organizing on its own. Although accurate membership figures are not available, the AFL unions probably enrolled more than 250,000 members by 1940, a 30 per cent increase since the founding of the CIO in 1935.[44]

The evolving status of the labor movement by 1940, then, was at least partially the product of changes within the labor movement itself. One source of change, industrial unionism, introduced organization to thousands of previously unorganized workers. Change was also a product of the state's industrial development and the changing leadership of the labor movement. Despite the varying quantity and quality of change, however, there was a remarkable continuity in the political behavior of Missouri's organized labor movement during the depression decade.

43. For example, MSFL, *Proceedings, 1936*, p. 95; *1937*, p. 47; *The Labor Herald,* July 24, 1936; September 13, 1940; *St. Louis Post-Dispatch,* August 10, 1936; *Minutes of St. Louis Central Trades and Labor Union,* December 11, 1936, in the Lloyd C. Stark, Papers; *St. Louis Labor Tribune,* March 17, 1938; July 27, 1940.

44. AFL membership in Missouri in 1940 was distributed in approximately the following manner: Saint Louis, 125,000; Kansas City, 45,000; the railroad brotherhoods, 55,000; and outstate unions, 35,000.

Chapter IX

LABOR, THE DEMOCRATS
AND THE PENDERGAST MACHINE

By the end of the thirties, Missouri labor leaders could feel some satisfaction with their decision to align labor's political fortunes with the Democratic party. On the national level, Franklin Roosevelt's New Deal administration had enacted many reforms long sought by the labor movement. Although congratulating itself for the successful association with the Democratic party on the national level, labor found the advantages on the state level less obvious. Their primary grievances were disappointment with local administration of New Deal programs and the reluctance of the Democratically controlled state legislature to enact reforms similar to those passed in Washington. Nevertheless, the achievements of Democrats nationally assured labor's continuing loyalty to the Democratic party in the state. The generous distribution of state and local patronage also guaranteed the loyalty of labor leaders.

Although the sincerity of Franklin D. Roosevelt's dedication to the interests and objectives of the organized labor movement has been seriously challenged, he, more than any other individual, cemented the alliance between organized labor and the Democratic party in Missouri. His programs for emergency relief and recovery were similar to those advocated by Missouri labor and produced a devoted and loyal labor following, even though initially Roosevelt's nomination in 1932 inspired little enthusiasm among Missouri labor leaders. Missouri labor's objections to the ways in which New Deal programs were administered, moreover, never led them to question the intentions of New Deal leadership.[1] The feelings of most Missouri trade unionists were summed up by Martin Dillmon, influential state labor leader and vigorously independent editor of the *St. Louis Union Labor Advocate,* who in 1940 "looking back over the past seven years," felt that "Divine Providence must have had something to do with giving Franklin D. Roosevelt to the United States of America as Chief Executive."[2]

On the local and state levels, the appointment of labor leaders to political positions also served to assure labor's continuing loyalty to

1. For examples of labor's attitude toward Roosevelt and the New Deal see the MSFL, *Proceedings, 1933–1940.*
2. Martin Dillmon to Stark, June 18, 1940, Lloyd C. Stark, Papers.

145

the Missouri Democratic party. The desire to place representatives of labor on agencies and boards concerned with the administration of labor laws was understandable. These positions were important to achieving the goals of the labor movement, but the apparent willingness to leave positions devoted to the advancement of the unions for public office suggests that the dedication to the labor movement was qualified by personal ambitions.

Shortly after the 1932 elections, the scramble for political office became so intense that the State Federation of Labor called a meeting on December 10 in Jefferson City to try to select a slate of candidates for political appointment. The leaders met all day, through the night, and into the next morning before agreeing on a slate of candidates.[3] This avid concern with political appointments continued throughout the decade.

So rapid was the exodus of labor leaders into political positions that nearly all top-rank offices of the unions were vacated. In addition to Reuben Wood, who went to Congress, the State Federation also lost several vice-presidents and executive board members.[4] Nearly all major officers of the Building Trades Councils in Saint Louis and Kansas City received political appointments, while leaders of a number of specialized unions such as the barbers, embalmers, and miners were swept into patronage positions. Outstate labor leaders in such cities as Saint Joseph, Springfield, and Sedalia also participated in the patronage carnival.[5]

Labor officials accepted patronage from all levels of government. On the federal level, they became postmasters, conciliators in the Department of Labor, and WPA administrators. The most cherished positions on the state level included the Department of Labor and Industrial Inspection, the Division of Workmen's Compensation, the Unemployment Compensation Commission, and the Bureau of Mines. Locally, patronage was distributed through appointments to various specialized boards and agencies.

The participation of Missouri labor leaders in political patronage inevitably brought them into close contact with Kansas City's Tom Pendergast, who was a powerful influence in dispensing patronage

3. *The Labor Herald,* May 28, 1937.

4. Among the MSFL officials receiving appointments were: Jack Yost, Kansas City Regional Labor Board; Richard Johnson, police commissioner, Saint Joseph; Emmett Sullivan, postmaster, Sedalia; A. R. Hendricks, WPA administrator; and Jesse L. Rogers, unemployment compensation commissioner.

5. Officials of the Building Trades Councils appointed to political positions include: Thomas Quinn, Governor's Advisory Council on Unemployment Compensation; Frank Lahey, workmen's compensation; Maurice Cassidy, Saint Louis Efficiency Board; Jesse Rogers, Unemployment Compensation Commission. Among the appointments in special areas were Paul A. Shanklin, State Board of Embalming; Arnold Griffith, chief mine inspector; J. Frank Davis and J. H. Skaggs, State Board of Barber Examiners.

in the state. Indeed, much of the story of labor's involvement in Democratic politics during the thirties is closely related to the activities, successes, and failures of the Kansas City politico. Moreover, as was the case with other elements of Missouri society, Pendergast was often a divisive influence in the labor movement. Labor leaders in western Missouri maintained extremely close ties with the Kansas City organization, while in the eastern half of the state, labor often supported candidates who were opposed to Pendergast.

The divisive influence of the Kansas City political boss in the labor movement was reflected in many of the political campaigns of the 1930s. These campaigns also evidence not only the labor movement's increased interest in national political affairs but also the importance of patronage to maintaining labor's continuing loyalty to the Democratic party in spite of the labor lobby's inability to gain major reform legislation on the state level.

In the off-year elections of 1934 two major contests absorbed labor's interest, Reuben Wood's race in the Sixth Congressional District and the election of a United States senator. Under a new redistricting plan finally worked out by the legislature, Wood, who had run at large in 1932, faced two other incumbents in the reorganized Sixth District. Although not expected to win, Wood waged a vigorous campaign that was financed by the labor movement. Union members, both resident and nonresident of the Sixth District, participated vigorously in the campaigning. Appealing on his voting record to both the farmer and labor vote, Wood ran well in the rural areas of the district, but his urban support ensured him his victory in the primary. Most political observers in Missouri assumed that a large labor vote could be credited with sending Wood back to Congress.[6]

The race for the Democratic nomination for United States senator reflected labor's continuing inability to act with unity during primary campaigns, although it remained loyally Democratic. Three candidates vied for the nomination: Harry S. Truman, Pendergast's choice; Jacob L. Milligan, a Richmond Congressman strongly supported by Sen. Bennett Clark; and John J. Cochran, a popular congressman from Saint Louis. Most Missouri labor organizations could support either Truman or Cochran. Only the Brotherhood of Railroad Trainmen, which had just removed officials loyal to Pendergast, supported Milligan. Although the new chairman of the brotherhood, H. W. Wooden, claimed to have delivered 75 per cent of the trainmen's vote to Milligan, he undoubtedly exaggerated.[7]

Of the other two candidates, Cochran had the better reputation

6. MSFL, *Proceedings, 1934,* pp. 55, 56, 58. *The Labor Herald,* June 29, 1934. *The Missouri Democrat,* August 17, 1934. *Official Manual, 1935–1936,* p. 387.

7. H. W. Wooden to Stark, October 27, 1935; D. W. Gramling to Stark, September 18, 1935, Lloyd C. Stark, Papers.

for backing labor. The Saint Louis congressman diligently cultivated and actively supported the labor movement and was described as the "best friend labor ever had" by Saint Louis labor leaders who vowed to support him for any office he might seek.[8]

Harry Truman did not have such close ties with the labor movement in Kansas City, but his labor record was acceptable. Labor had usually endorsed his candidacy for the Jackson County Court, and he maintained good labor relations as Missouri's Reemployment Director.[9] Nevertheless, minor blemishes spotted Truman's labor record. While he was presiding judge, he had employed convict labor on a road project in Jackson County and, according to Kansas City labor leaders, had treated organized labor unfairly when he supervised the construction of the Jackson County Court House.[10]

Kansas City labor's endorsement of Truman only shortly before the primary election was inspired more by loyalty to Boss Pendergast than to Truman. Earlier in the year, the Kansas City Union Labor Democratic Club, an organization formed in the early thirties by representatives of the Kansas City Central Labor Union and Building Trades Council, declared that the Kansas City Democratic organization had been fair to organized labor, and it vowed to support all Pendergast candidates. Although Truman was described as having been "loyal to labor in its entirety in all respects and had gone out of his way to help organized labor," Kansas City labor's participation in the campaign was not enthusiastic.[11] Some of the outstate union movements in western Missouri supported Truman more zealously. Reuben Wood, who nominally remained neutral in such contests, undoubtedly aided Truman in the Sixth District, which included Springfield and Sedalia. Both Truman and Pendergast were strong in the district, and the Kansas City organization supported Wood in his primary fight; it seems unlikely that Wood would have risked offending the Kansas City boss even if so inclined.[12] Moreover, Truman's campaign manager in northwestern Missouri, A. R. Hendricks, was a close friend of Wood. Hendricks, a Saint Joseph labor leader and

8. *The Labor Herald,* June 24, 1932. *St. Louis Labor Tribune,* August 1, October 15, 1938.

9. For labor's opinion of Truman's conduct as county judge, see *The Labor Herald,* October 29, 1926; August 3, 1928; June 5, 1931. For information concerning Truman's activities as state reemployment director, see "Documents Relating to Harry S. Truman from the Records of the United States Employment Service," Box #1, Truman Library.

10. *Kansas City Labor News,* October 17, 24, 31, 1924. *The Labor Herald,* December 29, 1933. See also, Edward A. Rogge, "The Speechmaking of Harry S. Truman," p. 211.

11. *The Labor Herald,* March 16, August 3, 1934.

12. For a discussion of Truman and Pendergast's strength in the outstate area, see Eugene F. Schmidtlein, "Truman the Senator," pp. 66–68; Lyle W. Dorsett, *The Pendergast Machine,* pp. 148–52, 191, 192.

member of the executive board of the State Federation of Labor, had successfully managed Wood's campaign for Congress in 1932. In the 1934 primary, he was credited with carrying Saint Joseph and Buchanan County for Truman. Later Hendricks organized the Andrew Jackson Democratic Club in Saint Joseph, which was modeled after the Kansas City organization, and became an important force in the Democratic party's affairs in the city. The leaders of the United Mine Workers also supported Truman's candidacy. T. W. Griffith, a UMW official and the brother of Arnold Griffith, whom Governor Park had appointed Chief Mine Inspector, met with Pendergast and promised to deliver at least ten thousand votes for Truman from the state's miners.[13]

In the primary election, Truman predictably received a substantial number of votes in Kansas City, while Cochran carried Saint Louis. Truman picked up enough outstate support to win the nomination, however, and coasted to an easy victory in the general election over the crusty, anti-New Deal Republican incumbent, Roscoe Patterson.[14]

In Missouri, as elsewhere, Franklin Roosevelt's campaign for reelection in 1936 dominated the national political scene. In state politics labor concentrated upon Wood's campaign for reelection and the gubernatorial bid of Lloyd C. Stark. As was usually true in the thirties, labor expended its major effort on the primary campaigns because prospective candidates most eagerly sought labor's endorsements at this level.

Reuben Wood won the Democratic nomination for Congress in the Sixth District only after an especially bitter and abusive campaign that, according to Senator Truman, was caused by his own belligerence. "He had been in the habit of using bricks and sticks and stones in his labor fights, and he has not learned to use sugar in his political ones."[15] Truman's analysis undoubtedly had some validity. Wood's fiery temperament limited his ability to use "political sugar," but the divided Sixth District had other, special problems. Wood's Democratic opposition was strongly anti-Pendergast and generally hostile toward most New Deal reforms. Wallace Crossley, one of the major spokesmen for the opposition faction, consistently disputed Wood's views and denounced Pendergast in the columns of his *Warrensburg Star-Journal*. The anti-Wood faction was close to Sen. Bennett Clark politically and ideologically and represented Clark's attempt to build up his own political capital by defeating Wood in the district.[16]

By 1936 Wood had a fairly effective political organization in the

13. Clipping from *Democracy,* August 20, 21, 1935; T. W. Griffith to Stark, October 11, November 18, 1935; April 8, 1936, Lloyd C. Stark, Papers.

14. *Official Manual, 1935–1936,* pp. 385, 410, 411.

15. Truman to James A. Farley, August 8, 1936, Truman–Farley Correspondence Folder, Senatorial Papers, Truman Library.

16. *Warrensburg Star-Journal,* May 18, June 23, 27, 1936. E. S. Turner,

Sixth District and worked closely with Pendergast. The Congressman, who stated that effective political power in the district was held by a combination of his supporters and Pendergast people, apparently had no illusions or qualms about Pendergast's influence. Despite the bitter campaign, Wood won the nomination rather easily and was reelected in the fall.[17]

Labor became most absorbed with the fight for the Democratic nomination for governor between Lloyd Stark and William Hirth. A former military officer and manager of a well-known nursery and apple orchard near Louisiana, Missouri, Stark had long participated in Democratic politics in Missouri and had even considered entering the race for governor in 1932. By 1936, he had considerable support all over the state including Pendergast's blessing during the primary campaign.[18]

Stark's major opponent, William Hirth, was a founder and head of the Missouri Farmers' Association. He also edited the *Missouri Farmer,* a semimonthly newspaper that was distributed to members of the association. Hirth ran as the farmer's friend but pitched much of his campaign to the boss issue. Vehemently anti-Pendergast, he pictured Stark as the stooge of a corrupt urban political machine.[19]

Because Stark was certain of losing farm votes to Hirth, he decided to seek the support of urban labor. Perhaps no gubernatorial candidate in the history of the state made a more diligent effort to cultivate the friendship of labor and won such unanimous and enthusiastic support from them, even though he promised few concrete benefits.

Stark began building his political fences in the labor movement long before the 1936 campaign. He gained Reuben Wood's friendship by supporting his candidacy in the 1932 Democratic primary,[20] and thereafter, studiously maintained his contact with the Missouri congressman and labor leader.[21] Early in 1935, he began extending his contacts in the labor movement in preparation for the 1936 campaign. He opened a correspondence with B. F. Brown, labor editor from Hannibal, and in the Stark tradition, sent him a box of apples as a token of esteem. In Saint Joseph he sought the support of Tru-

Jr., to Stark, May 16, 1936; William Ledbetter to Stark, January 10, 1936, Lloyd C. Stark, Papers. *The St. Joseph Union-Observer,* March 2, 1934. *The Labor Herald,* March 16, 1934. R. T. Wood to Park, July 8, 1935, Guy B. Park, Papers.

17. Wood to Stark, January 25, 1936, Lloyd C. Stark, Papers. *Official Manual, 1937–1938,* pp. 337, 363.

18. Dorsett, *Pendergast,* pp. 150, 204.

19. David D. March, *A History of Missouri,* pp. 1374, 1385.

20. Wood to Stark, August 8, September 10, 1932; Stark to Wood, June 7, 1932; Stark to Gramling, September 23, 1935, Lloyd C. Stark, Papers.

21. For example, Stark to Wood, March 14, 1933; December 30, 1935; January 14, 1936, *ibid.*

man's campaign manager, A. R. Hendricks, telling him, "Harry Truman is one of the best friends I have in the world . . . I think he is going to make a fine Senator—one of the best the State has ever had." Stark also contacted Edward Mullaley, a leader of the labor movement in Sedalia, and received his endorsement.[22]

In a similar fashion, Stark successfully gained the support of the railroad brotherhoods and miners' unions. He went to the home of the chairman of the Missouri Division of the Brotherhood of Locomotive Engineers, D. W. Gramling, where after a lengthy conference, Gramling gave his support to Stark on the condition that Roy McKittrick, the state's attorney general and long-time friend of the labor movement, did not enter the race. Stark also obtained the endorsement of H. W. Wooden, chairman of the Brotherhood of Railroad Trainmen, and T. W. Griffith, an official of the United Mine Workers, who promised to conduct an active campaign for Stark in the state's mining areas.[23]

Perhaps Stark's greatest assurance of being backed by the labor movement was the commitment of William Barkley, a lawyer and a legal counselor for most labor organizations in Saint Louis, to support him. Barkley, who had considerable influence in the labor movement, arranged a meeting between Saint Louis labor leaders and Stark in late January, promising the candidate there would be no attempt to quiz him on specific issues. Barkley told Stark all he had to promise these labor leaders was a "fair deal."[24]

Stark's managers arranged similar meetings with labor leaders in other Missouri cities, and the candidate also attended the annual convention of the State Federation of Labor. After addressing the convention, he personally talked with each delegate. In this way Stark met most of the prominent labor leaders in the state prior to the primary election. Having lined up the support of most labor leaders, Stark's managers next moved toward the rank-and-file unionists with Stark for Governor clubs. William Barkley and P. J. Morrin, a prominent Saint Louis labor leader and president of the International Association of Bridge, Structural and Ornamental Iron Workers, agreed to initiate the movement, and the clubs they organized became important elements of Stark's campaign. Each club raised money through

22. Stark to Brown, January 5, 24, 1935; Stark to A. R. Hendricks, February 11, 1935; Edward Mullaley to Stark, March 4, 1935, *ibid.*

23. Memorandum, "Conference with Dave Gramling," July 20, 1935; Stark to Gramling, July 23, 1935; Gramling to Stark, September 18, 1935; Wooden to Stark, October 27, 1935; Stark to Griffith, November 14, 1935; Griffith to Stark, October 11, 1935; April 8, May 11, 1936, *ibid.*

24. Stark to William Barkley, July 31, 1935; Ledbetter to Stark, January 25, 1936, *ibid.*

membership dues and contributions from labor unions, printed and distributed literature, and actively campaigned for Stark.[25]

Only two minor incidents threatened to disturb Stark's smooth campaign in the labor movement. One involved the printing done by the Stark Nursery that did not bear the union label. The other was a circular written by William Walden of Slater, Missouri, who was a representative of the Brotherhood of Locomotive Firemen and Enginemen. Distributed in labor centers by Stark's opponents, the circular claimed that laborers in the Stark Nursery were grossly underpaid and that the nursery's managers exploited woman and child labor. Stark's managers decided that these charges could be most effectively repudiated by labor leaders, themselves, and the candidate never publicly commented on them.[26] Thus, by the time Stark formally opened his campaign in early May, he had already obtained almost unanimous support from organized labor in the state.

Stark's highly successful maneuvers illustrated two important trends. The first was the growing influence of the labor movement in the affairs of the Missouri Democratic party in the thirties. Whether or not labor leaders actually could deliver a labor vote in the primary, Democratic politicians thought they could. Moreover, labor leaders could provide campaign funds, large numbers of campaign workers, and a momentum and winner's image so important to a successful campaign.

Reuben Wood's successful campaign in the at-large elections of 1932 and his unexpected victory in 1934 contributed greatly to the increased interest in the labor vote. Pendergast's newspaper, the *Missouri Democrat,* concluded that Wood won in 1934 because labor voters turned out to support their leader.[27] Ninth District Congressman Clarence Cannon, while discussing Stark's possible candidacy in early 1934, told the future governor to enlist Wood's support in the race. "Inasmuch as he is president of the Missouri State Federation of Labor and practically controls the labor vote in Missouri to a man, his support means a great deal more than the average district leader."[28] Apparently agreeing with Cannon's appraisal, the Stark

25. Stark to Frank Middleton, April 25, 1936; Ledbetter to Barkley, March 30, 1936, *ibid. The Labor Herald,* July 10, 1936. W. L. Bouchard to P. J. Morrin, March 28, 1936; Ledbetter to Barkley, March 30, 1936; Barkley to Ledbetter, May 23, 1936; Morrin, May 15, 1936; clipping from *The Ellington Press,* October 8, 1936, in Lloyd C. Stark, Papers.

26. Ledbetter to Stark, January 10, 1936; Barkley to Ledbetter, July 29, 1936; circular entitled, "Will You Think and Act or Will You Sink?" n.d.; Barkley to Ledbetter, July 29, 1936; Barkley to Frank J. Murphy, July 29, 1936; Morrin to Saint Louis Central Trades and Labor Union, September 17, 1936; Stark to Democratic County Chairman, October 27, 1936, *ibid.*

27. *The Missouri Democrat,* August 17, 1934.

28. Clarence Cannon to Stark, February 22, 1935, Lloyd C. Stark, Papers.

forces discussed various ways of gaining Wood's endorsement in such a manner that it could not easily be repudiated later. As a means of securing his unqualified support, they seriously considered attempting to clear the way for Wood's unopposed renomination in the Sixth District, but, concluding that factional strife ran too deeply in the district, they did not pursue that tactic.[29]

The second trend that was revealed by Stark's candidacy was his ability to gain the near unanimous endorsement of organized labor without committing himself to support any specific objectives of the labor movement. Unlike earlier years when labor leaders demanded that candidates seeking labor support take a specific stand on certain matters of special interest to the labor movement, Stark simply told labor leaders he believed in the principle of collective bargaining, endorsed the labor plank adopted by the Democratic party, and would give them a "square deal."[30]

Only two labor leaders seriously attempted to commit Stark on specific issues before the general elections, and both of these instances were essentially motivated by specific interests of individual unions. David Gramling of the Brotherhood of Locomotive Engineers wanted Stark's assurance that he would not reappoint the State Insurance Commissioner, Emmett O'Malley, who had sponsored legislation that would have seriously weakened the fraternal insurance plans carried by a number of railroad brotherhoods. The other instance involved Warren Welsh of the Saint Joseph Central Labor Union, who was interested in certain political appointments and the use of union labor on highway projects.[31]

Stark easily won the nomination in the primary election. Labor's efforts in behalf of Stark during the general election campaign were merged with its campaign to reelect Roosevelt. The Missouri branch of Labor's Non-partisan League, dedicated to the reelection of Roosevelt, often held joint rallies with Stark for Governor clubs in particular locales, and the leadership of the two organizations was often interchangeable. As the Democrats swept to victory in 1936, it became clear that it was a Democratic year in the state and in the nation.[32]

In comparison to previous Missouri governors, Stark treated organized labor relatively well during his four years in office. At the end of his term, he could claim that he had fulfilled his pledges to

29. Ledbetter to Stark, March 5, 1935; January 10, 1936, *ibid.*

30. "Statement of Major Stark to Organized Labor," n.d., *ibid.*

31. Gramling to Stark, March 15, April 25, July 28, 1936; Warren Welsh to Stark, October 3, 1936, *ibid.*

32. John P. Nick to Stark, July 7, 1936; Barkley to Andrew J. Murphy, September 26, 1936; clipping from *The Ellington Press,* October 8, 1936, *ibid. Official Manual, 1937–1938,* pp. 334, 335.

treat labor fairly, and whenever labor leaders had called upon him, they had found him sympathetic and understanding.[33] Moreover, his supporters argued that Stark's full recognition of organized labor was demonstrated by his appointment policy. According to a pro-Stark pamphlet, he had appointed

> at least six Department heads who are members of various labor organizations, in addition to many men and women in key positions. Altogether the records show more employees on the payroll who are connected with organized labor than ever before in the history of Missouri. Nearly every trade and craft, both A. F. of L. and C. I. O. are represented in this group.[34]

While few of the reforms desired by organized labor were achieved during his administration, Stark actively supported such labor measures as minimum wage laws for women and children, convict labor legislation, amendments to the workmen's compensation law, and mine safety legislation.[35]

Nevertheless, during his term of office, Stark alienated a large portion of the labor movement. It was not the Governor's policies that provoked the dissatisfaction, however, but his politics. Early in his term, Stark broke with the Pendergast organization and became one of its most resourceful antagonists. The break with Pendergast alienated those labor leaders who had been closely allied with the Kansas City organization.

The conflict began when Pendergast complained that the Governor was not consulting him on appointments and that many deserving Democrats were being neglected. In the spring of 1937 a series of scandals occurred in Kansas City involving frauds during the previous year's elections, and as a result, Stark further antagonized the Kansas City politico by ignoring his advice on appointments to the Kansas City Election Board. The final break between Stark and Pendergast came when the Governor decided to dismiss the controversial State Insurance Commissioner, Emmett O'Malley.[36]

The first test of strength between the two Democratic leaders occurred in the spring of 1938 when Pendergast threw his support behind the candidacy of James V. Billings in a contest for the state

33. Pamphlets entitled, "Stark, the Friend of Labor," n.d., and "Stark's Fair Labor Record," n.d., Lloyd C. Stark, Papers. See also Stark's opening address of his campaign for the United States Senate delivered in Mexico, Missouri, May 18, 1940, Lloyd C. Stark, Papers.

34. Pamphlet entitled, "Stark, the Friend of Labor," n.d., *ibid.*

35. Pamphlet entitled, "Stark's Fair Labor Record," n.d., *ibid.* MSFL, *Proceedings, 1937,* pp. 108, 112, 113. E. E. Murphy to Stark, October 5, 1936, Lloyd C. Stark, Papers.

36. Dorsett, *Pendergast,* pp. 205–18.

Supreme Court.[37] The incumbent, James M. Douglas, had been appointed by Stark to fulfill an unexpired term and opposed Billings in the primary. The contest indicated the way the labor movement would react to the growing conflict between Stark and Pendergast. Unions in the eastern half of the state generally supported Douglas and, in effect, Stark, while unions in the west favored the Pendergast candidate.[38] In a formal statement, the Union Democratic Club in Kansas City euphemistically declared that the reason for its opposition to Douglas was that he was "hand picked by Mayor Dickmann the head of the greatest political machine that has ever been built in St. Louis since the days of Harry Hawes and Butler." Billings, they argued, had never been under the influence of any political organization.[39]

The defeat of the Pendergast candidate to some extent portended the direction of events to follow. As District Attorney Maurice Milligan and Stark continued their relentless attacks on the Kansas City organization, it began to crumble, and by the end of 1939, a number of the organization's major figures including Pendergast, O'Malley, and WPA Administrator Murray were sentenced to prison terms.[40]

Nevertheless, Pendergast's allies in the labor movement remained loyal to the Kansas City organization. Kansas City labor opposed a reform–fusion ticket in the municipal elections of 1938, arguing that the "fusionists had hedged in their answers to directed questions and had preferred to deal in such generalities as a 'fair deal for labor.' "[41] Again in the municipal elections of 1940, the Kansas City labor movement endorsed the slate of candidates drawn by the remnants of the once-powerful Pendergast organization.[42]

Labor's fidelity to the Kansas City organization cannot be explained in terms of policy. Labor's discontent with their programs was strikingly revealed in a speech by Cliff Langsdale, the legal counsel for most Kansas City labor unions and the State Federation of Labor. Langsdale told the delegates of the Central Labor Union:

Now we have gone along—I have, all of you have—with the Democratic organization in this town. Most of us are Democrats.

37. *Ibid.,* pp. 218–23.
38. For information concerning labor's support of Douglas, see *The Hannibal Labor Press,* July 15, 1938; *St. Louis Labor Tribune,* July 14, August 1, October 15, 1938.
39. *The Labor Herald,* May 13, 1938.
40. Dorsett, *Pendergast,* pp. 226, 227.
41. *The Labor Herald,* March 25, 1938.
42. *The Kansas City Labor Herald,* March 15, 1940. See also, Shannon C. Douglass to Truman, March 13, 1940; V. Messall to Edward Keating, March 22, 1940, Labor Newspapers Folder, Senatorial Papers, Truman Library.

I know I am. I think the greatest public official who has ever served the people in the United States is Franklin Roosevelt, and for that reason I remain a Democrat. But it seems strange to me that all of the trouble that we have had in the last several years in Kansas City has come through this very organization that we have followed and gone along with.

It is time for you to rise up on your hind legs and say to your critics and these people in this Democratic organization who would put you in bad with the public of Kansas City, and wrongfully so, that you are not going to follow them any more if they don't give you a fair deal . . .[43]

Labor's loyalty to the Kansas City machine continued predominately because many labor leaders in the western half of the state were themselves integral members of the Democratic organization. Their loyalty to the organization had been secured through patronage, and as Governor Stark began to replace those labor leaders who were loyal to Pendergast with others who supported his own administration, he alienated a significant portion of the labor movement's leadership.

The conflicting loyalties within the labor movement were obvious in the 1940 contest for the Democratic nomination for the United States Senate. The contest pitted the incumbent, Harry Truman, against Governor Stark and Maurice Milligan, both of whom had been instrumental in the destruction of the Democratic organization in Kansas City. Labor leaders, generally ignoring Milligan, concentrated their attention and efforts on the contest between Truman and Stark.

Most commentators on this primary election have emphasized the support that Truman received from the labor movement during the campaign. While Truman did receive substantial support from labor, Stark also had important allies in that group. Both candidates pledged their loyalty to Roosevelt and the New Deal; both had favorable records for supporting and promoting issues concerning labor, and organized labor could expect a sympathetic hearing from either candidate.[44]

Truman obtained his most substantial labor support from railroad unions, which were indebted to him for his opposition to a 15 per cent wage reduction that had been proposed as a means of alleviating some of the financial problems of the nation's railroads. The support of the brotherhoods was also a reward for Truman's favorable voting

---

43. *The Labor Herald,* June 23, 1939.
44. Alfred Steinberg, *The Man From Missouri: The Life and Times of Harry S. Truman,* p. 174. Jonathan Daniels, *The Man of Independence,* pp. 203, 204. Schmidtlein, "Truman the Senator," pp. 218–20.

record and his sympathetic activities on the Senate Interstate Commerce Committee.[45]

The railroad brotherhoods conducted an active campaign in Truman's behalf. They sponsored mass rallies in both Saint Louis and Kansas City, flooded the state with campaign literature, and raised a large percentage of the money needed to finance the campaign. The Brotherhood of Railroad Trainmen was especially active in the campaign and worked closely with Truman's campaign headquarters in Sedalia and Saint Louis.[46]

It seems doubtful, however, that Truman would have received as much support from the brotherhoods in Missouri as he did if the national executives of the railroad unions had not advocated his candidacy with such vigor. As governor, Stark built considerable support among Missouri railroad union leaders. His dismissal of Insurance Commissioner O'Malley and his endorsement of their legislative goals in the General Assembly greatly pleased the brotherhoods. In the spring of 1939 the chairmen of the legislative boards of the Missouri Brotherhoods of Locomotive Engineers, Locomotive Firemen and Enginemen, and Railroad Trainmen issued a joint public statement praising Stark and strongly endorsing his labor record. Despite the strong endorsement of Truman by the national officers of the brotherhoods, several local unions in Missouri pledged their support to Stark, including the federated shop committee of six railroad shop craft unions in Sedalia, and the locals of the Brotherhood of Railway and Steamship Clerks in Hannibal.[47]

The Governor's greatest boosters in the Missouri railroad brotherhoods, however, were D. W. Gramling and James Miller, chairman and vice-chairman of the Missouri Division of the Brotherhood of

45. "Minutes of Meeting of Railroad Labor Organizations of Missouri on Behalf of the Candidacy of Senator Harry S. Truman," July 3, 1940; "Resolutions," n.d., Lloyd C. Stark, Papers. Schmidtlein, "Truman the Senator," pp. 179, 200.

46. "Memorandum," by David Gramling, n.d., Lloyd C. Stark, Papers. Messall to Wear, n.d., pamphlet entitled, "Mammoth Rally for Senator Truman," n.d., Truman for Senator Folder, Sam Wear, Papers. R. H. Wadlow, *et al.* to Franklin D. Roosevelt, July 28, 1940; David Berenstein to Edwin M. Watson, August 9, 1940, microfilm concerning Truman from the Franklin D. Roosevelt Library, Reel No. 1, Truman Library. *The Kansas City Labor Herald,* August 2, 1940. *St. Louis Labor Tribune,* August 3, 1940. Oral History Interview, Mildred Lee Dryden, September 26, 1963, Truman Library.

47. For labor's attitude toward the dismissial of O'Malley see *St. Louis Labor Tribune,* October 15, 1937; Gramling to Stark, April 12, 1939; "Statement of the Chairman of the Legislative Board of the Brotherhood of Locomotive Engineers, Brotherhood of Locomotive Firemen and Enginemen and Brotherhood of Railroad Trainmen, Relating to the Labor Record of Governor Lloyd C. Stark," n.d.; M. D. Hale to Stark, June 12, 1940; J. H. Pittman to Stark, September 22, 1939, Lloyd C. Stark, Papers.

Locomotive Engineers. Gramling's office distributed thousands of pieces of literature promoting Stark. The railroad union official argued that Truman's voting record was less favorable than usually pictured, and in supporting his contention, he noted that Truman had voted against a bill to limit the length of railroad trains and had opposed labor's interests in six other votes during his first term. Gramling and Miller actively campaigned for Stark in the railroad centers of the state.[48]

With the exception of the railroad brotherhoods, Truman seems to have received his backing by labor largely because of older loyalties to the Pendergast organization. Although two prominent Saint Louis labor leaders, Joseph Clark of the Central Trades and Labor Union and John Church of the Building Trades Council, endorsed Truman, most of his support came from the western half of the state. Kansas City labor, both AFL and CIO, strongly supported Truman along with Reuben Wood and the Springfield Central Labor Union.[49]

Stark received the endorsement of many of those Saint Louis labor leaders who had supported him four years earlier in his gubernatorial campaign. These labor leaders, moreover, blocked an attempt to endorse Truman at the May convention of the State Federation of Labor. William Barkley, the labor lawyer from Saint Louis, again played an important role in mobilizing labor support for Stark's candidacy, and such influential Saint Louis labor leaders as William Brandt, Martin Dillmon, Mary Ryder, Frank Lahey, and Joseph Hauser all endorsed Stark. He also received the support of the Saint Louis CIO Industrial Council, and the leadership of the Missouri Industrial Council appears to have favored his candidacy, although it did not formally endorse him.[50]

Besides his generally favorable labor record, Stark's support in the labor movement resulted from his own distribution of patronage, which he had funneled into the eastern half of the state, and the general skepticism of Saint Louis labor leaders toward labor's attachment to the Pendergast organization. Left-wing unionists also appreciated Stark's favorable recommendation of George Duemler, a Socialist lawyer, as regional attorney for the wage and hour division of the Department of Labor. Sen. Bennett Clark strongly opposed Duemler's

48. Gramling to Stark, March 30, 1940; Gramling to Officers and Members of all Sub-Divisions, Brotherhood of Locomotive Engineers in Missouri, July 20, 1940; Gramling to Stark, August 8, 1940, Lloyd C. Stark, Papers.

49. Harrol King to John Kirkpatrick, April 4, 1940, *ibid. The Kansas City Labor Herald,* July 26, 1940. *Union Labor Record,* June 26, 1940.

50. Stark to Barkley, Brandt, House, Ryder, and Lahey, May 26, 1940 (five letters); Stark to Dillmon, June 26, 1940; Luther M. Slinkard to Stark, August 13, 1940; "Memorandum," February 21, 1940; Stark to Walter Shannon, August 1, 1940; Stark to Barkley, May 26, 1940, Lloyd C. Stark, Papers.

appointment, and the radical lawyer probably would not have been appointed without Stark's strong endorsement.[51]

In general terms, the Truman–Stark contest split the labor movement into an east and west, pro- and anti-Pendergast, and left- versus right-wing struggle. Truman received the support of the western, pro-Pendergast, conservative faction of the labor movement. After he won the party nomination in a close contest, the labor movement quickly united to back Truman's successful candidacy in the general elections.

The campaigns and elections of 1940 marked the end of a political era for the Missouri labor movement. The New Deal, which had effected so many changes in the labor movement, was all but dead. A similar fate had befallen the Pendergast organization. State Federation of Labor President Reuben Wood failed in his effort for reelection to Congress after having served four terms, and the year also marked a revival, albeit short, of the Republican party in Missouri. A Republican won the gubernatorial election for the first time since 1928, and the Republican vote in other contests grew substantially.[52]

In assessing the significance of the Democratic–labor alliance during the decade of the 1930s, it is apparent that while labor's attachment to the national party paid important dividends in terms of social and economic reform, on the state level the alliance was less fruitful. Nevertheless, the political marriage to the state Democratic party held firm, primarily because of the distribution of patronage to labor leaders. Everything considered, labor leaders did not appear to regret their decision to abandon political nonpartisanship and join forces with the Democratic party.

51. *St. Louis Labor Tribune,* September 6, 1937; April 8, 29, November 18, 1939. Gramling to Stark, June 13, August 20, November 17, 1939, Lloyd C. Stark, Papers.

52. *Official Manual, 1941–1942,* pp. 239–47, 346.

Conclusion

TOWARD A NEW VIEW
OF LABOR AND POLITICS

ASSUMPTIONS about the uniqueness of the American environment have provided persistent themes in the studies of the American trade union movement. It is argued that labor leaders recognized that the American milieu differed substantially from that of Europe and, therefore, they realized that to succeed the labor movement would have to evolve a philosophy commensurable to peculiar American conditions. Unlike the more stable, class-oriented societies of Europe, the United States had a highly mobile population characterized by a constant immigration and internal migration that continually disrupted the labor market. This condition, along with a high degree of socioeconomic mobility and an inordinately large middle class, inhibited the development of a rigid class structure or a meaningful sense of class consciousness. Moreover, a highly decentralized political structure loosely bound together by an extremely flexible two-party system impeded the growth of radical political parties in the United States.[1]

The genius of the American labor movement, according to this theory, was its pragmatic adjustment to these peculiar American conditions and its corresponding rejection of the irrelevant doctrinaire Marxism of European trade unions. That adjustment embodied a voluntaristic philosophy of trade unionism under which the labor movement accepted and committed itself to working within an individualistic, *laissez faire* capitalistic economy. Voluntarism, as it was styled, was essentially an antistatist, apolitical policy placing its emphasis upon the potential economic power of the trade union movement. Government assistance was neither to be sought nor accepted on either the administrative or legislative levels.[2] Consequently, labor's political activity was limited and its political objectives essentially negative. Labor wanted a neutral government, one that would not interfere in the economic struggles between labor and manage-

1. Originally derived from Frederick Jackson Turner's frontier thesis, the most influential treatment of this argument is contained in Selig Perlman's *A Theory of the Labor Movement,* Chap. 5. See also Gerald N. Grob, *Workers and Utopia: A Study of Ideological Conflict in the American Labor Movement, 1865–1900.*

2. David J. Saposs, "Voluntarism in the American Labor Movement," pp. 967, 968.

161

ment. The political strategy adopted to produce this type of governmental neutrality was nonpartisanship. Labor unions were to support their friends and defeat their enemies regardless of party affiliation.[3]

While the foregoing analysis rather accurately described the philosophy of AFL leaders, it had only limited applicability to organized labor in Missouri. Compared to the more passive political attitude of the AFL leadership, Missouri labor leaders were political activists, who, having a more positive view of the possibilities of political action, rejected antistatist, voluntaristic assumptions. They considered the exercise of economic power important, but Missouri labor leaders repeatedly expressed the conviction that the successful exercise of economic power had to be accompanied by political action. As a result they often became disillusioned and dissatisfied with the AFL's political strategy, and, at least until the La Follette–Wheeler campaign of 1924, viewed an independent labor party as a viable alternative to the nonpartisan tactics of the AFL leadership. After the failure of the third-party movement, Missouri labor, still dubious about the effectiveness of nonpartisanship, gradually began to move into an active alliance with the Democratic party, hoping to operate more effectively as a pressure group inside the party system.

Missouri labor's seemingly divergent behavior gives rise to broader questions about the political attitudes and behavior of the American labor movement. Was the Missouri experience unique? How pervasive were voluntarist assumptions in the labor movement? If the Missouri experience was not uncommon, of what significance is it to a better understanding of the political behavior of American labor? Why did differences of attitude and policy exist?

AFL Voluntarism

Although voluntarism is generally applauded by labor historians as a realistic adjustment to special American conditions, both the philosophy and the favorable appraisals of the system are established upon questionable assumptions. Conclusions about the special character of the United States have never been supported thoroughly by well-documented research; indeed, the weight of recent scholarship challenges the foundation upon which such theories were built.[4] In-

3. Marc Karson, *American Labor Unions and Politics, 1900–1919,* Chap. 6, *et passim.*

4. The "frontier thesis" upon which so many assumptions of American uniqueness have been built has been attacked by many historians. See, for example. Richard Hofstadter, "Turner and the Frontier Myth." The argument that the American environment was inhospitable to a political party with a radical ideology has been effectively challenged by James Weinstein, "Big Business and the Origins of Workmen's Compensation." Both Isaac Hourwich, *Immigration and Labor,* and Philip S. Foner, *History of the Labor Movement in the United States,* dispute the contention that immigration seriously under-

dividualism and *laissez faire,* if ever part of the American scene, were becoming less meaningful at the very time that the AFL emerged.[5] Thus, grounded upon an essentially unrealistic view of the economy, the labor philosophy of voluntarism was obsolete at the time it was formulated. Nevertheless, it had surprising longevity. Voluntarism remained the formal dogma of the AFL until the mid-1930s, and even then, many prominent labor leaders viewed its passing with alarm.[6]

Michael Rogin, in a provocative essay entitled, "Voluntarism: The Political Functions of an Antipolitical Doctrine," provided one explanation for the labor movement's tenacious subscription to voluntarism. Rogin contends that voluntarism served the purposes of the leadership of the AFL in two vital ways: First, it helped ensure the internal survival and supremacy of the existing leadership of the labor movement; second, it helped to assure the external supremacy of the craft union movement. Voluntarism, Rogin argues, "was above all an organization ideology, serving organizational needs." It served the purposes of the trade union hierarchy through its acceptance of the existing distribution of power within the labor movement and its denial of differing points of view. The AFL's policy of nonintervention in the affairs of affiliates was in actuality based upon a recognition of existing power realities within the labor movement but ideologically justified in terms of freedom, the abstract disavowal of the use of force or coercion.[7] Theoretically, force was not used because it was not necessary, and, because the unions would be essentially homogeneous, internal dissension or conflict could not exist. This belief had the effect of recognizing the union leader as the only legitimate spokesman for the group; consequently, those criticizing the existing leadership, in effect, attacked the union itself rather than the wisdom or decisions of its leaders. In Rogin's words, "voluntarism, by ignoring the problems of power in the name of an abstract defense of freedom, legitimized the existing power distribution and attacked the legitimacy of attempts to change it."[8]

mined unionization. A number of historians have challenged older assumptions about class consciousness and social and economic mobility. See, for example, Stephen Thernstrom *Poverty and Progress: Social Mobility in a Nineteenth Century City,* and Staughton Lynd, *Class Conflict, Slavery and the United States Constitution.*

5. See Robert A. Lively, "The American System: A Review Article," pp. 81–96.

6. George G. Higgins, *Voluntarism in Organized Labor in the United States, 1930–1940,* pp. 77, 81, 82, *et passim.*

7. Michael Rogin, "Voluntarism: The Political Functions of an Antipolitical Doctrine," pp. 525–27, 535. In reality this injunction applied only to the larger and more powerful nations. AFL officials often intervened in the affairs of smaller unions, especially if they appeared to be challenging the claimed prerogatives of larger or more favored unions.

8. *Ibid.,* p. 529.

During its early years, the greatest internal criticism of the labor movement's leadership came from Socialist trade unionists. It is one of the apparent ironies of traditional interpretations of American labor history that the supposedly rigid and doctrinaire Socialists should have interpreted "peculiar" American conditions in a more "practical" way than the pragmatic and nonideological AFL leadership. The Socialist advocates of social-welfare legislation, industrial unionism, and political activism were, after all, the true prophets of the labor movement, although their views were only accepted after literally being forced on the labor movement by internal and external conditions in the 1930s.[9] It appears that rather than a pragmatic response to special American conditions, the philosophy of voluntarism, as it evolved, was, in part at least, the established labor leadership's reaction to its own doctrinaire anti-Socialist biases. AFL leaders almost automatically opposed anything the Socialists advocated—to have accepted the legitimacy of Socialist criticism would have been a tacit recognition of the heterogeneity of the labor movement and would have destroyed the euphemism that power and coercion were unnecessary. Moreover, it would have opened the door to questions about the distribution of power within the labor movement.

If voluntarism was self-serving, organization-centered, and unrealistic how, then, did the AFL leadership convince the labor movement of its wisdom. The conclusion that lower level unions accepted voluntarism implicitly assumes that the policy of the AFL leadership was the policy of its constituent unions. Many historians concur on this assumption. In the most definitive available study of AFL voluntarism, George Higgins calls it "the keystone of the philosophy of Samuel Gompers and of the movement which he was leading." David Saposs agrees. He declares that during World War I the labor movement temporarily abandoned voluntarism, but "with the advent of peace and the withdrawal of Government regulation of the economy of the country, the AFL, as a whole, reverted to voluntarism, to which it adhered consistently until the middle 1930's." In his study of labor and politics during the first two decades of the twentieth century, Marc Karson declares that the practical and materialistic outlook of pure and simple unionism "wove its way deeply into the fabric of the AF of L, its affiliated unions, and their rank and file."[10]

Like so many other conclusions about the pervasive influence of

9. Most American trade union Socialists were neither rigid nor extremely doctrinaire. Indeed one explanation of the failure of the Socialist party in America is that it was too flexible and nonideological. See Ira Kipnis, *The American Socialist Movement, 1897–1912,* passim.

10. Higgins, *Voluntarism in Organized Labor,* p. 41. Saposs, "Voluntarism in American Labor," p. 972. Karson, *American Labor Unions,* p. 118.

voluntarist assumptions, these statements are not only unsupported but also unsupportable. While no doubt accurately portraying the convictions of the AFL leadership, they largely fail to reflect the attitudes of local and state labor leaders. Evidence provided to support the widespread acceptance of voluntarism invariably consists of votes at AFL conventions favoring voluntaristic principles, especially as associated with social-welfare legislation such as maximum hour and minimum wage laws, social insurance.[11]

The validity of this evidence rests upon the assumption that AFL conventions effectively represented the labor movement at all levels. The AFL convention, in reality, was gerrymandered in such a way as to ensure the domination of the existing bureaucracy, while, at the same time, severely limiting the influence of state and local central bodies. Regardless of size, each central body had only one delegate at annual conventions of the AFL. By contrast, national and international unions had one delegate for every four thousand members, and on rollcalls they cast one vote for every one hundred members, while the representatives of the central bodies still had only one vote. This constitutional arrangement had the effect of denying the labor organizations that were most influential on the local level the power in the national organization to which the size of their constituencies entitled them.[12]

Many local trade union leaders (including non-Socialists) recognized and resented the unrepresentative and tightly controlled character of AFL conventions. In 1906 the West Virginia State Federation of Labor, objecting to the secondary role accorded state federations at national conventions, passed a resolution urging the American Federation of Labor "to adopt a 'one-man, one-vote' system and the use of the referendum on all questions and in the election of officers." In a letter to Gompers discussing the dissatisfaction of local labor central bodies, the secretary of the New Hampshire State Federation of Labor commented, "in the past at the conventions of the A. F. of L. the effort to gain consideration at the hands of the convention by the various State bodies . . . has been given but scant consideration." The correspondent went on to criticize the way in which the officials of international unions controlled and directed convention proceedings for their own selfish purposes.[13] Perhaps a conservative Missouri trade unionist made the most introspective comment on an

11. See, for example, Karson, *American Labor Unions,* pp. 128–30, *et passim;* Philip Taft, *The A. F. of L. in the Time of Gompers,* p. 366, *et passim;* Higgins, *Voluntarism in Organized Labor,* pp. 8–55.

12. AFL, *Constitution,* Article XI, Section 5.

13. Evelyn L. K. Harris and Frank Krebs, *From Humble Beginnings: West Virginia State Federation of Labor, 1903–1957,* p. 29. D. W. Finn to Gompers, April 17, 1908, AFL, Papers, Series 117A, File 11A.

AFL convention when he concluded his report as the Missouri State
Federation of Labor delegate to the national convention with the following observations:

> In conclusion, I wish to deal briefly with a subject that is more or
> less personal to us. To begin with, in rendering the foregoing re-
> port, it is not my desire to create an impression that your delegate
> was conspicuously prominent in the deliberations of labor's highest
> tribunal. Rather, I confess my unimportance; but in doing so it
> is with the full knowledge that mine was the common fate of all
> who for the first time are honored with a place in that convention.
> There, as almost everywhere, an apprenticeship must be served.
> To the uninitiated there appears to be a code of ethics that ex-
> cludes the stranger from the councils of the high and mighty
> leaders—some of them self-constituted leaders—of our destinies.
> There may even arise in the mind of the frail and timid a suspicion
> that he is being tolerated so long as he remains good, with the
> alternative that if he misbehaves he may be crushed by a gigantic
> steamroller—a form of punishment that is merciless in its Jugger-
> naut-like qualities and from which there is no escape; and, now
> and then, it may even number among its victims an innocent hav-
> ing the courage of his convictions.[14]

Some students of the American labor movement have recognized
the limited applicability of the pronunciamentos of the AFL. As John
Shover phrased it, "the political decisions of national conventions of
the parent AFL or the constituent unions . . . have had little significance in shaping political policies at the local level." In a somewhat different vein, Philip Taft asserts that "the failure of European
and American writers to recognize the significance of the state federation of labor as a political institution is perhaps the chief reason for
their inability to understand American labor's political behavior."
Nevertheless, labor historians have paid little attention to the social
convictions of labor at the local level.[15]

Furthermore, the significance of antivoluntarist impulses in the
labor movement have been greatly diluted by placing them into the
broader conflict between Socialist and non-Socialist trade unionists.
Although no doubt an accurate appraisal of Gompers's view of the
critics of his policies, in fact, many non-Socialists in the labor movement criticized voluntarist assumptions. While some of these critics
existed in the upper echelons of the hierarchy of the labor movement,
the vast majority are to be found at the lower levels of the labor

14. MSFL, *Proceedings, 1909*, p. 23.
15. John L. Shover, review of Taft, *The California State Federation of
Labor, The Journal of American History* (March, 1969), p. 888. Philip Taft,
Labor Politics American Style: The California State Federation of Labor,
p. 5.

movement. Indeed, little evidence exists to suggest local labor leaders thought in voluntaristic terms at all. The term or the concept seldom appears in the speeches, records, minutes, or convention proceedings of state and local unions. Moreover, local labor movements promiscuously violated most of the cardinal tenets of voluntarism.

Although not having received sufficient study, the forces that caused the AFL's eventual break with voluntarism during the thirties are important to better understanding the political behavior of organized labor. To be sure, the Great Depression and the New Deal helped direct the national leadership of the labor movement toward a new ideological position, but considerable pressure for change also emanated from within labor's ranks. It certainly seems significant that the national leaders of the labor movement never found it necessary to explain or justify their repudiation of voluntarism to their local affiliates. There is abundant evidence to indicate that within the lower echelons of the labor movement, voluntarism had long since ceased to inspire any intellectual allegiance, if, indeed, local labor leaders had ever been convinced of its merit.

The Rejection of Voluntarism and the Promotion of Reform

A survey of available studies of state and local labor movements and the convention proceedings of selected state federations of labor reveals that unlike the apolitical, antistatist attitude of the national leadership of the labor movement, labor at the local level advocated a program of legislated social reform approximating the welfare or guarantor state.[16] The reforms sought by these local labor movements can be divided into four general classifications: (1) reform of the political system; (2) social insurance; (3) social-welfare legislation; and (4) governmental reforms directly affecting the trade union movement. In most instances these reform objectives antedated World War I and were continually maintained until their ultimate acceptance and enacted into law.[17]

16. After his study of the California State Federation of Labor, Philip Taft asserts, "The record of the California State Federation of Labor is impressive, and a large body of legislation assuring the collection of wages, safety, days of rest, and a multitude of regulations affecting the workers in virtually all phases of his working life have been directly due to his efforts." *Ibid.,* p. 7.

17. Available studies of local labor movements during this period include: Grace Heilman Stimson, *Rise of the Labor Movement in Los Angeles;* Louis B. Perry and Richard S. Perry, *A History of the Los Angeles Labor Movement, 1911–1941;* Thomas W. Gavett, *Development of the Labor Movement in Milwaukee;* Harry Seligson and George E. Bardwell, *Labor-Management Relations in Colorado* (Denver, 1961); Leo Troy, *Organized Labor in New Jersey;* Eugene Staley, *A History of the Illinois State Federation of Labor;* Irwin Yellowitz, *Labor and the Progressive Movement in New York State, 1897–1916;* George W. Lawson, *Organized Labor in Minnesota;* Doris B.

An important illustration of the differing assumptions of local labor leaders regarding the importance of political involvement is reflected by the vigor with which they fought for various types of reforms of the political system. Direct legislation most excited the imagination of local labor leaders. While the AFL leadership perfunctorily endorsed the provisions for initiative, referendum, and recall, labor leaders at the state and local levels advocated these measures with an obsessive zeal. They often wrote the bills providing for direct legislation, arranged for their introduction, and lobbied for their approval both in the state legislatures and with the general electorate. Labor leaders naively assumed that the passage of these reforms would enable labor to enact through the initiative procedure all of the reform legislation frustrated in state legislatures. Conversely, anti-labor legislation making its way through state legislatures could be defeated in referendum elections. The faith in the common man, so manifest in the fight for direct legislation, was also attested by labor's support of such political reforms as direct primaries, municipal home rule, direct election of senators, and woman suffrage.[18]

Thus in the area of political reform, organized labor not only participated in the national Progressive movement in the late years of the nineteenth and early years of the twentieth centuries but also sometimes led the forces of reform at both the state and local level. Labor did not confine its energies to the reform of political practices, however; political reform was a means rather than an end. Local labor leaders, profoundly interested in many of the programs associated with the social-justice wing of progressivism, hoped that a reformed political system would bring about the passage of social-welfare legislation. In their pursuit of reform legislation, labor leaders

---

McLaughlin, *Michigan Labor: A Brief History from 1818 to the Present;* Taft, *California State Federation of Labor;* Harris and Krebs, *From Humble Beginnings.*

The AFL–CIO Library in Washington has a collection of state federation of labor convention proceedings. Proceedings of the meetings of the federations of labor in the following states were used in this survey: Washington, Ohio, Pennsylvania, and Colorado.

18. Harris and Krebs, *From Humble Beginnings,* pp. 30, 31, 32, 39ff, 59. Taft, *California State Federation of Labor,* pp. 43, 44. Stimson, *Labor Movement in Los Angeles,* pp. 128, 178, 307, 357. Yellowitz, *Labor and the Progressive Movement,* pp. 172, 173. Staley, *Illinois State Federation,* pp. 146, 166, 167, 168, 293, 294, 295, 430. Lawson, *Labor in Minnesota,* pp. 18, 163, 169, 171, 172, 183–202, 210–15ff. Frederick M. Heath, "Labor and the Progressive Movement in Connecticut," p. 62. See also the proceedings of the annual conventions of the following state federations of labor for the dates indicated: Washington (1903), p. 28; (1904), pp. 25, 28, 31; (1906), p. 47; (1907), pp. 14, 15; (1909), p. 85; (1912), p. 107; Pennsylvania (1904), pp. 13, 42; (1907), pp. 37, 44, 45, 46; Colorado (1902), pp. 11, 35; (1905), n.p.; (1906), n.p.; Missouri (1903), p. 15.

often cooperated with or actively joined various social progressive organizations. While labor leaders and social progressives sometimes disagreed on tactics, emphasis, and the nature of proposed reforms, the areas of agreement generally far outweighed those of disagreement.[19]

The importance of this working-class contribution to the Progressive movement has been the subject of considerable study and comment,[20] but its significance to a better understanding of the political behavior of the American labor movement has been virtually ignored. The major thrusts of the social progressives and AFL voluntarists were, after all, largely antithetical. Voluntarism was a throwback to the nineteenth-century concepts of society and government that the social progressive ultimately rejected. Consequently, if local labor leaders advocated social reform, they did so at the expense of AFL voluntarism.

Perhaps local and national labor leaders' differing attitudes toward government are nowhere better illustrated, than in their respective convictions regarding social insurance. Samuel Gompers clearly outlined the official attitude of the AFL toward social insurance and welfare reforms in general:

> Sore and sad as I am by the illness, the killing, the maiming of so many of my fellow workers, I would rather see that go on for years and years, minimized and mitigated by the organized labor movement, than give up one jot of the freedom of the workers to strive and struggle for their own emancipation through their own efforts.[21]

Most labor leaders who accepted and advocated various types of social insurance as a legitimate means of promoting the economic security of the working class rejected this reasoning.

Gompers and voluntarism to the contrary, workmen's compensation became the first of many social insurance schemes to gain wide acceptance in the labor movement. The agitation for a system of industrial accident insurance grew out of earlier attempts to reform existing employer liability laws by eliminating traditional common-law defenses. Although both of these desired reforms were sought

19. Yellowitz, *Labor and the Progressive Movement,* has the most comprehensive study of the relationship between labor and the progressive reformers. For other examples, see Heath, "Labor in Connecticut"; Keith L. Bryant, "Labor in Politics: The Oklahoma State Federation of Labor during the Age of Reform"; Gavett, *Labor Movement in Milwaukee,* Chap. 8.

20. See, for example, Yellowitz, *Labor and the Progressive Movement;* Heath, "Labor in Connecticut"; Bryant, "Labor in Politics"; John L. Shover, "The Progressives and the Working Class Vote in California," pp. 584–601; J. Joseph Huthmacher, "Urban Liberalism and the Age of Reform."

21. Bernard Mandel, *Samuel Gompers: A Biography,* p. 185.

through political action, they involved fundamentally different solutions to the problem of industrial accidents. Employer liability reform clearly conformed to the philosophical assumptions of voluntarism, but workmen's compensation, which anticipated permanent government involvement, directly violated the most fundamental tenets of the AFL philosophy. Characteristic of their lack of concern for the niceties of voluntarism, local labor leaders often advocated both reforms simultaneously. When workmen's compensation appeared most likely to win the approval of state legislators, however, labor began to emphasize the compensation method and quickly assumed a leadership role in the campaign for workmen's compensation throughout the nation.[22]

One reflection of local labor's fundamentally more optimistic view of government than that of the national leadership of the trade unions can be seen in the type of compensation program favored by local labor leaders. A major area of controversy in the compensation campaign involved the question of who would administer the program and how the industrial insurance would be carried. Local labor leaders almost universally advocated a system of monopolistic state insurance, or, if that proved unattainable, a system of competitive state insurance.[23] This willingness to give government a predominant role in financing and administering the program suggests that labor leaders considered government more sensitive than private industry to pressure from labor organizations. Perhaps because of the strength of the workmen's compensation movement, the AFL leadership ultimately found it impossible to oppose this reform, even though it had to be considered a fundamental divergence from voluntarist policies.

While the AFL leadership may have compromised with local sentiment in supporting workmen's compensation, it doctrinairely refused to support other forms of social insurance. When unemployment insurance received serious consideration during the economic recession of 1914–1915, Gompers responded with a series of negative pronouncements:

When the government undertakes the payment of money to those who are unemployed, it places in the power of the government

22. Taft, *California State Federation of Labor,* pp. 44, 54. Yellowitz, *Labor and the Progressive Movement,* pp. 30, 31, 107–18, 155, 156. Harris and Krebs, *From Humble Beginnings,* pp. 40, 54, 55, 57, 58, 66, 67. Gavett, *Labor Movement in Milwaukee,* pp. 107, 108. George E. Bardwell and Harry Seligson, *Organized Labor and Political Action in Colorado,* pp. 87–89, 108–19. Robert F. Wesser, "Conflict and Compromise: The Workmen's Compensation Movement in New York, 1890s–1913." Cf. Weinstein, "Big Business and the Origins"; Roy Lubove, "Workmen's Compensation and the Prerogatives of Voluntarism."
23. Taft, *The California State Federation of Labor,* p. 54. Yellowitz, *Labor and the Progressive Movement,* pp. 113–15. Wesser, "Conflict and Compromise," pp. 345–72.

the lives and the work and the freedom of the workers . . . it is paternalism that will destroy initiative and encourage dependency.

. . . . .

[Such laws] are not advocated for the good of the workers. They are advocated by persons who know nothing of the hopes and aspirations of labor which desires opportunities for work, not for compulsory unemployment insurance.

. . . . .

[Under such a system] the labor movement would lose its voluntary character and its effectiveness, and there would be brought about a condition of affairs in our country whereby the toilers would be rendered ineffective in their work for the protection and promotion of their rights and interests.[24]

The American Association for Labor Legislation assumed the early leadership in the campaign for unemployment insurance, but United States involvement in World War I and the return to full employment temporarily diverted interest from unemployment compensation.[25] After the war, however, that interest revived, and at this time many state and local labor groups joined the movement.[26] Nevertheless, not until 1933, after being prodded during several acrimonious debates in AFL conventions, did the national leaders of the labor movement endorse unemployment insurance.[27]

The first unemployment insurance bill in the United States was introduced in the Massachusetts state legislature in 1916; it had the

24. Taft, *A. F. of L. in the Time of Gompers,* pp. 364–66.

25. Irwin Yellowitz, "The Origins of Unemployment Reform in the United States," pp. 338–60. Daniel Nelson, *Unemployment Insurance: The American Experience, 1915–1935,* Chap. 1.

26. In his study of the origins of unemployment insurance, Daniel Nelson states that the local labor movements did not enthusiastically support the unemployment compensation movement. Yet, he does not contend that local labor movements opposed the principle of unemployment insurance but argues instead that they did not support reformers interested in unemployment compensation as enthusiastically as they might have. Nelson does not seem to fully appreciate the fact that unemployment insurance was only one of a number of legislative objectives of organized labor. Because of its controversial nature and the unlikelihood of its winning the approval of state legislators, unemployment insurance was often given a rather low priority by labor lobbyists. Actually, because Nelson's study demonstrates that so many local unions endorsed the principle of unemployment insurance, it provides considerable support for the argument presented here. In the final analysis, as Nelson concedes, no unemployment insurance program was enacted without the active support of organized labor. Nelson, *Unemployment Insurance,* pp. 18, 70, 71, 155–58, 160, 170, 175, 178, 189, 190, *et passim.* See also Taft, *California State Federation of Labor,* p. 364; Staley, *Illinois State Federation,* pp. 276, 492; Lawson, *Organized Labor,* pp. 70, 72, 76, 80, 374, 375, 399; Gavett, *Development of the Labor Movement,* pp. 112, 115.

27. Taft, *A. F. of L. in the Time of Gompers,* pp. 365, 366.

support of the Massachusetts State Federation of Labor. The first unemployment insurance plan to be accepted in the United States was enacted in Wisconsin in 1932; it had the support of the Wisconsin State Federation of Labor. Between those two dates many influential state federations and city central organizations endorsed the principle of unemployment insurance. Actually, similar to their campaign for industrial accident reform, local labor leaders simultaneously supported two different plans to provide for the unemployed during hard times. While accepting the principle of unemployment insurance, they also advocated a governmental public works program. This opportunistic behavior characterized many local labor leaders who refused to quibble over the means through which their needs were maintained and had few ideologically inspired apprehensions about a loss of individual freedom or the collapse of voluntary associations.[28]

Labor on the local level again rejected the principles espoused by the national leadership of the labor movement when it endorsed a system of old-age pensions and health and sickness insurance. Local labor organizations had made their commitment to the principle of old-age pensions before World War I. The interest in old-age security began with an effort to establish a pension fund for widowed mothers. After the campaign to establish the mothers' pension met with considerable success, acquiring pensions for federal employees became the primary objective. Ultimately, labor expanded its interest in old-age pensions to include all citizens. Ohio is the only state in which the old-age pension issue appears to have provoked serious controversy. Significantly, however, Ohio labor leaders did not debate the principle of old-age pensions in voluntarist terms but rather argued about the type of system most desirable and how it should be financed.[29]

Closely related to the support of old-age pensions was an interest in a health and sickness insurance system.[30] Characteristically, this proposed reform received the support of labor on the local level but

28. Nelson, *Unemployment Insurance,* pp. 18, 156, Chaps. 4, 6.
29. Harris and Krebs, *From Humble Beginnings,* pp. 127, 135. Taft, *California State Federation of Labor,* p. 56. Staley, *Illinois State Federation,* pp. 279, 367, 430, 495–99. Lawson, *Organized Labor,* pp. 70, 376, 400, 409–12. See also, the proceedings of the annual conventions of the following state federations of labor for the dates indicated: Washington (1913), p. 32; (1914), pp. 32, 139; (1915), p. 134; Ohio (1911), p. 50; (1915), pp. 59, 112; (1917), pp. 13, 59, 88–96.
30. Harris and Krebs, *From Humble Beginnings,* p. 125. Taft, *A. F. of L. in the Time of Gompers,* p. 56. Yellowitz, *Labor and the Progressive Movement,* pp. 137, 138. Staley, *Illinois State Federation,* pp. 367, 499, 500. Lawson, *Labor in Minnesota,* pp. 39, 40, 364. *Proceedings of the Pennsylvania State Federation of Labor, 1917,* p. 101. Mandel, *Samuel Gompers,* pp. 184, 185.

encountered opposition on the national level. In Gompers's opinion the assumption that

> the state should provide sickness insurance for workers is funda-
> mentally based upon the theory that these workers are not able
> to look after their own interests and the state must interpose its
> authority and wisdom to assume the relation of parent or guardian.
> There is something in the very suggestion of this relationship and
> this policy which is repugnant to a free born citizen. It seems to
> be at variance with our concept of voluntary institutions and of
> freedom for individuals.[31]

Thus labor at the local level overwhelmingly rejected the voluntaristic assumptions of the national labor leadership as they effected
social insurance and positive state action. If local labor leaders did
not aggressively pursue all of these reforms in state legislatures, it
was not because they believed some of the reforms were less valuable
but because as practical men they usually emphasized those reform
objectives they felt had the most realistic chance of enactment.[32]

The national movement did offer at least token support to local
labor leaders in some areas of social-welfare reform. Woman and
child labor reform constituted one of the most important of these
programs. The labor movement at all levels advocated and supported
maximum hour legislation for women and children, restrictions from
hazardous occupations, compulsory school attendance, and free textbooks for the public schools. Although invariably justified in humanitarian terms, this legislation had significant economic implications
that were realized by labor leaders, especially those in affected occupations.[33] Labor at all levels also supported convict labor reform in
an effort to eliminate competition between the goods produced by
convict labor and those of free labor. Labor leaders advocated the
state-use system under which convicts devoted their labor to the task
of producing items needed by state institutions. As true of woman
and child labor reform, advocates of convict labor legislation in the
labor movement advanced both economic and humanitarian arguments to justify this legislation.[34]

The general aura of agreement between the AFL and state and
local groups characterizing these two areas of reform dissolved on

31. Mandel, *Samuel Gompers*, pp. 184, 185. Taft, *A. F. of L. in the
Time of Gompers*, p. 364.

32. Harris and Krebs, *From Humble Beginnings*, pp. 133, 134. Taft, *California State Federation of Labor*, pp. 6–8, 41. Yellowitz, *Labor and the
Progressive Movement*, pp. 25, 26.

33. Taft, *A. F. of L. in the Time of Gompers*, pp. 12, 71, 289, 370.
Karson, *American Labor Unions*, pp. 18, 81, 85, 86, 115, 217.

34. Taft, *A. F. of L. in the Time of Gompers*, pp. 289, 290.

the question of maximum hour–minimum wage legislation. First advocated for women and children and then gradually broadened to include many exclusively or predominantly male occupations, the question of a legal eight-hour day was as old as the modern labor movement and a generally accepted objective of the labor movement in all but the highest councils of the AFL.[35] Even local labor leaders who normally dismissed or simply ignored Gompers's obstinate opposition were disgruntled with his attitude toward maximum hour legislation because they considered this reform well within the realm of the possible. They blamed Gompers's public declarations against legislated maximum hours for adult male workers for the defeat of referendums on the eight-hour day in Washington, California, and Oregon. A delegate at the Illinois State Federation of Labor convention in 1915 declared during a debate on an eight-hour law that the "convention ought to go on record opposing such tomfoolery as goes on in the American Federation of Labor." Despite the vigorous opposition of the influential, hard-line voluntarist Matthew Woll, the convention delegates did so, declaring in favor of the eight-hour day "by any means we can get it," and ordering their delegate to the AFL convention to support the principle of a legislated eight-hour day.[36]

The question of minimum wage legislation created more controversy. Labor leaders appeared at all levels who, along with Gompers, feared that the minimum would become the maximum wage. Nevertheless, the predominant sentiment of labor at the local level appears to have been in favor of some form of minimum wage legislation. Even the AFL president's personal involvement in the controversy over minimum wage legislation in New York failed to deter the New York State Federation of Labor and the Brooklyn Central Labor Union from endorsing and campaigning for a minimum wage law. Gompers also intervened, more successfully, in a minimum wage controversy in California, where a minimum wage law was enacted in

35. Taft, *California State Federation of Labor,* pp. 9, 78. Harris and Krebs, *From Humble Beginnings,* pp. 8, 128. Gavett, *Labor Movement in Milwaukee,* pp. 79–81. Stimson, *Labor Movement in Los Angeles,* pp. 128, 200, 294, 357. Bryant, "Labor in Politics," pp. 266, 268, 274. Bardwell and Seligson, *Organized Labor in Colorado,* pp. 84, 87, 89. Yellowitz, *Labor and the Progressive Movement,* pp. 135, 136. Heath, "Labor in Connecticut," p. 58. Lawson, *Labor in Minnesota,* pp. 21, 163, 171, 177. Staley, *Illinois State Federation,* pp. 33, 474, 475. See also the proceedings of the annual conventions of the following state federations of labor for the dates indicated: Washington (1903), p. 17; (1907), pp. 45, 46; (1910), pp. 95, 97; (1914), p. 36; Pennsylvania (1907), pp. 36, 37; Ohio (1911), p. 30; (1914), p. 79; Colorado (1898), pp. 16, 17; (1902) p. 11; (1905), n.p.; Oregon (1912), p. 23; (1919), p. 24.

36. Staley, *Illinois State Federation,* p. 474.

1913. By 1919 thirteen states, the District of Columbia, and Puerto Rico had established minimum wage legislation, in most cases with the active support of organized labor.[37]

Local labor movements also supported an array of reforms which, rather than emphasizing a negative government, provided for positive government intervention in behalf of the safety and welfare of the working class. These reforms included government regulation of working conditions through mine safety inspection, minimum safety standards on construction work, and a comprehensive system of factory inspection. Perhaps the most dramatic illustration of local labor's rejection of the AFL's apolitical, antistatist philosophy was reflected by the widespread enthusiasm at the local level for government ownership of public utilities, mines, and railroads.[38] Labor leaders assumed that government would be a more enlightened employer than private interests and that their political leverage with government would be more effective in raising wages and improving working conditions than their economic leverage had been with private employers. Although certainly in the minority, a number of state and local labor movements even expressed a willingness to accept the Socialist alternative of government ownership of the means of production and distribution.[39]

A final area of labor's legislative objectives directly involved the activities of organized labor. Like their national counterparts, local labor leaders strongly advocated legislation to end the arbitrary and

37. Thomas J. Kerr IV, "The New York Factory Investigating Commission and the Minimum-Wage Movement," pp. 373–91. Taft, *A. F. of L. in the Time of Gompers*, pp. 32, 33, 54–56. Harris and Krebs, *From Humble Beginnings*, p. 128. Gavett, *Labor Movement in Milwaukee*, pp. 110, 143. Stimson, *Labor Movement in Los Angeles*, p. 293. Yellowitz, *Labor and the Progressive Movement*, pp. 135, 136. Staley, *Illinois State Federation*, pp. 273–76, 367. Lawson, *Labor in Minnesota*, p. 215. *Proceedings of the Washington State Federation of Labor, 1913*, pp. 21, 29; *1914*, p. 42. *Proceedings of the Ohio State Federation of Labor, 1911*, p. 39; *1912*, pp. 103, 105.

38. Harris and Krebs, *From Humble Beginnings*, pp. 32, 123, 142, 143. Gavett, *Labor Movement in Milwaukee*, pp. 88, 89, 96, 97, 109. Taft, *A. F. of L. in the Time of Gompers*, pp. 46, 77, 78. Stimson, *Labor Movement in Los Angeles*, pp. 57, 128, 150, 178, 216, 230, 305, 346. Yellowitz, *Labor and the Progressive Movement*, pp. 172, 173. Staley, *Illinois State Federation*, pp. 141, 144, 145, 152, 153, 174, 264–69, 301, 367. Lawson, *Labor in Minnesota*, pp. 18, 171, 172, 355. Bardwell and Seligson, *Organized Labor in Colorado*, p. 89. Bryant, "Labor in Politics," pp. 266, 268, 272, 274. See also the proceedings of the annual conventions of the following state federations of labor for the dates indicated: Washington (1906), pp. 13–16; (1911), p. 22; Pennsylvania (1904), pp. 13, 42; (1906), p. 58; (1907), pp. 45, 46; (1912), p. 56; (1914), pp. 125, 130, 131; Colorado (1898), p. 22; (1905), p. 78; (1907), p. 45.

39. Weinstein, *Decline of Socialism*, pp. 29–53.

excessive issuance of injunctions during labor disputes.[40] To complement this provision, they also urged legislated governmental recognition of the legitimacy of the picket line and boycott. Local labor leaders, however, desired that more extensive powers be allowed trade unions. They not only advocated legislation to provide for government recognition of the legitimacy of union organizations and the use of their major economic weapons but also promoted a measure to eliminate a series of unfair business practices that anticipated much of the labor legislation enacted during the 1930s.

Despite opposition from the AFL leadership, many local labor leaders advocated and sought legislation assuring the right of workers to join a labor union for collective bargaining purposes and making it illegal to discriminate against any worker because of his union affiliation. When the secretary of the Missouri State Federation of Labor sent the AFL president a copy of such legislation approved for introduction in the state legislature, Gompers responded with the following admonitions:

> I want to say that I doubt the wisdom of trying to secure the passage of a bill interfering with the right of an employer to discharge an employee . . . If we secure the enactment of a law making that act unlawful our enemies will certainly argue that the right to quit work singly or collectively (that is as a union) for any certain reasons ought to be made unlawful and they will endeavor to secure the enactment of a law to that effect.[41]

Despite the AFL chieftain's qualms, many local labor movements continued to advocate such legislation until its ultimate acceptance.[42]

Local labor movements, moreover, advocated a long list of reforms designed to protect and promote the interests of organized labor. Although rigidly opposed to compulsory arbitration, most state labor leaders supported the creation of state arbitration and conciliation boards to mediate labor disputes. They advocated laws to control advertising practices during strikes, to prohibit the interstate transportation of strikebreakers, and to regulate private detective agencies. In a related area, local labor leaders sought legislation to curb the

---

40. To the AFL leadership, this was the most important legislative item affecting the labor movement. Taft, *A. F. of L. in the Time of Gompers,* pp. 293, 403.

41. Gompers to Charles Fear, March 29, 1909, Gompers, Letterbooks.

42. Bryant, "Labor in Politics," pp. 272, 273. Gavett, "Labor Movement in Milwaukee," p. 154. Heath, "Labor in Connecticut," p. 55. Staley, *Illinois State Federation,* pp. 367, 434–40. Taft, *California State Federation of Labor,* pp. 9, 29. See also, the proceedings of the annual conventions of the following state federations of labor for the dates indicated: Pennsylvania (1907), pp. 37, 76; (1914), p. 126; Washington (1910), p. 101; Ohio (1912), p. 51.

activities of private employment agencies. Labor opposed these agencies, in part, because it considered their fees a tax on work, but more importantly, the private employment agencies were viewed as essentially strikebreaking institutions. Realizing the useful purposes such agencies could serve, however, local labor leaders endorsed the principle of a free employment service controlled and operated by government. Finally, a great many occupational groups—barbers, plumbers, stationary engineers, steamfitters, electricians, miners, etc.—vigorously sought to control entry into their professions through a system of government licensing. Although these regulations were usually justified by arguments that such licensing was necessary for the safety of workers and the general public, it seems clear that they were primarily motivated by hopes of acquiring through governmental intervention the control over the number and requirements of people who entered their trades that they had not been able to acquire through union activity.[43]

Independent Political Action

Thus important differences did exist within the structure of the labor movement. Nevertheless, few of these differences concerned the objectives of trade union activity; disagreements were over means. Rather than the antistatist attitude of the national labor leadership, local labor movements vigorously advocated political action and positive government intervention in all areas of working-class life. Because they placed so much emphasis on and assigned such importance to political activity, many local labor leaders inevitably became disillusioned with the seeming ineffectiveness of the AFL's nonpartisan political program. They were political activists deeply involved in local politics, and when they found their efforts to accomplish legislative objectives continually frustrated, their thoughts often turned to the possibility of organizing a labor party. The apparent

43. Harris and Krebs, *From Humble Beginnings,* pp. 54, 125, 135, 213, 219, 275–77. Gavett, *Labor Movement in Milwaukee,* pp. 88, 89, 110, 134, 142, 143. Taft, *California State Federation of Labor,* pp. 47, 52, 55, 77, 84. Bardwell and Seligson, *Organized Labor in Colorado,* pp. 87, 88, 89. Bryant, "Labor in Politics," pp. 273, 274. Heath, "Labor in Connecticut," pp. 55, 58. Stimson, *Labor Movement in Los Angeles,* pp. 57, 58, 128, 129, 200, 357. Staley, *Illinois State Federation,* pp. 33, 34, 142, 162, 163, 268, 281–83, 284–86, 489, 491, 503–5. Lawson, *Labor in Minnesota,* pp. 70, 162, 164, 165, 172, 174, 175, 176, 183, 220, 371, 378, 379. Yellowitz, *Labor and the Progressive Movement,* p. 143. See also the proceedings of the annual conventions of the following state federations of labor for the dates indicated: Washington (1903), p. 17; (1904), pp. 23, 27; (1905), p. 28; (1907), pp. 14, 15; (1908), p. 77; (1911), p. 86; Ohio (1911), p. 47; (1912), p. 88; (1913), p. 40; (1914), p. 83; Colorado (1898), p. 28; (1907), p. 45; Pennsylvania (1913), p. 26; (1914), pp. 119, 132.

success of labor parties in Europe, especially Great Britain, only served to heighten this interest.

During the first two decades of the twentieth century, most of the state and local labor movements in a survey of state and local labor movements either endorsed or actively participated in an independent political movement.[44] Although such activity, of course, proved ephemeral, in a practical sense, it reveals to the researcher a significant amount of enthusiasm for political action at the lower levels of the labor movement. This is all the more surprising when considering that not only the national leadership of the labor movement adamantly opposed independent political action, but so also did radical unionists who saw no need for another labor party with the Socialist party on the ballot and available to the union labor movement.

Although much has been written regarding the failure of a labor party to emerge in America, too little attention has been paid to the institutional structure of the American labor movement and the resourcefulness with which its leaders defused and frustrated those advocates of independent political action in the lower echelons.[45] The AFL leadership's activities associated with the 1906 political program (discussed earlier) provides one example. The failure of a conference of state federations of labor called by J. Harvey Lynch, a voluntary AFL organizer in Oklahoma, provides another. The Oklahoma labor movement had been extremely active politically, and its diligence was rewarded with considerable influence in the state's initial constitutional convention and later with the elected administration and state legislature.[46] Based upon organized labor's success in Oklahoma, Lynch wrote the officials of the various state federations of labor requesting their views regarding the possibility of holding a national conference of state federations to formulate a platform of labor demands and to devise a plan for securing pledges of support from congressmen and state legislators. After receiving favorable responses from twenty-seven state organizations, Lynch issued a call for the conference to meet in Springfield, Illinois in the late spring of 1908.[47]

In the meantime, AFL President Samuel Gompers began a

44. See, for example, Harris and Krebs, *From Humble Beginnings,* pp. 174–77; Gavett, *Labor Movement in Milwaukee,* pp. 73, 131, 133, 172; Stimson, *Labor Movement in Los Angeles,* pp. 295, 304–9, 352, 353; Yellowitz, *Labor and the Progressive Movement,* pp. 171–78, 203, 204, 206–10; Foner, *History of the Labor Movement,* pp. 287–97; *Proceedings of the Washington State Federation of Labor, 1910,* p. 90; *1911,* pp. 23, 24, 97, 98.

45. Rogin, "Voluntarism," pp. 527–30.

46. Bryant, "Labor in Politics," pp. 259–76.

47. Foner, *History of the Labor Movement,* pp. 347, 348. J. Harvey Lynch to W. E. Bryan, April 1, 1908, AFL, Papers, Series 117A, File 11A.

vigorous counteroffensive against what he regarded as a challenge to the AFL's integrity and authority. He first wrote Lynch advising him to call off the convention, which, he argued, could only "show to those who are hostile to the cause of labor something that would bring glee and unction to their souls, demonstrating that there is neither unity, or spirit, or purpose among the organized workers of the country." Rejecting the logic of Gompers's argument, Lynch persisted. The AFL president then sent a confidential letter to the members of the executive council warning them of Lynch's plans and suggesting that in reality the Oklahoma labor leader wanted to initiate a third-party movement. He then communicated with the officers of the various state federations expressing his official disapproval of the proposal.[48]

Gompers's opposition proved decisive. The proposed conference was cancelled. The response to Gompers's letter of opposition, however, could not have been entirely satisfactory to the AFL chieftain. Most of the correspondents, while not denying Gompers's reasoning, expressed their convictions regarding the importance of political action and their dissatisfaction with the labor movement's political accomplishments. Some labor leaders suggested that if the labor movement did not soon achieve a greater measure of political success, they would in the future favor a conference such as Lynch had proposed. Moreover, the president of at least one international union, W. D. Mahon of the Amalgamated Association of Street and Electric Railway Employees of America also questioned the adequacy of the AFL political program and suggested a conference to formulate a specific labor platform along with a more coherent plan to exercise labor's political influence.[49]

Assuming that events are not predestined by the fact of their having happened and that men do make conscious decisions from existing alternatives, one needs at least to contemplate the questions: Did American labor have to develop the political policies it did? Did viable alternatives exist to the AFL program? If the leadership of the AFL and the international unions had endorsed political activism with the same enthusiasm as state and local labor leaders, would the

48. Gompers to Lynch, April 14, 1908; Gompers to Executive Council, April 15, 1908, AFL, Papers, Series 117A, File 11A. There are numerous examples of this correspondence in the AFL, Papers, Series 117A, File 11A.

49. See, for example, P. H. Connolley to Gompers, May 9, 1908; Howard O. Smith to Gompers, April 26, 1908; F. N. Graves to Gompers, n.d.; J. H. Strief to Gompers, April 27, 1908; W. E. McEwen to Gompers, April 22, 1908; H. Moore to Gompers, April 20, 1908; Smith to Gompers, April 26, 1908; Graves to Gompers, April 27, 1908; W. D. Mahon to Gompers, May 12, 27, 1908; Gompers to Mahon, May 16, June 9, 1908, AFL, Papers, Series 117A, File 11A.

story of American labor and politics have been significantly different? Conclusive answers to these questions are difficult, perhaps impossible, to determine, but the questions are important and legitimate. Although it is not within the purview of this monograph to speculate about these matters, the study does suggest that there is much about the political behavior of American labor that has yet to be studied and explained.

The historical fact remains, however, that American labor did not evolve a labor party but instead eventually allied itself with the Democratic party. Among other state and local labor movements, indications of the rejection of voluntarism and third-party interest were relatively obvious, but ascertaining how unusual Missouri labor's alliance with the Democratic party during the 1920s was proved a much more difficult task. Like the Missouri movement, most labor bodies on the state level at least rhetorically continued to practice the nonpartisan political strategy. Although labor endorsements of Democratic candidates greatly exceeded those for Republicans, any definitive conclusions concerning the relationship between labor and the Democratic party in other states would require an extensive investigation of the political affairs of those states.[50]

Differences in the Labor Movement

The divergent political behavior of labor at the local and national level appears to have resulted from several circumstances. Besides those institutional factors discussed earlier, disparate constituencies at different levels of organization encouraged differing outlooks. The AFL owed its origin and continued existence to the several international union bureaucracies that had confederated at its formation. The international union bureaucracy had a vested interest in maintaining the *status quo;* innovation was dangerous, and any challenge to the adequacy of the bureaucracy as then constituted was anathema. It was this constituency to which the AFL leadership felt responsible. State and local central bodies, on the other hand, served a much different clientele. Their support came primarily from individual union locals. Local central bodies were voluntary associations of local trade unions; and that association, which included financial sacrifices, was unlikely to be continued if the central body did not serve the needs and reflect the desires of its affiliated local unions.

The political behavior of labor at the local and national levels also diverged because the leadership at the varying levels was so different.

50. The labor movements in Colorado and Missouri apparently experienced very similar situations. See Seligson and Bardwell, *Labor-Management Relations in Colorado,* pp. 89, 94–96.

Socialists, single-taxers, and other radical unionists who played an important leadership role in many local central bodies had almost no influence in the AFL hierarchy. Indeed, AFL officials appear to have devoted considerable time and energy to the task of undermining nonconforming union leaders. Because they came to the labor movement from such divergent backgrounds, local labor leaders assumed a much more expansive role as spokesmen for the entire working class rather than just for those few who were organized. Although AFL leaders also professed to speak for the working class, they were more concerned with the primacy and survival of the organization. Perhaps this conflict of purpose is nowhere better evidenced than in the AFL's endorsement, and local labor's rejection, of the selfish and organization-centered ideal of voluntarism.[51]

A final explanation for the differing political attitudes of labor at the local and national levels resulted from their varying perspective. Local labor was much closer to the immediate economic and political realities of working-class America. Unlike the national leaders of organized labor, they tended to react to immediate problems and seldom thought in long-range terms or in terms of the labor movement as a whole. They were more pragmatic and less inclined to react to various situations and events from any preconceived theory of the role and place of organized labor in larger American society. Moreover, in a very literal sense, local labor organizations were much more democratic than either the AFL or the various international union bureaucracies. If an old-age pension system seemed a reasonable and desirable reform to local union members, that interest was soon expressed in the meetings of local central bodies. By the time it had moved upward through the various union bureaucracies into an AFL convention, however, it could be (and often was) squashed easily by Gompers and like-minded union leaders.[52]

Despite any myopic perspective that local labor leaders may have had, the future certainly appears to have been theirs. Within a little over a decade after Gompers's death, most of the concepts upon which he had built his philosophy of trade unionism were being challenged or overthrown; voluntarism expired peacefully during the New

51. Rogin, "Voluntarism," pp. 521–35. Henry Pelling, *American Labor*, p. 140.

52. Pelling, *American Labor*, pp. 527–30, *et passim*. William Leiserson has described numerous ways in which the leadership of an international union can maintain its position regardless of the accuracy with which it represents its membership. *American Trade Union Democracy*, Chap. 6, *et passim*. Philip Taft has commented on the grass-roots character of the state federation of labor, *California State Federation of Labor*, p. 3, and Daniel Nelson has also noted the effectiveness of grass-roots pressure on state federations, *Unemployment Insurance*, pp. 160, 183.

Deal; nonpartisanship became a virtual dead letter as labor's fortunes were more and more closely tied to that of the Democratic party; craft organizing gave way in many industries to industrial organization; and during the 1930s and 1940s, labor's political passivity on the national level was replaced by an aggressive political activism. A more thorough investigation of organized labor at all levels would reveal that these developments were not as great a break with the earlier practices of the labor movement as a whole as has been assumed.

APPENDIXES

THE LABOR LOBBY
ITS SUCCESSES AND FAILURES

MUCH of the analysis of the political effectiveness of the trade union movement in the preceding pages is based upon the perceptions of the Missouri labor leaders. Because causation is largely the product of a conception of reality rather than of reality itself, the emphasis in this monograph has been upon the interpretation that labor unionists imposed upon the forces, people, and events affecting them and the trade union movement. At some point, however, it is necessary to divorce myth from reality. Did Missouri labor leaders realistically evaluate their political accomplishments? Were their policies and programs based upon a valid assessment of political reality? In answering these questions, the voting record of the Missouri General Assembly provides a useful point of reference. It was in the state legislature that many of the labor movement's political efforts were either crowned with achievement or frustrated by defeat.

An analysis of roll-call voting in the General Assembly reveals that while labor did score some legislative victories, its power and influence were severely limited. The legislative environment in which the labor lobby functioned was simply not very sensitive to working-class pressures. Although labor lobbyists were considerably successful in influencing roll-call voting, most measures in which labor was most interested failed to reach the roll-call stage. Everything considered, the analysis suggests that labor leaders were justified in being disappointed and disillusioned with their legislative lobbying efforts.

The Method

In the effort to measure and describe with some degree of precision the success and failures of the labor lobby in the Missouri General Assembly, several statistical devices were employed to analyze roll-call voting. One of the most important of these methods is Guttman scale analysis, the best available technique for ordering and arranging roll-call votes into meaningful patterns of roll-call behavior on a specific type of issue. The device has several advantages. It isolates roll-call votes into substantially unidimensional issue areas, the procedure is extremely valuable to the researcher who is attempting to study voting reactions on a single dimension of legislation—for example, voting behavior on labor measures. It eliminates roll calls that do not conform to the particular variable under study and votes in which cross pressures are strong enough to disqualify the vote on a single issue as a meaningful measure of behavior. After isolating those roll-call votes that reflect behavior in a substantially unidimensional issue area, the scaling procedure then provides a method for ranking the reactions of legislators on roll calls to certain types of legislation along a "positive" to "negative" continuum.

It also permits the identification of various voting blocs and alignments, which can then be compared in a systematic way.[1]

A preliminary universe of roll-call votes for this study was established by identifying every measure in which the labor movement exhibited an active interest that was voted upon between the years 1907 and 1939 in either branch of the Missouri General Assembly. For the first ten years of the period, this process was subjective and eclectic. The procedure consisted of a perusal of labor documents and publications as a means of identifying the measures in which the labor movement exhibited a strong interest. A survey of the *Journals* of the House and Senate facilitated the location of roll-call votes on those measures. The research process became more precise for data after 1917 through the availability of reports published by the State Federation of Labor's legislative committee that detailed the labor-oriented measures considered by the General Assembly. These legislative reports were published in the annual convention proceedings of the State Federation of Labor.

This procedure produced a preliminary universe of 117 roll-call votes for the House of Representatives and 85 for the Senate. In establishing these universes, all votes of a near-unanimous character (over 90 per cent positive or negative) were eliminated. The scaling procedure produced 18 separate scales for the House and 17 for the Senate. Each scale had a coefficient of reproducibility in excess of 0.90. A coefficient of reproducibility measures the proportion of responses on the scale items that could be accurately predicted from a knowledge of the legislator's scale scores. It is calculated by dividing the number of responses that could be predicted by the total number of responses. In general terms, the scales fell into two distinct categories. The first includes issues that directly affected workers and labor unions, such as mine safety measures, maximum hour–minimum wage legislation, and anti-injunction laws. The second category includes more broadly gauged social-welfare measures (old-age pensions, tax measures, child labor, etc.).

In this study, the primary emphasis was placed upon voting behavior in legislative districts rather than that of individual legislators. The locations of state senate districts were divided into three general classifications: (1) metropolitan districts in Kansas City and Saint Louis; (2) semiurban districts that include such cities as Saint Joseph, Springfield, and Sedalia; and (3) rural districts without a significant urban population. The locations of house districts were divided into four classifications: (1) Kansas City and Saint Louis metropolitan districts; (2) districts in which more than half of the population was urban; (3) semiurban districts in which at least 25 per cent of the population lived in an urban area; and (4) rural districts containing an urban population of less than 25 per cent. Legislative districts with a substantial mining or railroad interest also were identified. These classifications were based

1. For an explanation of Guttman scaling, see Samuel Stouffer, Louis Guttman, *et al., Measurement and Prediction: Studies in Social Psychology in World War II,* pp. 247–80; Lee F. Anderson, *et al., Legislative Roll-Call Analysis,* pp. 89–94; George Belknap, "A Method for Analyzing Legislative Behavior," pp. 377–402; Duncan MacRae, Jr., *Dimensions of Congressional Voting;* Charles Dollar and Richard Jensen, *Historians Guide to Statistics,* Chap. 4. For a critical discussion analyzing roll-call voting, see Duncan MacRae, Jr., *Issues and Parties in Legislative Voting: Methods of Statistical Analysis* (Chicago, 1970).

upon the 1910 census, and although changes occurred during the remaining thirty years of the period, those changes did not distort the data enough to override the obvious advantages of continuity in maintaining a single classification system. Legislative districts were reapportioned in 1923, and while this change did affect the continuity of Senate districts, it did not substantially alter the basis of representation in the House. (The population characteristics of the House districts are reported in Table 1–B.)

Individual scale scores for each legislative district were determined by collapsing the scales into percentile rankings. In this way the rankings of any individual legislative district can be traced over time. The voting behavior of the previously identified district classification groups was also compiled by averaging the mean percentile rankings. An illustration of this procedure is provided in the sample scale reproduced in Table 1–A. Scale scores on labor issues for the House and Senate are reported in Tables 2–B, 3–B, and 4–B.

Another statistical device used in this study was the computation of a labor lobby success score. This measure is an adaptation of Robert Dahl's initial effort to define and measure relative power among individual members of a legislative body by determining who won on roll-call votes. Although the success score as an adequate measure of relative power has been effectively challenged, it still provides a useful method of measuring relative success in converting policy preferences into law at the roll-call stage. In this case, however, rather than measuring the success of an individual legislator, the success score has been adjusted to determine the effectiveness of a legislative pressure group. The success score is computed by dividing the difference between the "wins" and "losses" by the total number of votes cast. If there are more wins than losses, the result will be a positive score ranging from 0.00 to 1.00. When the labor lobby lost more votes than it won, the success score was positioned in the negative success range from 0.00 to -1.00.[2]

In an effort to identify and analyze voting tendencies and patterns of a particular party, indexes of party cohesion and likeness were constructed. The most commonly used measure of intragroup agreement is the Rice Index of Cohesion. Cohesion as defined according to this index reflects the extent to which the distribution of the votes of a single group (Democrats or Republicans) varies from the distribution that would be expected if all forces operated in a completely random fashion (a fifty–fifty split). Thus if a group divides its votes equally on both sides of an issue there would be minimum cohesion. Conversely, if all votes were cast on one side of the issue it would represent maximum cohesion. The Rice Index is derived by finding the percentage in favor of and against a measure and subtracting the larger percentage from the smaller. The index is the absolute difference between the two percentage figures.[3]

The most widely used measure of intergroup difference is the index of likeness. It measures the differing responses of two groups to a roll-call vote or a series of votes. Computationally, it is derived by determining

2. Robert Dahl, "The Concept of Power," pp. 201–15. Duncan MacRae, Jr., and Hugh Price, "Scale Positions and 'Power' in the Senate." William Riker, "Some Ambiguities in the Notion of Power," pp. 341–49. Richard Jensen, "Power and Success Scores," pp. 1–6.

3. Anderson, *Legislative Roll-Call Analysis,* pp. 32–35.

Table 1–A. Voting behavior of Missouri State Senate districts on legislation affecting miners in 1921.

Dist. No.	Dist. Character	1	2	3	1	2	3	Percentile Ranking of Voting Blocks
15	Semiurban	R	R	R				
17	Rural	R	R	R				
34	Metro.	R	R	R				0.0 (0 ÷ 31)
21	Semiurban	R	A	R				
9	Metro.	R	R	A				
18	Rural		R	R	A			
19	Rural		R	R	A			
26	Rural		D	D	A			
29	Metro.		R	R	A			1.93 (6 ÷ 31)
1	Rural		R	R	R			
14	Semiurban		D	D	D			
16	Rural		R	R	R			
22	Rural		D	D	D			
25	Semiurban		R	R	R			
27	Metro.		R	R	R			
30	Metro.		R	R	R			
32	Metro.		R	R	R			
28	Metro.		R	A	R			
8	Rural				D	D	D	
12	Rural				D	D	D	
13	Rural				D	A	D	
24	Rural				D	A	D	6.13 (19 ÷ 31)
31	Metro.				D	A	D	
4	Rural	(R)				R	R	
3	Metro.				D	A	D	
6	Rural				A	D	D	7.74 (24 ÷ 31)
20	Semiurban				A	D	D	
23	Rural				D	A	D	
7	Metro.				R	R	R	
10	Rural				D	D	D	
11	Semiurban				D	D	D	

Unclassified (Absences)

2	Semiurban	R = Republican
5	Metro.	D = Democratic
33	Metro.	A = Absence

Roll Call Identification:
1. Vote on a measure to require the construction of bathhouses in mine fields.
2. Same as above.
3. Vote on a measure concerning the ventilation and inspection of coal mines.

the percentage of positive votes cast by each group, subtracting the smaller percentage from the larger, and subtracting the result from 100. The index ranges from 0 to 100—0 reflects absolute difference and 100 represents minimum differences.[4] (Success scores and index scores are listed in Tables 5–B and 6–B.)

4. *Ibid.*, pp. 44, 45.

Legislative Success and Failure

As a pressure group attempting to influence votes on issues debated and voted upon in the Missouri General Assembly, the labor lobby had a significant degree of success. Legislators in both houses of the legislature supported labor's position on well over two-thirds of the measures concerning labor that were submitted to a roll-call vote, and the labor lobby was only slightly less successful on nonlabor measures in which it took an active interest. The labor lobby had somewhat more success in the House of Representatives than the Senate. In the House the Democratic party supported labor at a higher level than the Republicans, but in the Senate the labor lobby had nearly the same degree

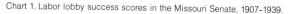

Chart 1. Labor lobby success scores in the Missouri Senate, 1907–1939.

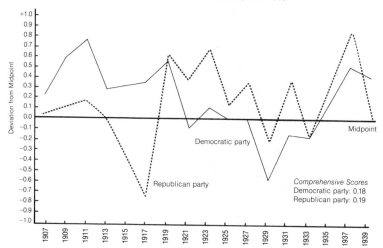

Chart 2. Labor lobby success scores in the Missouri House of Representatives, 1907–1939.

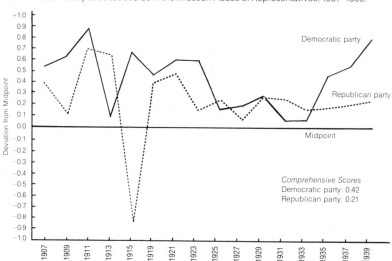

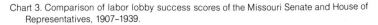

Chart 3. Comparison of labor lobby success scores of the Missouri Senate and House of Representatives, 1907–1939.

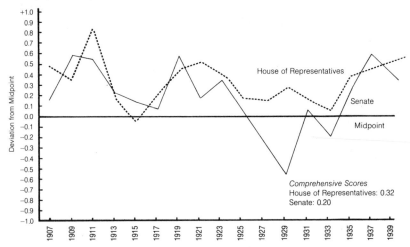

of success with both parties. Thus at the roll-call stage of the legislative process the labor lobby appears to have been a highly successful pressure group (see Charts 1–3). Once committed to vote for or against a measure of interest to the labor movement, most legislators responded in a manner that was satisfactory to the labor lobbyists. Labor's influence at this stage of the legislative process is further evidenced by the tactic adopted by a number of legislators: The practice of changing their votes from the negative to the positive after a measure had received a majority during a roll call. Another commonly used device that particularly annoyed labor lobbyists was the legislators' practice of leaving the legislative chamber during a vote to avoid having their position on an issue recorded. Under the rules of the General Assembly, a measure had to receive an absolute majority vote of the legislative chamber before enactment; consequently, in some cases an absence or an abstention was the equivalent of a "nay" vote, which, in effect, provided the legislator with a means of opposing a measure without being recorded as such.[5]

Labor's influence at this stage of the legislative process, however, fails to provide an adequate measure of its over-all effectiveness as a legislative pressure group. Only slightly more than 20 per cent of the measures labor advocated were submitted to a vote in both branches of the legislature. For the period 1933–1939, for example, the labor lobby actively supported 139 measures, but only 30 of these bills were voted upon by both houses of the legislature. The labor group had more success in getting votes in the House of Representatives where ballots were taken on 50 of the measures, but in the Senate only 31 of the bills reached the roll-call stage.[6] Companion bills introduced in both houses gave each an equal opportunity to express a preference on the particular bill in question. Included in those measures never

5. See the Legislative Reports of the Missouri State Federation of Labor's legislative committee, which are printed in the MSFL, *Proceedings*.

6. This information was gathered from a survey of the MSFL Legislative Reports and the *Journals* of the General Assembly.

reaching the floor of the legislature, moreover, were many of the measures labor considered most vital. Anti-injunction legislation provides an illustration. In almost every session of the General Assembly from 1907 to 1939, anti-injunction bills were introduced. Only one reached the roll-call stage in either house of the legislature. The labor lobby failed almost as often in its attempts to reform the convict labor system, enact an effective maximum hour–minimum wage law, amend the workmen's compensation law, enact a "little Wagner Act," and bring about other important reforms.

The labor lobby's ineffectiveness at this stage of the legislative process largely resulted from circumstances over which the labor lobbyists had little or no control. The absence of continuity in legislative membership from session to session presented one major problem. Because senators served for four years, half of their terms expired every two years. During the fifteen sessions of the General Assembly that are covered in this study, more than 70 per cent of the senators served only one term in office. This percentage was even higher for the House, where a large turnover occurred every two years rather than four years as in the Senate.[7]

The small number of legislators who accumulated considerable longevity in the state legislature acquired considerable influence and power because of the transient character of the majority of representatives. In the Senate they took over leadership roles and chaired many of the important standing and *ad hoc* committees. If one of these legislators opposed a measure, it was very unlikely to be voted upon. Sens. Michael Kinney of Saint Louis and Michael Casey of Kansas City were both prime examples of men who served for long periods and had extensive power. Both acquired an effective immunity to pressure exerted by interest groups (including labor), and they supported such groups only when it served their purposes.

A substantially different situation existed in the House, where legislators with the longevity of a Casey or Kinney did not emerge. Instead the House turnover in leadership was almost as great as that of the general membership. Freshman representatives often chaired major standing committees, while it was somewhat unusual for a speaker of the house to succeed himself.[8]

The discontinuities in the membership of the General Assembly had important repercussions on the labor lobby because this condition diminished the chances of building up a permanent labor bloc. In each session the labor lobby confronted a majority of new faces, most of whom had no apparent plans to seek reelection, thus negating any electoral pressures that a large working-class movement might have had upon legislative behavior. As a consequence, the process of educating legislators to the needs and desires of the working class had to be started anew at each session of the General Assembly.

Another circumstance operating against the effective operation of the labor lobby involved the character of those elected to the General Assembly. In most cases public service necessitated financial sacrifices that effectively excluded from service many potential candidates from the working classes. Recognizing this problem, the labor lobby consistently

7. This information is available for each session of the General Assembly in the *Official Manual*.
8. *Ibid.*

advocated increased compensation and benefits for legislators. These financial advantages would have permitted broader class and occupational representation in the General Assembly and encouraged more legislators to seek reelection, thus promoting continuity in legislative representation. As it was, the majority of legislators represented a very selective portion of the general population. Lawyers predominated in the Senate controlling, on the average, between one-half and two-thirds of the Senate seats. Businessmen and merchants constituted the next largest occupational group, followed by farmers and professional people. Seldom did the working class have more than one representative in the Senate. In the House, representation was more evenly balanced between farmers, lawyers, professionals, and businessmen. During the first three decades of the twentieth century, farmers as a group were dominant in the House, but by the thirties, representation among farmers declined and lawyers emerged as the largest occupational group. During the entire period, substantial numbers of businessmen and professionals served in the House, where representation of the working class was also very limited. In an average session of the General Assembly, between five and six working-class representatives served in the state legislature, many of them union business agents who were, in effect, financially subsidized by their unions.[9]

Few members of the General Assembly appear to have been interested in pursuing a political career. The retired businessman or lawyer more commonly appeared in the legislature than the ambitious young man moving upward in politics. Many members of the General Assembly were small-town lawyers, apparently anxious to acquire the prestige and professional advantages that service in the state legislature could provide. In other cases election to the General Assembly appears to have been a reward for loyal party work.[10]

Another circumstance influencing labor's lobbying activity at the state legislature resulted from the near absence of any party unity in the General Assembly.[11] This situation especially prevailed in regard to labor issues. Scores on the index of cohesion were low for both parties, especially in the Senate, while scores on the index of likeness were relatively high. Both measures reflect an absence of commitment by either party to support or oppose the causes of labor. In the House, Democrats tended to support labor at slightly higher levels than Republicans, and in the Senate, the reverse was true.[12] For the labor lobby the absence of party voting had both positive and negative results. Legislators unable to rely upon the party for guidance on complex or unfamiliar issues sought voting clues elsewhere. Here the large, active labor lobby could,

9. See *ibid.*, 1907–1939, for occupational listings.

10. For a discussion of types of representatives in the various state legislatures, see James D. Barber, *The Lawmakers: Recruitment and Adaptation to Legislative Life.* See also Robert H. Salisbury, *Missouri Politics and State Political Systems;* David R. Derge, "Metropolitan and Outstate Alignments in Illinois and Missouri Legislative Delegations," *The American Political Science Review,* pp. 1051–65; Robert F. Karsch, *The Standing Committees of the Missouri General Assembly;* John Wohlke, *et al. The Legislative System;* David A. Leuthold, *The Missouri Legislature: A Preliminary Profile.*

11. See Tables 5–B and 6–B. Malcolm E. Jewell, *The State Legislature: Politics and Practice* (New York, 1964), pp. 51–53, 58–60.

12. See Table 6–B.

and often did, play an important role. On the other hand, this condition also had the effect of increasing the power and influence of other pressure groups, some of which opposed the goals of the labor movement. The absence of allegiance to party also enhanced the influence of legislators with long service, who were the men most inclined to be hostile toward a labor lobby, which they may have viewed as either a potential or actual competing power broker.

Labor suffered the greatest disadvantages from the absence of party discipline during the decade of the 1930s. Having forged a firm alliance with the Democratic party on the state and national level, labor expected to profit from the overwhelming Democratic control of both houses of the General Assembly. To its disappointment, labor experienced little more success in the thirties than previously.[13] Had a more responsible party system predominated, the Democratic party would have been more conscientious in fulfilling its platform promises to the labor movement.

Thus the labor lobby functioned in a legislative environment often extremely personal and rigid but also capable of being impersonal and anarchic. In the absence of party leaders who were able to consistently deliver a large bloc of votes, the labor lobbyists devoted much of their energy during each session of the General Assembly to the task of building coalitions of sympathetic legislators. One indication of their success in this area of activity is provided by their ability to identify their measures as labor measures. Almost all labor measures during a session of the General Assembly scaled, which reflects the lobby's success in eliminating potential cross pressures on labor measures. The labor lobby's effort to create a favorable labor coalition in the state legislature was greatly facilitated by labor movements in individual legislative districts that had developed a good working relationship with local political interests.

In their attempts to build a labor bloc in the General Assembly, labor lobbyists could not depend upon a large bloc of metropolitan legislators from Kansas City and Saint Louis to support consistently their legislative program. Some legislators from those districts did compile very positive labor voting records, but they were offset by an almost equal number of senators and representatives having little sympathy for labor's legislative objectives. When scale scores (percentile rankings on the scales) are averaged over time, senators from metropolitan districts had a labor voting record only slightly more positive than the voting record of legislators from essentially rural legislative districts. In the House, representatives from metropolitan districts accumulated a substantially more positive labor voting record (see Charts 4 and 5).

The labor lobby did have one group of legislators it could usually count upon to support its interests. This group consisted of the senators and representatives sent to the General Assembly by Missouri's larger outstate cities. In the House, legislators from Springfield, Saint Joseph, and Hannibal accrued outstanding labor records through the years. In the Senate, legislators from districts that included Springfield, Saint Joseph, and Sedalia most consistently supported labor's legislative program. As indicated by Charts 4 and 5, the outstate urban areas supported labor at significantly higher levels than any other general population group. (For a more detailed breakdown of voting behavior of these groups, see Tables 3–B and 4–B.)

13. See Charts 4 and 5.

Chart 4. Comprehensive scale scores of the Missouri Senate on issues concerning labor, 1907–1939.

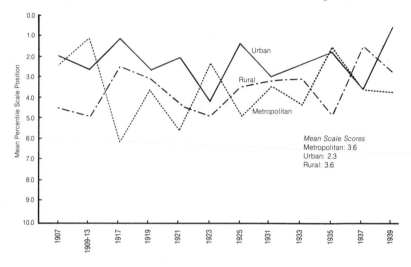

Mean Scale Scores
Metropolitan: 3.6
Urban: 2.3
Rural: 3.6

The reasons for labor's extraordinary success with these outstate legislators are not easily apparent, although they did have several conditions in common. Labor movements in the smaller cities had a highly motivated leadership that devoted considerable effort and energy to political affairs at the local level. Perhaps the best example is provided by Springfield, the hometown of Reuben Wood. The Springfield labor movement actively participated in local politics and was considered a force to be reckoned with by politicos of the city.[14]

Another factor the outstate cities had in common was a large group of railroad workers. The well-organized railroad unions had always been politically conscious because of the public nature of the railroad industry, and their influence extended well beyond the cities into the smaller railroad towns of the state such as Moberly (Randolph County), Macon (Macon County), Brookfield (Linn County), and Desoto (Jefferson County). Finally, socialism and Socialists had played a role in the labor movements of most of the outstate cities, instilling a political consciousness that survived long after the Socialists had ceased to play a significant role in their union labor movements.

While rural or predominantly rural legislators had the poorest voting record from a labor standpoint, rural legislators did not exhibit the hostility to labor's legislative objectives that might be anticipated. In the Senate, rural legislators developed labor voting records comparable to those from metropolitan districts. The coalition on labor and nonlabor issues that developed in each session of the General Assembly always contained significant numbers of rural legislators. Undoubtedly, this situation partially resulted from the absence of any extensive polarization between metropolitan and outstate legislators in the state legislature.[15]

14. There are numerous examples in the Ewing Y. Mitchell, Papers and the Sam Wear, Papers.

15. Derge, "Metropolitan and Outstate Alignments." Malcolm E. Jewell, *The State Legislature: Politics and Practice,* pp. 58, 59. Salisbury, *Missouri Politics.*

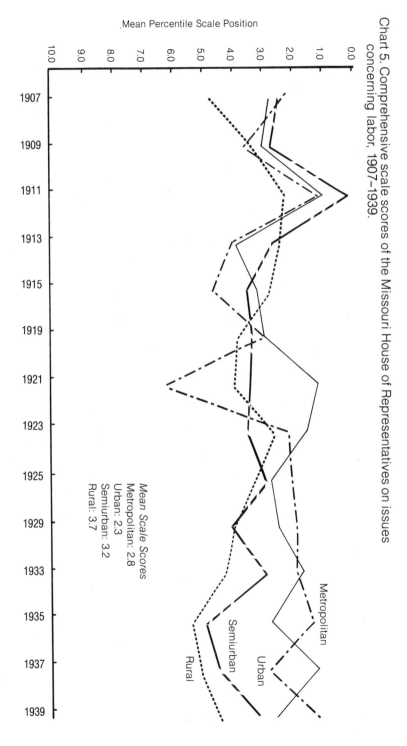

Chart 5. Comprehensive scale scores of the Missouri House of Representatives on issues concerning labor, 1907–1939.

Mean Percentile Scale Position

Mean Scale Scores
Metropolitan: 2.8
Urban: 2.3
Semiurban: 3.2
Rural: 3.7

Metropolitan
Semiurban
Urban
Rural

195

Consequently, a labor issue did not necessarily or automatically become an urban issue. A number of these rural legislators no doubt were influenced also by older Populist prejudices against big business and supported labor measures as one means of striking out at business interests. Finally, much of the state was underlaid by significant deposits of various minerals. Organizations of miners probably influenced the favorable voting records of representatives from such important mining districts as Saint Francois, Washington, Madison, Audrain, Lafayette, and Randolph counties. There were twenty House districts having a significant degree of commercial mining activity. These mining districts (excluding Henry, Franklin, and Crawford, which had no union organizing activity) had a mean comprehensive scale score on labor issues of 2.6, a more favorable labor record than that registered by metropolitan legislators. As true of other politically successful labor groups, the miners' unions had an important socialist heritage and politically were highly visible and active.

The Labor Lobby in Retrospect

Any attempt to evaluate the successes and failures of the labor lobby in the Missouri General Assembly must take into account the environment in which it functioned. Because of the circumstances discussed above, the labor lobby dealt with a group of legislators who in the strictest sense were both politically and representationally irresponsible. Moreover, institutional factors mitigated against effective pressure group activity. The constitutional provisions requiring an absolute majority to pass a bill, rather than a majority of those voting, cost labor several legislative victories. In the same vein, labor lost on numerous measures that a majority of legislators appear to have favored because strong-willed committee chairmen bottled up measures in committee and prevented a general vote of the chamber. The state legislature also operated under a time restriction that worked against the labor lobby. The Missouri General Assembly usually proceeded at a rather leisurely pace until the last few days of a session, when in a feverish burst of activity, legislators strained to enact necessary legislation before the Assembly adjourned. As a result, many of labor's legislative objectives, previously receiving favorable consideration, died on the House or Senate Calendar at the end of the session. This rather typical legislative scenario, of course, partially resulted from the absence of continuity in legislative membership and leadership, but it does not appear to have been wholly unintentional or unconscious. Delaying final action until the end of a session provided an effective means of killing the legislation a committee chairman or chamber leader opposed.

Perhaps the principle of inertia applies to the activities of the Missouri General Assembly. The introduction and successful enactment of a substantial, new piece of legislation was an extremely tenuous proposition, and even when achieved, it most likely was the result of several legislative sessions rather than a single session. This not only held true for the labor lobby but also generally characterized the experience of other legislative pressure groups in the General Assembly. This legislative inertia forced labor leaders to turn more and more to the Congress for reforms they felt vital.

While initiating new legislation in the General Assembly was an arduous and usually frustrating task, opposing legislation proved more rewarding. In this case the general inertia of the state legislature worked to the advantage of the obstructionists. In this role, the labor lobby was most effective. If labor intensely opposed a measure, it seldom received favorable consideration from the state legislature. In the period between 1919 and 1939, only three out of fifty measures in the General Assembly that the labor lobby opposed received favorable majorities in both houses of the legislature. One of the three received a gubernatorial veto, and of the remaining two, one involved tax matters and the other prevented consideration of the child labor amendment to the United States Constitution. The labor lobby defeated all attempts to establish a court of compulsory arbitration, abolish the state primary law, subject labor unions to taxation, create a state police force, and other measures that both directly and indirectly would adversely affect labor.

Thus, when all circumstances are considered, the labor lobby operated within a legislative environment in which the "possible" was not infinite. Instead, it was very limited, and labor's success or lack of it must be measured within that range. Given this condition, the labor lobby was considerably successful. To be sure, labor lobbyists had failures due to circumstances over which they did have some degree of control. Internal divisions over policy issues, poorly drafted legislation, tactless dealings with legislators, and ignorance of legislative processes all qualified the labor lobby's achievements. For the most part, however, the labor representatives were hard-working and conscientious men who compensated for their lack of lobbying skills and political leverage with a dedication to the interests of the working class that, in many ways, made the labor lobby a people's lobby.

APPENDIX B

STATISTICAL TABLES

Table 1–B. Population characteristics in districts of the Missouri House of Representatives in 1914.

Rural Districts (75%–100% rural)

District	Urban Pop.	Rural Pop.	Major Urban Area	Industry
Andrew	0	15,282	–	–
Atchison	0	13,604	–	–
Barton	2,700	14,047	Lamar	coal
Benton	0	14,881	–	–
Bollinger	0	14,576	–	–
Caldwell	0	14,605	–	–
Camden	0	11,582	–	–
Carroll	3,452	19,646	Carrollton	–
Carter	0	5,504	–	–
Cass	0	22,973	–	–
Cedar	2,503	13,577	Stockton	–
Chariton	0	23,503	–	–
Christian	0	15,832	–	–
Clark	0	12,811	–	–
Clinton	2,980	12,317	Plattsburg	–
Crawford	0	13,576	–	iron
Dade	0	15,613	–	–
Dallas	0	13,181	–	–
Daviess	0	17,605	–	–
DeKalb	0	12,531	–	–
Dent	0	13,245	–	iron
Douglas	0	16,664	–	–
Dunklin	3,033	27,295	Kennett	–
Franklin	3,670	26,160	Washington	lead, baryte, pyrite, etc.
Gasconade	0	12,847	–	–
Gentry	0	16,820	–	–
Harrison	0	20,466	–	–
Henry	4,992	22,250	Clinton	coal
Hickory	0	8,741	–	–
Holt	0	14,539	–	–
Howard	2,586	13,067	Fayette	–
Howell	2,914	18,151	West Plains	–
Iron	0	8,563	–	–
Johnson	4,689	21,603	Warrensburg	–
Knox	0	12,403	–	–
Laclede	0	17,363	–	–
Lawrence	4,148	22,435	Mt. Vernon Pierce City	–
Lewis	0	15,514	–	–
Lincoln	0	17,033	–	–
McDonald	0	13,539	–	–
Macon	3,584	27,284	Macon	coal
Maries	0	10,088	–	–
Mercer	0	12,335	–	–
Miller	0	16,717	–	–
Mississippi	3,144	11,413	Charleston	–
Moniteau	0	14,375	–	–
Monroe	0	18,304	–	–
Montgomery	0	15,604	–	–
Morgan	0	12,863	–	–

Table 1–B. Population characteristics in districts of the Missouri House of Representatives in 1914. (*Continued*)

Rural Districts (75%–100% rural) (*Continued*)

District	Urban Pop.	Rural Pop.	Major Urban Area	Industry
New Madrid	0	19,488	–	–
Newton	3,661	23,475	Neosho	–
Nodaway	4,762	24,071	Maryville	–
Oregon	0	14,681	–	–
Osage	0	14,283	–	–
Ozark	0	11,926	–	–
Pemiscot	3,655	15,904	Caruthersville	–
Perry	0	14,898	–	–
Phelps	0	15,796	–	–
Pike	4,454	18,102	Louisiana	–
Platte	0	14,429	–	–
Polk	0	21,561	–	–
Pulaski	0	11,438	–	–
Putnam	0	14,308	–	–
Ralls	0	12,913	–	–
Ray	3,664	17,787	Richmond	coal
Reynolds	0	9,592	–	–
Ripley	0	13,099	–	–
St. Claire	0	16,412	–	–
Ste. Genevieve	0	10,607	–	–
Schuyler	0	9,062	–	–
Scotland	0	11,869	–	–
Scott	3,327	19,045	Sikeston	–
Shannon	0	11,443	–	–
Shelby	0	14,864	–	–
Stoddard	0	27,807	–	–
Stone	0	11,559	–	–
Sullivan	0	18,598	–	–
Taney	0	9,134	–	–
Texas	0	21,458	–	–
Warren	0	9,123	–	–
Washington	0	13,378	–	lead, baryte
Wayne	0	15,181	–	–
Webster	0	17,377	–	–
Worth	0	8,007	–	–
Wright	0	18,315	–	–

Semiurban Districts (25%–50% urban)

District	Urban Pop.	Rural Pop.	Major Urban Area	Industry
Adair	6,347	16,353	Kirksville	coal
Audrain	5,939	15,748	Mexico	coal
Barry	4,177	19,692	Monett	railroads
Bates	5,648	20,220	Butler Amsterdam	coal
Boone	9,662	30,533	Columbia	–
Butler	6,916	13,708	Poplar Bluff	–
Callaway	5,228	19,172	Fulton	–
Cape Girardeau	8,475	19,146	Cape Girardeau Jackson	–
Clay	6,880	13,422	Excelsior Springs Liberty	–

Table 1–B. Population characteristics in districts of the Missouri House of Representatives in 1914. (*Continued*)

Semiurban Districts (25–50% urban) (*Continued*)

District	Urban Pop.	Rural Pop.	Major Urban Area	Industry
Cooper	4,252	16,059	Boonville	–
Grundy	5,656	11,088	Trenton	–
Jefferson	7,277	20,601	Desoto	lead, zinc, copper, railroads
Lafeyette	7,870	22,784	Lexington	coal
Linn	9,669	15,584	Brookfield	coal, railroads
Livingston	6,265	13,188	Chillicothe	–
Madison	2,632	8,461	Fredericktown	lead
Randolph	10,923	15,259	Moberly	coal, railroads
St. Charles	9,437	15,258	St. Charles	–
St. Francois	7,725	28,013	Bonne Terre, Flat River, Desloge	lead, copper, baryte, iron
St. Louis	23,539	58,878	Clayton, Kirkwood, Kinlock, etc.	–
Saline	8,107	21,341	Marshall	–
Vernon	7,176	21,651	Nevada	–

Urban (50%–100% urban)

Buchanan	77,403	15,617	St. Joseph	railroads
Cole	11,850	10,107	Jefferson City	railroads
Greene	35,201	28,630	Springfield	railroads
Jasper	57,912	31,761	Joplin, Carthage Webb City	zinc lead
Marion	18,341	12,231	Hannibal	–
Pettis	17,822	16,091	Sedalia	railroads

Metropolitan

Jackson	258,240	25,282	Kansas City	railroads
St. Louis City	750,000	0	–	railroads

Table 2–B. Comprehensive scale scores of the Missouri Senate, 1907–1921.

Dist. No.	Dist. Character	Scale Position by Year (Range—0.0 to 10.0)					Comp.
		1907	09–13	1917	1919	1921	
15	Urban-Rural	0.0	4.4	0.0	0.0	0.0	0.9
20	Urban-Rural	3.6	0.0	0.0	0.0	1.2	1.0
2	Urban-Rural	0.0	0.0	0.0	5.2	1.2	1.3
17	Rural	3.6	6.9	0.0	0.0	0.0	2.1
29	Metro. (StL)	0.0	0.0	6.1	0.0	4.2	2.1
24	Rural	0.0	0.0	4.5	0.0	7.0	2.3
23	Rural	0.0	0.0	0.0	5.2	7.0	2.4
26	Rural	0.0	6.9	4.5	0.0	1.2	2.5
6	Rural	5.7	0.0	6.1	0.0	1.2	2.6
30	Metro. (StL)	0.0	0.0	6.1	A*	4.2	2.6
22	Rural	5.7	4.4	0.0	0.0	3.3	2.7
9	Rural	3.6	4.4	0.0	5.2	1.2	2.9
16	Rural	5.7	4.4	0.0	0.0	4.2	2.9
32	Metro. (StL)	0.0	0.0	6.1	5.2	4.2	3.1
10	Urban-Rural	0.0	4.4	0.0	8.3	4.2	3.4
7	Metro. (KC)	0.0	0.0	6.1	5.2	6.7	3.6
8	Rural	8.4	0.0	6.1	0.0	4.2	3.7
21	Rural	5.7	4.4	0.0	8.3	0.0	3.7
28	Urban-Rural	5.7	4.4	6.1	0.0	3.3	3.9
33	Metro. (StL)	8.4	0.0	A	0.0	7.0	3.9
31	Metro. (StL)	0.0	0.0	6.1	5.2	9.4	4.1
34	Metro. (StL)	A	9.1	6.1	0.0	1.2	4.1
25	Rural	8.4	0.0	6.1	5.2	0.9	4.1
11	Rural	0.0	A	4.5	5.2	7.0	4.2
4	Rural	3.6	9.1	4.5	0.0	4.2	4.3
27	Rural	3.6	8.4	0.0	A	6.4	4.6
13	Rural	5.7	9.1	0.0	0.0	8.8	4.7
14	Rural	3.6	8.4	0.0	A	7.0	4.8
18	Rural	9.9	4.4	0.0	A	A	4.8
12	Rural	5.7	6.9	0.0	5.2	9.4	5.4
1	Rural	5.7	6.9	6.1	9.0	1.2	5.8
19	Rural	3.6	6.9	6.1	9.3	3.3	5.8
5	Metro. (KC)	8.4	0.0	6.1	9.3	7.0	6.2
3	Rural	5.7	A	4.5	A	8.8	6.3

Comprehensive (1907–1921)

	Rural	4.5	4.8	2.5	3.1	4.3	3.8
	Urban-Rural	1.9	2.6	1.2	2.7	2.0	2.1
	Metro.	2.4	1.1	6.1	3.6	5.5	3.7
	Kansas City	4.2	0.0	6.1	7.3	6.9	4.9
	St. Louis	1.7	1.5	6.1	2.1	5.0	3.3

*A = Absent

Table 3–B. Comprehensive scale scores of the Missouri Senate, 1923–1939.

Dist. No.	Dist. Character.	Scale Position by Year (Range–0.0 to 10.0)							
		1923	1925	1931	1933	1935	1937	1939	Comp.
25	Urban-Rural	3.8	0.0	0.0	0.0	0.0	0.0	0.0	0.5
26	Rural	0.0	6.9	A*	A	0.0	0.0	0.0	1.3
14	Urban-Rural	3.8	0.0	A	0.0	5.2	0.0	0.0	1.5
3	Metro. (KC)	5.6	0.0	0.0	0.0	0.0	6.1	0.0	1.7
17	Rural	0.0	6.2	0.0	0.0	7.4	0.0	0.0	1.9
23	Rural	8.8	0.0	0.0	3.0	0.0	A	0.0	1.9
15	Rural	0.0	0.0	4.5	3.0	7.4	0.0	0.0	2.1
28	Urban-Rural	0.0	0.0	0.0	5.7	0.0	9.5	0.0	2.2
32	Metro. (StL)	0.0	5.3	3.4	A	0.0	0.0	4.4	2.2
19	Rural	3.8	6.9	0.0	0.0	0.0	0.0	4.4	2.5
20	Urban-Rural	6.6	0.0	5.8	0.0	0.0	6.1	0.0	2.6
21	Urban-Rural	A	0.0	5.8	5.7	0.0	0.0	4.4	2.7
11	Urban-Rural	6.6	6.2	3.4	A	0.0	0.0	0.0	2.7
6	Rural	5.6	A	A	5.7	A	0.0	0.0	2.8
30	Metro. (StL)	0.0	6.9	A	5.7	0.0	0.0	4.4	2.8
1	Rural	0.0	0.0	0.0	3.0	7.4	6.1	4.4	3.0
29	Metro. (StL)	3.8	0.0	4.5	5.7	0.0	0.0	8.2	3.2
9	Metro. (KC)	3.8	0.0	0.0	3.0	5.2	6.1	4.4	3.3
16	Rural	3.8	0.0	5.8	5.7	A	0.0	4.4	3.3
18	Rural	0.0	4.7	5.8	A	5.2	0.0	4.4	3.4
33	Metro. (StL)	0.0	6.9	5.8	5.7	5.2	0.0	0.0	3.4
10	Rural	7.8	0.0	5.8	3.0	9.9	0.0	0.0	3.8
4	Rural	6.6	6.9	0.0	5.7	0.0	0.0	8.2	3.9
5	Metro. (KC)	0.0	6.9	A	9.9	0.0	0.0	8.2	4.1
22	Rural	8.8	6.9	5.8	0.0	7.4	0.0	0.0	4.1
2	Urban-Rural	A	0.0	5.8	3.0	7.4	9.5	0.0	4.3
7	Metro. (KC)	6.6	5.6	3.4	0.0	0.0	6.1	8.2	4.3
8	Rural	8.8	0.0	5.8	5.7	5.2	0.0	4.4	4.3
12	Rural	7.8	4.7	0.0	0.0	7.4	6.1	4.4	4.3
27	Metro. (StL)	0.0	6.9	5.8	3.0	5.2	6.1	4.4	4.5
34	Metro. (StL)	0.0	6.9	4.5	5.7	0.0	6.1	8.2	4.5
31	Metro. (StL)	5.6	6.9	4.5	5.7	A	6.1	4.4	5.5
13	Rural	7.8	5.6	5.8	5.7	7.4	6.1	4.4	6.1
24	Rural	8.8	A	5.8	3.0	5.2	6.1	8.2	6.2

Comprehensive (1923–1939)

	Rural	4.9	3.5	3.2	3.1	4.9	1.6	2.9	3.4
	Urban-Rural	4.2	1.4	3.0	2.4	1.8	3.6	0.6	2.4
	Metro.	2.4	4.8	3.5	4.4	1.6	3.6	3.8	3.4
	Kansas City	4.0	3.1	1.1	3.2	1.3	4.6	5.2	3.2
	St. Louis	1.3	5.7	4.7	5.2	1.7	2.6	4.9	3.7

Comprehensive (1907–1939)

	Rural	–	–	–	–	–	–	–	3.6
	Urban-Rural	–	–	–	–	–	–	–	2.3
	Metro.	–	–	–	–	–	–	–	3.6
	Kansas City	–	–	–	–	–	–	–	4.1
	St. Louis	–	–	–	–	–	–	–	3.5

* A = Absent

Table 4–B. Comprehensive scale scores of Missouri House of Representatives, 1907–1939.

County[b]	X	Scale Position By Year Range: 0.0–10.0[a]													
		07	09	11	13	15	19	21	23	25	29	33	35	37	39
Buchanan (4)(U)[c]	0.3	0.0	A	0.0	A	1.4	0.0	0.0	–	–	–	–	–	–	–
Greene (2)(U)	1.0	0.0	0.0	0.0	0.0	5.9	2.6	A	0.0	9.0	A	0.0	0.0	0.0	0.0
Pemiscot (R)	1.0	5.9	0.0	0.0	0.0	1.4	0.0	0.0	0.0	2.7	0.0	0.0	A	3.3	A
Greene (1)(U)	1.1	A	0.0	0.0	2.9	0.0	A	0.0	0.0	2.7	1.8	0.0	2.6	0.0	4.5
Marion (U)	1.4	0.0	A	0.0	2.9	1.4	2.6	0.0	0.0	2.7	5.9	0.0	2.6	0.0	A
St. Francois (S)	1.5	0.0	–	–	0.0	5.9	0.0	7.2	0.0	0.0	1.8	0.0	2.6	1.8	0.0
Greene (3)(U)	1.6	–	A	0.0	–	–	–	–	A	0.0	0.0	3.5	A	0.0	4.5
Jackson (1)(M)	1.7	5.3	A	0.0	2.9	1.4	2.6	0.0	6.1	0.0	1.8	0.0	0.0	A	0.0
Macon (R)	1.7	2.3	0.0	0.0	2.9	1.4	2.6	0.0	0.0	2.7	0.0	0.0	2.6	3.3	4.5
St. Louis (3)(M)	1.7	A	0.0	0.0	2.9	1.4	0.0	5.2	0.0	2.7	0.0	0.0	0.0	0.0	0.0
St. Louis (3)(M)	–	A	0.0	–	2.9	5.1	A	5.2	A	2.7	1.8	0.0	0.0	1.8	0.0
St. Louis (3)(M)	–	A	–	0.0	2.9	A	A	9.4	A	2.7	A	3.5	0.0	A	0.0
Washington (R)	1.8	–	A	0.0	–	–	–	A	A	2.7	A	A	A	A	4.5
Buchanan (1)(U)	1.9	5.9	A	0.0	0.0	5.9	2.6	0.0	0.0	0.0	1.8	0.0	A	1.8	A
Linn (S)	2.0	0.0	0.0	0.0	8.2	1.4	5.7	0.0	0.0	2.7	1.8	0.0	2.6	0.0	0.0
Buchanan (2)(U)	2.2	5.9	A	0.0	2.9	0.0	5.7	0.0	6.1	2.7	0.0	0.0	5.6	3.3	7.3
Jackson (10)(M)	2.2	0.0	–	0.0	0.0	1.4	5.7	2.9	0.0	2.7	A	0.0	2.6	4.6	0.0
Jasper (3)(U)	2.2	7.6	A	–	8.8	4.8	0.0	0.0	0.0	2.7	0.0	3.5	0.0	0.0	4.5
Saline (S)	2.2	2.3	0.0	0.0	2.9	0.0	5.7	0.0	0.0	2.7	1.8	4.5	5.6	4.6	4.5
Scott (R)	2.2	2.3	0.0	0.0	0.0	1.4	5.7	0.0	0.0	2.7	1.8	4.5	A	U	0.0
St. Louis (5)(M)	2.2	5.9	A	7.9	0.0	5.9	0.0	7.2	6.1	2.7	0.0	3.5	0.0	1.8	0.0
St. Louis (5)(M)	–	5.9	4.0	A	2.9	5.6	0.0	2.9	0.0	0.0	0.0	0.0	0.0	0.0	0.0
St. Louis (5)(M)	–	–	–	–	–	–	–	–	A	2.7	1.8	A	2.6	3.3	0.0
St. Louis (5)(M)	–	–	–	–	–	–	–	–	A	2.7	1.8	A	2.6	3.3	A
Buchanan (3)(U)	2.3	2.3	4.0	0.0	0.0	5.7	5.6	A	0.0	A	1.8	0.0	4.9	3.3	0.0
Caldwell (R)	2.4	0.0	A	0.0	2.9	5.3	2.6	0.0	0.0	2.7	A	0.0	8.4	4.6	A

205

Table 4–B. Comprehensive scale scores of Missouri House of Representatives, 1907–1939. (*Continued*)

County[b]	X	Scale Position By Year Range: 0.0-10.0[a]												
		07	09	11	13	15	19	21	23	25	29	33	35	37	39
Randolph (S)	2.4	0.0	0.0	0.0	2.9	1.4	0.0	2.9	0.0	2.7	1.8	4.5	9.0	7.7	0.0
Ripley (R)	2.4	2.3	0.0	0.0	2.9	0.0	5.7	0.0	0.0	9.0	1.8	4.5	7.7	0.0	0.0
Worth (R)	2.4	2.3	6.6	0.0	2.9	0.0	2.6	2.9	6.1	2.7	A	0.0	2.6	3.3	0.0
Holt (R)	2.5	0.0	A	0.0	0.0	5.9	2.6	0.0	0.0	9.0	1.8	0.0	5.6	A	4.5
Jackson (5)(M)	2.5	0.0	A	0.0	2.9	4.8	9.3	0.0	0.0	2.7	1.8	0.0	U	1.8	4.5
Madison (S)	2.5	0.0	A	0.0	2.9	5.9	5.7	0.0	0.0	0.0	5.9	4.5	2.6	4.6	0.0
Pike (R)	2.5	5.3	0.0	0.0	0.0	1.4	2.6	0.0	6.1	2.7	A	0.0	6.9	4.6	A
Audrain (S)	2.6	5.9	0.0	0.0	2.9	1.4	2.6	0.0	A	A	9.0	4.5	0.0	0.0	7.3
Lafayette (S)	2.6	2.3	4.0	0.0	2.9	1.4	0.0	0.0	0.0	2.7	5.9	0.0	0.0	5.6	9.2
Perry (R)	2.6	2.3	A	0.0	0.0	5.9	9.3	A	A	2.7	0.0	0.0	U	5.6	A
St. Louis (1)(M)	2.6	0.0	0.0	0.0	0.0	5.1	0.0	7.2	0.0	2.7	0.0	0.0	0.0	1.8	0.0
St. Louis (1)(M)	—	2.3	4.0	0.0	8.2	5.9	0.0	7.2	0.0	2.7	1.8	3.5	0.0	1.8	0.0
St. Louis (1)(M)	—	A	6.6	0.0	8.2	5.9	0.0	8.7	6.1	2.7	1.8	3.5	0.0	1.8	0.0
St. Louis (1)(M)	—	—	—	—	—	—	—	A	A	2.7	1.8	A	A	3.3	4.5
Barry (S)	2.7	A	4.0	0.0	0.0	5.9	2.6	0.0	A	0.0	0.0	0.0	8.6	5.6	A
Dent (R)	2.7	A	0.0	0.0	0.0	1.4	0.0	9.2	6.1	8.4	1.8	4.5	7.7	1.8	0.0
Lincoln (R)	2.7	8.9	0.0	0.0	2.9	1.4	2.6	0.0	0.0	0.0	8.4	4.5	0.0	3.3	0.0
Pettis (U)	2.7	5.3	6.6	0.0	2.9	0.0	5.7	A	6.1	0.0	5.9	0.0	A	0.0	0.0
Jefferson (S)	2.8	2.3	A	0.0	8.2	5.9	5.7	A	6.1	0.0	A	4.5	0.0	1.8	A
Johnson (R)	2.8	2.3	A	0.0	0.0	1.4	5.7	A	0.0	2.7	5.9	4.5	6.9	4.6	0.0
Mercer (R)	2.8	7.6	A	0.0	0.0	4.8	0.0	0.0	A	2.7	0.0	4.5	A	U	8.3
Ray (R)	2.8	5.3	6.6	7.9	0.0	1.4	5.7	0.0	0.0	A	1.8	4.5	2.6	0.0	0.0
Clinton (R)	2.9	0.0	6.6	0.0	0.0	0.0	5.7	5.2	0.0	9.0	1.8	4.5	A	3.3	4.5
Cole (U)	2.9	5.9	4.0	7.9	0.0	0.0	0.0	2.9	0.0	2.7	1.8	4.5	2.6	5.6	0.0
Jackson (9)(M)	2.9	—	—	—	—	—	—	0.0	9.3	2.7	1.8	0.0	0.0	1.8	4.5
Monroe (R)	2.9	2.3	A	0.0	2.9	1.4	9.3	2.9	A	0.0	0.0	8.2	A	7.7	0.0
Ste. Genevieve (R)	2.9	2.3	4.0	0.0	8.2	5.9	2.6	0.0	0.0	2.7	1.8	4.5	0.0	3.3	A
St. Louis (4)(M)	3.0	0.0	0.0	0.0	0.0	5.9	0.0	5.2	0.0	2.7	0.0	3.5	2.6	0.0	0.0
St. Louis (4)(M)	—	0.0	6.6	0.0	2.9	5.9	0.0	7.2	0.0	2.7	1.8	3.5	2.6	1.8	0.0

St. Louis (4)(M)	—	5.9	6.6	7.9	8.8	5.9	0.0	9.4	6.1	2.7	A	3.5	4.9	1.8	A
St. Louis (4)(M)	—	—	—	—	—	—	—	—	6.1	A	A	3.5	A	3.3	A
Clay (S)	3.0	2.3	6.6	0.0	2.9	0.0	5.7	5.2	0.0	A	1.8	4.5	6.5	A	0.0
Jackson (3)(M)	3.0	0.0	0.0	A	2.9	1.4	5.7	9.4	0.0	0.0	A	A	A	7.7	A
Jackson (6)(M)	3.0	0.0	A	0.0	0.0	1.4	8.7	7.2	0.0	2.7	A	0.0	5.6	7.7	0.0
Stone (R)	3.0	A	6.6	0.0	2.9	0.0	A	A	A	0.0	1.8	8.2	9.6	5.6	A
Chariton (R)	3.1	2.3	A	7.9	0.0	0.0	5.7	5.2	0.0	0.0	9.0	4.5	0.0	1.8	4.5
Gentry (R)	3.1	2.3	0.0	A	2.9	5.9	2.6	2.9	0.0	0.0	1.8	4.5	7.7	5.6	0.0
Vernon (S)	3.1	2.3	0.0	0.0	2.9	1.4	5.7	2.9	9.3	9.0	A	4.5	9.3	A	0.0
Callaway (S)	3.2	2.3	0.0	0.0	2.9	1.4	2.6	5.2	6.1	2.7	5.9	4.5	U	7.7	0.0
Cooper (S)	3.2	0.0	4.0	0.0	2.9	5.9	2.6	5.2	0.0	2.7	1.8	0.0	5.6	3.3	0.0
Jackson (8)(M)	3.2	—	—	—	0.0	—	—	—	A	0.0	5.9	A	2.6	7.7	7.3
McDonald (R)	3.2	8.9	9.5	0.0	0.0	0.0	0.0	2.9	0.0	0.0	1.8	8.2	A	A	0.0
St. Claire (R)	3.2	7.6	A	0.0	2.9	1.4	2.6	5.2	0.0	2.7	9.0	4.5	9.9	U	0.0
Shannon (R)	3.2	2.3	0.0	0.0	8.8	5.9	0.0	5.2	0.0	0.0	5.9	4.5	6.6	0.0	0.0
Stoddard (R)	3.2	2.3	0.0	0.0	2.9	1.4	2.6	8.9	0.0	9.0	A	4.5	0.0	7.7	A
Wayne (R)	3.2	5.9	0.0	0.0	8.2	1.4	5.7	0.0	6.1	2.7	5.9	8.2	2.6	A	A
Lawrence (R)	3.3	2.3	4.0	0.0	2.9	5.9	9.2	0.0	A	2.7	0.0	0.0	0.0	0.0	7.3
New Madrid (R)	3.3	0.0	7.9	2.9	1.4	A	5.2	6.1	0.0	5.9	1.8	0.0	A	A	A
Osage (R)	3.3	2.3	6.6	6.6	8.2	0.0	2.6	5.2	0.0	2.7	A	4.5	7.4	5.6	0.0
Pulaski (R)	3.3	2.3	4.0	0.0	2.9	1.4	5.7	7.2	0.0	0.0	5.9	8.2	2.6	5.6	A
St. Louis (3)(U)	3.3	—	—	—	—	—	—	—	0.0	2.7	A	3.5	A	3.3	4.5
Adair (S)	3.4	0.0	6.6	0.0	2.9	5.9	0.0	2.9	6.1	2.7	A	4.5	4.9	9.1	4.5
Dallas (R)	3.4	0.0	A	0.0	0.0	5.3	5.7	A	0.0	2.7	1.8	8.2	5.6	1.8	A
Jasper (1)(U)	3.4	7.6	6.6	0.0	2.9	5.9	2.6	0.0	9.3	2.7	1.8	A	2.6	U	8.3
Jasper (2)(U)	3.4	5.9	4.0	0.0	8.8	4.8	2.6	0.0	0.0	2.7	1.8	4.5	A	0.0	0.0
Knox (R)	3.4	2.3	6.6	7.9	8.2	5.9	2.6	5.2	0.0	2.7	1.8	0.0	2.6	1.8	0.0
Laclede (R)	3.4	5.3	6.6	0.0	0.0	5.9	2.6	2.9	0.0	2.7	1.8	4.5	0.0	5.6	9.2
Lewis (R)	3.5	5.3	4.0	0.0	2.9	1.4	5.7	7.2	6.1	2.7	0.0	4.5	2.6	9.1	4.5
Newton (R)	3.5	2.3	0.0	0.0	2.9	1.4	2.6	2.9	A	2.7	1.8	8.2	2.6	5.6	9.2
Schuyler (R)	3.5	2.3	0.0	9.8	2.9	0.0	0.0	0.0	6.1	2.7	5.9	4.5	7.5	5.6	4.5
Bates (S)	3.6	2.3	4.0	0.0	0.0	1.4	0.0	2.9	6.1	9.0	5.9	0.0	6.9	4.6	7.3
Cass (R)	3.6	7.6	6.6	0.0	2.9	1.4	2.6	5.2	6.1	0.0	A	0.0	4.9	5.6	4.5
DeKalb (R)	3.6	0.0	A	0.0	2.9	1.4	A	9.4	6.1	0.0	9.0	0.0	A	5.6	4.5

Table 4–B. Comprehensive scale scores of Missouri House of Representatives, 1907–1939. (*Continued*)

County[b]	X						Scale Position By Year Range: 0.0–10.0[a]									
		07	09	11	13	15	19	21	23	25	29	33	35	37	39
Iron (R)	3.6	2.3	0.0	0.0	8.8	1.4	5.7	A	0.0	9.0	8.4	0.0	A	A	4.5
Jackson (4)(M)	3.6	A	6.6	0.0	2.9	5.6	5.7	A	6.1	0.0	A	A	A	1.8	A
Morgan (R)	3.6	5.9	6.6	0.0	0.0	5.9	5.7	2.9	0.0	2.7	5.9	4.5	A	A	A
Oregon (R)	3.6	7.6	0.0	0.0	2.9	0.0	5.7	A	0.0	8.4	0.0	8.2	6.9	7.7	0.0
St. Louis (1)(U)	3.6	0.0	0.0	7.9	2.9	5.3	5.7	A	0.0	2.7	5.9	4.5	4.9	3.3	4.5
St. Louis (2)(U)	3.6	0.0	6.6	0.0	8.2	A	A	7.2	0.0	2.7	A	4.5	2.6	0.0	7.3
Texas (R)	3.6	5.9	0.0	0.0	2.9	1.4	A	0.0	0.0	9.0	8.2	5.6	5.6	A	4.5
St. Louis (2)(M)	3.6	0.0	6.6	0.0	8.8	5.1	0.0	7.2	0.0	2.7	0.0	0.0	0.0	1.8	0.0
St. Louis (2)(M)	—	0.0	9.5	7.9	8.8	5.9	8.7	7.2	0.0	2.7	1.8	3.5	0.0	5.6	0.0
St. Louis (2)(M)	—	A	A	7.9	A	5.9	8.7	7.2	0.0	2.7	5.9	3.5	0.0	1.8	A
St. Louis (6)(M)	3.6	0.0	A	0.0	2.9	5.9	0.0	5.2	—	2.7	—	—	—	—	—
St. Louis (6)(M)	—	5.9	A	0.0	A	A	8.7	7.2	—	—	—	—	—	—	—
Barton (R)	3.7	0.0	0.0	0.0	2.9	1.4	0.0	A	9.3	2.7	9.0	4.5	9.0	4.6	4.5
Daviess (R)	3.7	2.3	A	0.0	2.9	1.4	2.6	2.9	0.0	8.4	9.0	0.0	4.9	5.6	8.3
Maries (R)	3.7	2.3	0.0	0.0	0.0	1.4	5.7	5.2	6.1	A	8.4	4.5	4.9	4.6	4.5
Phelps (R)	3.7	7.6	4.0	0.0	8.8	1.4	2.6	5.2	0.0	2.7	5.9	4.5	A	5.6	0.0
Putnam (R)	3.7	7.6	6.6	0.0	0.0	5.9	0.0	0.0	0.0	0.0	8.4	0.0	9.0	5.6	8.3
Carroll (R)	3.8	8.9	4.0	0.0	2.9	0.0	A	2.9	A	2.7	1.8	8.2	9.7	5.6	7.3
Polk (R)	3.8	5.9	4.0	0.0	2.9	5.9	2.6	0.0	0.0	2.7	1.8	4.5	9.7	5.6	4.5
Ralls (R)	3.8	2.3	4.0	0.0	2.9	1.4	5.7	5.2	6.1	2.7	5.9	0.0	8.6	A	0.0
Clark (R)	3.9	8.9	0.0	0.0	0.0	5.9	5.7	5.2	6.1	2.7	5.9	0.0	A	4.6	8.3
Dade (R)	3.9	8.9	A	A	2.9	5.9	2.6	0.0	6.1	2.7	1.8	0.0	7.7	A	A
Moniteau (R)	3.9	7.6	9.5	0.0	2.9	1.4	2.6	0.0	0.0	9.0	5.9	4.5	A	U	A
Shelby (R)	3.9	2.3	0.0	0.0	2.9	0.0	9.3	5.2	0.0	2.7	8.4	8.2	6.6	9.1	0.0
Bollinger (R)	4.0	9.9	6.6	7.9	0.0	0.0	0.0	2.9	6.1	A	0.0	8.2	6.5	A	0.0
Boone (S)	4.0	2.3	A	0.0	2.9	1.4	5.7	5.2	9.1	2.7	1.8	4.5	A	7.7	4.5
Butler (S)	4.0	0.0	A	0.0	A	5.9	2.6	7.2	0.0	8.4	1.8	0.0	8.4	A	9.2
Grundy (S)	4.0	5.9	A	7.9	0.0	5.9	0.0	2.9	9.3	0.0	1.8	4.5	A	5.6	A
Cedar (R)	4.1	7.6	4.0	0.0	2.9	5.6	8.7	7.2	0.0	0.0	A	A	0.0	9.1	A
Jackson (2)(M)	4.1	8.9	4.0	0.0	2.9	A	5.7	9.4	A	0.0	5.9	0.0	4.9	7.7	0.0

County														
Warren (R)	4.1	8.9	4.0	9.8	0.0	5.9	2.6	5.2	0.0	2.7	1.8	8.2	0.0	4.6
Atchison (R)	4.3	2.3	0.0	0.0	0.0	5.9	5.7	5.2	6.1	8.4	1.8	9.9	U	0.0
Carter (R)	4.3	2.3	0.0	7.9	8.8	1.4	2.6	2.9	0.0	9.0	5.9	4.5	7.5	7.7
Howard (R)	4.3	2.3	0.0	9.3	0.0	1.4	5.7	7.2	6.1	A	1.8	8.2	6.9	0.0
Camden (R)	4.4	5.9	A	0.0	0.0	5.9	9.7	8.7	0.0	2.7	A	4.5	0.0	5.6
Dunklin (R)	4.5	0.0	0.0	9.3	2.9	1.4	8.7	0.0	6.1	9.0	A	4.5	7.7	A
Henry (R)	4.6	5.9	6.6	0.0	2.9	0.0	2.6	9.4	9.3	2.7	1.8	4.5	6.6	7.7
Montgomery (R)	4.4	A	0.0	0.0	0.0	5.9	9.3	0.0	6.6	2.7	5.9	4.5	U	9.1
Platte (R)	4.6	5.3	A	0.0	2.9	1.4	5.7	9.0	6.1	2.7	A	4.5	5.6	3.3
Webster (R)	4.6	7.6	6.6	0.0	2.9	5.9	2.6	2.9	6.1	2.8	5.9	0.0	2.6	9.4
Harrison (R)	4.7	2.3	4.0	7.9	0.0	5.9	0.0	5.2	6.1	0.0	A	4.5	A	9.9
Miller (R)	4.7	2.3	6.6	0.0	2.9	5.1	5.7	7.2	6.1	8.4	0.0	4.5	U	7.7
Sullivan (R)	4.7	5.9	6.6	0.0	2.9	5.9	2.6	0.0	0.0	2.7	8.4	4.5	7.7	9.4
Nodaway (R)	4.8	8.9	9.4	7.9	0.0	5.9	5.7	9.2	0.0	0.0	1.8	4.5	7.5	0.0
Reynolds (R)	4.9	7.6	4.0	0.0	2.9	1.4	5.7	A	6.1	8.4	9.0	0.0	4.9	4.6
Scotland (R)	4.9	8.9	0.0	7.9	2.9	1.4	8.7	2.9	6.1	9.0	5.9	0.0	7.7	7.7
Franklin (R)	4.9	8.9	4.0	7.9	0.0	5.9	0.0	9.4	0.0	2.7	1.8	8.2	9.6	9.1
Benton (R)	5.0	7.6	6.6	0.0	8.8	5.9	8.7	5.2	6.1	0.0	1.8	0.0	6.9	5.6
Cape Girardeau (S)	5.0	8.9	4.0	0.0	2.9	5.9	2.6	8.9	9.1	A	5.9	8.2	2.6	0.0
Douglas (R)	5.0	A	4.0	7.9	2.9	5.9	2.6	5.2	A	A	0.0	3.5	5.6	5.6
Jackson (7)(M)	5.0	—	—	—	—	—	—	—	9.1	8.4	8.4	4.5	2.6	3.3
Andrew (R)	5.1	7.6	4.0	0.0	0.0	5.9	5.7	9.4	6.1	2.7	5.9	8.2	5.6	4.6
Christian (R)	5.1	A	6.6	9.3	0.0	5.9	0.0	8.7	9.3	0.0	A	4.5	0.0	5.6
Livingston (R)	5.1	5.3	6.6	0.0	2.9	5.9	9.7	A	6.1	0.0	9.0	4.5	2.6	5.6
Mississippi (R)	5.2	8.9	0.0	0.0	8.8	1.4	5.7	5.2	6.1	9.0	5.9	8.2	7.7	A
Crawford (R)	5.3	8.9	0.0	7.9	2.9	5.9	2.6	7.2	6.1	0.0	A	4.5	9.3	5.6
Howell (R)	5.3	5.9	4.0	9.3	8.8	5.9	0.0	8.7	0.0	0.0	5.9	8.2	A	7.7
Gasconade (R)	5.7	7.6	6.6	9.8	0.0	5.9	2.6	5.2	A	2.7	1.8	8.2	9.8	9.1
Ozark (R)	5.7	7.6	4.0	9.3	2.9	5.9	0.0	7.2	0.0	2.7	9.0	8.2	8.4	9.1
Wright (R)	5.9	5.9	6.6	0.0	0.0	5.9	2.6	2.9	6.1	9.0	9.0	8.2	9.3	5.6
St. Charles (S)	6.1	7.6	A	0.0	8.2	5.9	8.7	5.2	9.3	2.7	8.4	8.2	7.4	3.3
Taney (R)	6.1	A	6.6	9.3	8.8	5.9	2.6	2.9	0.0	2.7	5.9	8.2	9.0	7.7
Hickory (R)	6.3	5.9	6.6	9.3	0.0	5.9	2.6	5.2	A	2.7	9.0	8.2	9.0	9.9

Table 4–B. Comprehensive scale scores of Missouri House of Representatives, 1907–1939. (*Continued*)

County[b]	X	07	09	11	13	15	19	21	23	25	29	33	35	37	39
							Scale Position By Year Range: 0.0–10.0[a]								
Comprehensive															
Urban	2.3	2.7	3.2	1.1	4.0	2.9	3.2	1.3	1.6	2.8	2.6	1.8	2.8	1.4	2.7
Metropolitan	2.8	2.5	3.6	1.2	4.0	4.7	3.2	6.4	2.4	2.2	2.0	1.9	1.5	2.9	1.3
Semiurban	3.2	2.6	2.8	0.4	2.8	3.6	3.4	3.5	3.6	3.0	4.1	3.0	5.0	4.6	3.2
Rural	3.7	4.8	3.5	2.3	2.6	3.3	3.9	4.0	2.7	3.4	4.1	4.3	5.4	5.2	4.5

[a] See sample scale in Chapter XI.
[b] For county descriptions see Table 1.
[c] U = Urban
   S = Semiurban
   M = Metropolitan
   R = Rural

Table 5–B. Index scores for the Missouri Senate, 1907–1939.

Year	Labor Success Score (Democrats)	Labor Success Score (Republicans)	Labor Success Score (Comprehensive)	Index of Cohesion (Democrats)	Index of Cohesion (Republicans)	Index of Likeness
1907	.22	.04	.16	25.0	05.0	89.8
1909	.57	.55	.56	68.4	100.0	84.2
1911	.73	.17	.53	84.2	25.0	70.4
1913	.29	.00	.21	36.8	00.0	81.6
1917	.36	−.75	.07	40.4	75.0	42.3
1919	.55	.57	.56	63.8	70.8	96.5
1921	−.09	.38	.17	12.2	41.2	73.3
1923	.10	.64	.32	11.8	69.2	71.3
1925	.00	.11	.01	04.1	03.2	96.3
1927	.00	.33	.13	00.0	39.6	80.2
1929	−.59	−.22	−.53	68.0	50.0	91.0
1931	−.14	.34	.05	16.6	42.8	70.3
1933	−.17	−.20	−.20	22.2	40.0	91.1
1935	.23	.35	.24	26.8	42.8	92.0
1937	.50	.83	.56	64.7	100.0	82.3
1939	.39	.00	.36	49.4	00.0	75.3
X	.18	.19	.20	37.1	44.0	80.5

Table 6–B. Index scores for the Missouri House of Representatives, 1907–1939.

Year	Labor Success Score (Democrats)	Labor Success Score (Republicans)	Labor Success Score (Comprehensive)	Index of Cohesion (Democrats)	Index of Cohesion (Republicans)	Index of Likeness
1907	.52	.34	.45	.66	.46	.90
1909	.60	.11	.34	.82	.16	.68
1911	.86	.70	.79	.90	.78	.93
1913	.08	.61	.18	.28	.76	.66
1915	.66	−.85	−.03	.72	.96	.16
1919	.45	.38	.41	.58	.56	.98
1921	.59	.46	.49	.72	.54	.90
1923	.58	.13	.39	.76	.22	.87
1925	.14	.22	.18	.18	.32	.94
1927	.18	.05	.11	.22	.06	.92
1929	.26	.26	.26	.38	.36	.98
1931	.06	.23	.13	.10	.38	.86
1933	.04	.14	.05	.04	.16	.94
1935	.45	.16	.36	.64	.24	.81
1937	.51	.19	.42	.66	.28	.81
1939	.78	.21	.51	.90	.10	.60
X	.42	.21	.32	.53	.40	.81

BIBLIOGRAPHY

A. FEDERAL PUBLIC DOCUMENTS

United States Bureau of the Census. *Twelfth Census of the United States: 1900. Characteristics of the Population.* Vol. I, Part I. Washington, D.C.: Government Printing Office, 1901.

United States Bureau of Labor Statistics. *Bulletin No. 270.* Washington, D.C.: Government Printing Office, 1921.

————. *Bulletin No. 274.* Washington, D.C.: Government Printing Office, 1919.

United States Department of Labor. *Report of the Secretary of the National War Labor Board.* Washington, D.C.: Government Printing Office, 1920.

B. MISSOURI PUBLIC DOCUMENTS

Bureau of Labor Statistics and Inspection. Twenty-Third and Twenty-Fourth Annual Reports of the Bureau of Labor Statistics: 1901, 1902. Jefferson City: Tribune Publishing Company, n.d. (*The Missouri Red Book*).

Bureau of Labor Statistics. Twenty-Fifth to Forty-Third Annual Reports of the Bureau of Labor Statistics: 1904–1922. Jefferson City: The Hugh Stephens Printing Company, n.d. (*The Missouri Red Book*).

Messages and Proclamations of the Governors of the State of Missouri, Vols. IX, X, XI, XII. Eds. Floyd C. Shoemaker and Sarah Ginter. Columbia: The State Historical Society, 1926.

Messages and Proclamations of the Governors of the State of Missouri, Vol. XIII. Eds. Floyd C. Shoemaker and Buel Leopard. Columbia: The State Historical Society, 1947.

Official Manual of the State of Missouri for Years 1913–1914; 1915–1916; 1917–1918; 1921–1922; 1923–1924; 1925–1926: 1927–1928; 1929–1930. Jefferson City: The Hugh Stephens Press, n.d.

Official Manual for Years 1931–1932. Jefferson City: Botz Printing and Stationery Company, n.d.

Official Manual for Years 1933–1934; 1935–1936; 1937–1938; 1941–1942. Jefferson City: Midland Publishing Company, n.d.

Proceedings of the Missouri Constitutional Convention, 1922, 1923. *Journal and Debates,* Vols. I, II, III, IV.

Report of the Missouri Commission on Employers' Liability and Workmen's Compensation to the Governor and the Forty-Seventh General Assembly, January, 1913. Jefferson City: The Hugh Stephens Printing Company, n.d.

C. LABOR DOCUMENTS

Constitution. American Federation of Labor, 1944.

Constitution, By-Laws and Rules of Order. Missouri State Federation of Labor, 1911, State Historical Society of Missouri, Columbia.

Joint Labor Legislative Committee Report, 1907. State Historical Society of Missouri, Columbia.
Proceedings of the Colorado State Federation of Labor, 1893–1914. AFL–CIO Archives, Washington, D.C.
Proceedings of the Missouri State Federation of Labor, 1893–1941. State Historical Society of Missouri, Columbia.
Proceedings of the National Women's Trade Union League of America, 1911–1917. AFL–CIO Archives, Washington, D.C.
Proceedings of the Ohio State Federation of Labor, 1911–1917. AFL–CIO Archives, Washington, D.C.
Proceedings of the Oregon State Federation of Labor, 1909–1912. AFL–CIO Archives, Washington, D.C.
Proceedings of the Pennsylvania State Federation of Labor, 1903–1917. AFL–CIO Archives, Washington, D.C.
Proceedings of the Washington State Federation of Labor, 1903–1917. AFL–CIO Archives, Washington, D.C.
Women's Trade Union League, Official Minutes, June 9, 1910. AFL–CIO Archives, Washington, D.C.

D. MANUSCRIPTS

American Federation of Labor. Papers. State Historical Society of Wisconsin, Madison.
C. Jasper Bell. Papers. Western Historical Manuscripts Collection and State Historical Society of Missouri Manuscripts, Columbia.
Brewers and Maltsters, Minutes of Local Union No. 6, Saint Louis. Western Historical Manuscripts Collection and State Historical Society of Missouri Manuscripts, Columbia.
Clarence A. Cannon. Papers. Western Historical Manuscripts Collection and State Historical Society of Missouri Manuscripts, Columbia.
Mildred Lee Dryden, Oral History Interview. Harry S. Truman Library, Independence, Missouri.
Edward F. Goltra. Papers. Missouri Historical Society, Saint Louis.
Samuel Gompers. Letterbooks. Library of Congress, Washington, D.C.
William Green. Letterbooks. Library of Congress, Washington, D.C.
Herbert S. Hadley. Papers. Western Historical Manuscripts Collection and State Historical Society of Missouri Manuscripts, Columbia.
Charles M. Hay. Papers. Western Historical Manuscripts Collection and State Historical Society of Missouri Manuscripts, Columbia.
Gottlieb A. Hoehn. Papers. Western Historical Manuscripts Collection and State Historical Society of Missouri Manuscripts, Columbia.
Arthur M. Hyde. Papers. Western Historical Manuscripts Collection and State Historical Society of Missouri Manuscripts, Columbia.
Breckingridge Long. Papers. Library of Congress, Washington, D.C.
Ralph F. Lozier. Papers. Western Historical Manuscripts Collection and State Historical Society of Missouri Manuscripts, Columbia.
Ewing Y. Mitchell. Papers. Western Historical Manuscripts Collection and State Historical Society of Missouri Manuscripts, Columbia.
Guy B. Park. Papers. Western Historical Manuscripts Collection and State Historical Society of Missouri Manuscripts, Columbia.
Alroy S. Phillips. Papers. Missouri Historical Society, Saint Louis.
Lloyd C. Stark. Papers. Western Historical Manuscripts Collection and State Historical Society of Missouri Manuscripts, Columbia.

William Joel Stone. Papers. Western Historical Manuscripts Collection
and State Historical Society of Missouri Manuscripts, Columbia.
Documents Relating to Harry S. Truman Microfilmed at the Franklin
D. Roosevelt Library. Harry S. Truman Library, Independence,
Missouri.
Harry S. Truman Senatorial Papers. Harry S. Truman Library, Inde-
pendence, Missouri.
United States Employment Service. Papers. National Archives, Washing-
ton, D.C.
War Labor Policies Board. Papers. National Archives, Washington, D.C.
Sam Wear. Papers. Harry S. Truman Library, Independence, Missouri.
Francis M. Wilson. Papers. Western Historical Manuscripts Collection
and State Historical Society of Missouri Manuscripts, Columbia.
Works Progress Administration. Papers. National Archives, Washington,
D.C.

E. PERIODICALS

American Federationist, Vol. 13, 1906.
Democracy, August, 1935.
United States Department of Labor, Bureau of Labor Statistics, *Monthly
Labor Review,* Vol. 7, 1918.

F. NEWSPAPERS

Unless otherwise indicated, all newspapers listed below are on file in the
State Historical Society of Missouri, Columbia, Missouri.

Chillicothe Constitution, May 22, 1934.
Daily Capital City News (Jefferson City), September 17, 1939.
Democracy, August 20, 21, 1935. Clippings from Lloyd C. Stark, Papers.
Western Historical Manuscripts Collection and State Historical So-
ciety of Missouri Manuscripts, Columbia.
The Ellington Press, October 8, 1936. Clipping from Lloyd C. Stark,
Papers. Western Historical Manuscripts Collection and State Histori-
cal Society of Missouri Manuscripts, Columbia.
The Hannibal Labor Press, April 30, 1937–December, 1940.
The Kansas City Labor Herald, March, 1940–December, 1940.
Kansas City Labor News, October, 1924, November, 1925.
The Kansas City Star, March–April, 1904; September, 1910; February,
1913; January, 1917; March, 1918; October, 1926; December, 1936.
The Kansas City Times, December, 1918–January, 1919; August, 1922;
April, 1937.
The Labor Herald (Kansas City), 1911–1940.
The Missouri Democrat (Kansas City), August, 1934.
The Missouri Mule (Kansas City), 1919–1922.
Missouri Socialist (Saint Louis), March 16, 1901.
Missouri State Journal (Jefferson City), December 17, 1921.
Missouri Trades Unionist (Joplin), 1911–1916.
Moberly Monitor–Index, August 14, 1922.
The Progressive Press (Saint Louis), December, 1930–January, 1931.
Railway Federationist (Sedalia), June, 1917–September, 1919.
The Saint Joseph Union, 1916–1919.

St. Joseph Union–Observer, March 2, 1934.
St. Louis Globe-Democrat, July 9, 1906.
St. Louis Labor, 1906–1930.
St. Louis Labor Tribune, September, 1937–December, 1940.
St. Louis Post-Dispatch, January, April, November, 1911; February, 1913; August, 1917; February, April, 1919; January–February, 1921; January, 1922; April 18, 1930; June, 1932.
The St. Louis Republic, July 9, 1906.
St. Louis Star, March–April, 1918.
St. Louis Times, December 31, 1924. Clipping from the Alroy S. Phillips, Papers. Missouri Historical Society, Saint Louis.
The Springfield Laborer, September, 1916–June, 1917.
The Springfield Leader, October–November, 1916; May–June, 1917.
Springfield Union Labor Record, 1938–1940.
Warrensburg State–Journal, May–June, 1936.

G. BOOKS

Anderson, Lee F., Meredith W. Watts, Jr., and Allen R. Wilcox. *Legislative Roll-Call Analysis.* Evanston: Northwestern University Press, 1966.
Barber, James D. *The Lawmakers: Recruitment and Adaptation to Legislative Life.* New Haven: Yale University Press, 1965.
Bardwell, George E., and Harry Seligson. *Organized Labor and Political Action in Colorado, 1900–1960.* Denver: College of Business Administration, University of Denver, 1959.
Bedford, Henry F. *Socialism and the Workers in Massachusetts, 1886–1912.* Amherst: The University of Massachusetts Press, 1966.
Bing, Alexander M. *War-Time Strikes and their Adjustment.* New York: E. P. Dutton & Co., Inc., 1921.
Brown, Andrew T. *Frontier Community: Kansas City.* Columbia: University of Missouri Press, 1963.
———. *The Politics of Reform: Kansas City's Municipal Government, 1925–1950.* Kansas City: Community Studies, 1958.
Calkins, Fay. *The CIO and the Democratic Party.* Chicago: The University of Chicago Press, 1952.
Charles, Searle F. *Minister of Relief: Harry Hopkins and the Depression.* Syracuse: Syracuse University Press, 1963.
Crighton, John C. *Missouri and the World War, 1914–1917: A Study in Public Opinion.* The University of Missouri Studies Series, Vol. 21, No. 3. Columbia: University of Missouri, 1947.
Crossland, William A. *Industrial Conditions Among Negroes in St. Louis.* Saint Louis: Press of Mendle Printing Company, 1914.
Daniels, Jonathan. *The Man of Independence.* Philadelphia: J .P. Lippincott Company, 1950.
Dollar, Charles, and Richard Jensen. *Historian's Guide to Statistics.* New York: Holt, Rinehart, and Winston, Inc., 1971.
Dorsett, Lyle W. *The Pendergast Machine.* New York: Oxford University Press, 1968.
Dulles, Foster Rhea. *Labor in America.* New York: Thomas Y. Crowell Company, 1949.
Fine, Nathan. *Labor and Farmer Parties in the United States, 1828–1928.* New York: Russell & Russell, Inc., 1928.

216 • **Labor's Search for Political Order**

Foner, Philip S. *History of the Labor Movement in the United States.* Vol. 3. New York: International Publishers Co., Inc., 1964.
Galenson, Walter. *The CIO Challenge to the AFL.* Cambridge: Harvard University Press, 1960.
Gavett, Thomas W. *Development of the Labor Movement in Milwaukee.* Madison: The University of Wisconsin Press, 1965.
Geiger, Louis G. *Joseph W. Folk of Missouri.* The University of Missouri Studies Series, Vol. 25, No. 2. Columbia: University of Missouri, 1953.
Greenstone, J. David. *Labor in American Politics.* New York: Alfred A. Knopf, Inc., 1969.
Grob, Gerald N. *Workers and Utopia: A Study of Ideological Conflict in the American Labor Movement, 1865–1900.* Evanston, Ill.: Northwestern University Press, 1961.
Grubbs, Frank L., Jr. *The Struggle for Labor Loyalty: Gompers, the A. F. of L., and the Pacifists, 1917–1920.* Durham, N.C.: Duke University Press, 1968.
Gutman, Herbert G. "The Worker's Search for Power: Labor in the Gilded Age," in *The Gilded Age: A Reappraisal,* ed. H. W. Morgan, pp. 38–63. Syracuse: Syracuse University Press, 1963.
Harris, Evelyn L. K., and Frank J. Krebs. *From Humble Beginnings: West Virginia State Federation of Labor, 1903–1957.* Charleston: Labor History Publishing Fund, 1960.
Higgins, George G. *Voluntarism in Organized Labor in the United States, 1930–1940.* Washington, D.C.: The Catholic University of America Press, 1945.
Hourwich, Isaac. *Immigration and Labor.* New York: G. P. Putman's Sons, 1912.
Jewell, Malcolm E. *The State Legislature: Politics and Practice.* New York: Random House, Inc., 1962.
Karsch, Robert F. *The Standing Committees of the Missouri General Assembly.* Columbia: Bureau of Government Research, University of Missouri, 1959.
Karson, Marc, *American Labor Unions and Politics, 1900–1919.* Carbondale: Southern Illinois University Press, 1958.
Kipnis, Ira. *The American Socialist Movement, 1897–1912.* New York: Columbia University Press, 1952.
Klamon Joseph M., *et al. A Survey of the Labor Market in Missouri in Relation to Unemployment Compensation.* Washington Uiversity Studies, Series No. 5. Saint Louis: Washington University, 1937.
Laslett, John H. M. *Labor and the Left: A Study of Socialism and Radical Influences in the American Labor Movement, 1881–1924.* New York: Basic Books Inc., 1970.
Lawson, George W. *Organized Labor in Minnesota.* Saint Paul: Minnesota State Federation of Labor, 1955.
Leiserson, William. *American Trade Union Democracy.* New York: Columbia University Press, 1959.
Leuchtenburg, William E. *Franklin D. Roosevelt and the New Deal.* New York: Harper & Row, Publishers, 1963.
Leuthold, David A. *The Missouri Legislature: A Preliminary Profile.* Columbia: University of Missouri Research Center, School of Business and Public Administration, 1967.
Lorwin, Lewis. *The American Federation of Labor: History, Policies and Prospects.* Washington, D.C.: Brookings Institution, 1933.

Lynd, Staughton. *Class Conflict, Slavery and the United States Constitution.* Indianapolis: The Bobbs-Merrill Company, Inc., 1967.

MacKay, Kenneth. *The Progressive Movement of 1924.* New York: Columbia University Press, 1947.

MacLaughlin, Doris B. *Michigan Labor: A Brief History from 1818 to the Present.* Ann Arbor: Institute of Labor and Industrial Relations, The University of Michigan—Wayne State University, 1970.

MacRae, Duncan, Jr. *Issues and Parties in Legislative Voting: Methods of Statistical Analysis.* New York. Harper & Row, Publishers, 1970.

———. *Dimensions of Congressional Voting.* Los Angeles: University of California Press, 1958.

Mandel, Bernard. *Samuel Gompers: A Biography.* Yellow Springs, Ohio: The Antioch Press, 1963.

March, David D. *A History of Missouri,* Vol. 2. New York and West Palm Beach: Lewis Historical Publishing Company, 1967.

Mayer, George. *The Republican Party, 1854–1966.* New York: Oxford University Press, 1967.

McReynolds, Edwin C. *Missouri: A History of the Crossroads State.* Norman: University of Oklahoma Press, 1962.

Meyer, Duane G. *The Heritage of Missouri: A History.* Saint Louis: The State Publishing Company, 1963.

Mitchell, Franklin D. *Embattled Democracy: Missouri Democratic Politics, 1919–1932.* The University of Missouri Studies Series, Vol. 47. Columbia: University of Missouri Press, 1968.

Morris, James O. *Conflict within the AFL: A Study of Craft versus Industrial Unionism, 1901–1938.* Ithaca: Cornell University Press, 1958.

Nelson, Daniel. *Unemployment Insurance: The American Experience, 1915–1935.* Madison: The University of Wisconsin Press, 1969.

Newell, Barbara Warne. *Chicago and the Labor Movement: Metropolitan Unionism in the 1930's.* Urbana: University of Illinois Press, 1961.

Patterson, James T. *The New Deal and the States: Federalism in Transition.* Princeton: Princeton University Press, 1969.

Pelling, Henry. *American Labor.* Chicago: The University of Chicago Press, 1960.

Perlman, Mark. *The Machinists: A New Study in American Trade Unionism.* Cambridge: Harvard University Press, 1961.

Perlman, Selig. *A History of Trade Unionism in the United States.* New York: The Macmillan Company, 1922.

———. *A Theory of the Labor Movement.* New York: The Macmillan Company, 1928.

———, and Philip Taft. *History of Labor in the United States: Labor Movement, 1896–1932.* New York: The Macmillan Company, 1935.

Perry, Louis B., and Richard S. Perry. *A History of the Los Angeles Labor Movement, 1911–1941.* Berkeley and Los Angeles: University of California Press, 1963.

Quint, Howard H. *The Forging of American Socialism: Origins of the Modern Movement.* Columbia: University of South Carolina Press, 1953.

Reedy, William M. *The Story of the Strike.* Saint Louis: n.p., n.d.

Reid, Ira de A. *A Study of the Industrial Status of Negroes in St. Louis.* Saint Louis: Welfare Plan Council of St. Louis and St. Louis County, 1934.

Salisbury, Robert H. *Missouri Politics and State Political Systems.* Columbia: Bureau of Government Research, University of Missouri, 1959.

Shannon, David A. *The Socialist Party in America.* New York: The Macmillan Company, 1955.

Staley, Eugene. *A History of the Illinois State Federation of Labor.* Chicago: The University of Chicago Press, 1930.

Steinberg, Alfred. *The Man from Missouri: The Life and Times of Harry S. Truman.* New York: G. P. Putnam's Sons, 1962.

Stimson, Grace Heilman. *Rise of the Labor Movement in Los Angeles.* Berkeley: University of California Press, 1955.

Stouffer, Samuel, and Louis Guttman, *et al. Measurement and Prediction: Studies in Social Psychology in World War II,* Vol. 4. Princeton: Princeton University Press, 1950.

Taft, Philip. *The A. F. of L. in the Time of Gompers.* New York: Harper and Brothers, 1957.

————. *The A. F. of L. from the Death of Gompers to the Merger.* New York: Harper and Brothers, 1959.

————. *Labor Politics American Style: The California State Federation of Labor.* Cambridge: Harvard University Press, 1968.

Thernstrom, Stephen. *Poverty and Progress: Social Mobility in a Nineteenth Century City.* Cambridge: Harvard University Press, 1964.

Troy, Leo. *Organized Labor in New Jersey.* Princeton: D. Van Nostrand Company, 1965.

Vale, Vivian. *Labour in American Politics.* London: Routledge and Kegan Paul, Ltd., 1971.

Weinstein, James. *The Decline of Socialism in America, 1912–1925.* New York Monthly Review Press, 1967.

Wohlke, John, *et al. The Legislative System.* New York: John Wiley & Sons, Inc., 1962.

Yellowitz, Irwin. *Labor and the Progressive Movement in New York State, 1897–1916.* Ithaca: Cornell University Press, 1965.

Zieger, Robert H. *Republicans and Labor, 1919–1929.* Lexington: University of Kentucky Press, 1969.

H. ARTICLES

Belknap, George. "A Method for Analyzing Legislative Behavior." *Midwest Journal of Political Science,* 2 (November, 1958), 377–402.

Bryant, Keith L. "Labor in Politics: The Oklahoma State Federation of Labor during the Age of Reform." *Labor History,* 10 (Summer, 1970), 259–84.

Crockett, Norman L. "The 1912 Single Tax Campaign in Missouri," *Missouri Historical Review,* 56 (October, 1961), 40–52.

Dahl, Robert. "The Concept of Power." *Behavioral Science,* 2 (July, 1957), 201–15.

Derge, David R. "Metropolitan and Outstate Alignments in Illinois and Missouri Legislative Delegations." *American Political Science Review,* 52 (December, 1958), 1051–65.

Fink, Gary M. "The Paradoxical Experiences of St. Louis Labor During the Depression of 1837." *The Bulletin of the Missouri Historical Society,* 26:1 (October, 1969), 53–63.

————. "The Unwanted Conflict: Missouri Labor and the CIO." *Missouri Historical Review,* 64 (July, 1970), 432–47.

Heath, Frederick M. "Labor and the Progressive Movement in Connecticut." *Labor History,* 12 (Winter, 1971), 52–67.

Hofstadter, Richard. "Turner and the Frontier Myth." *The American Scholar,* 12 (Autumn, 1949), 433–43.

Huthmacher, J. Joseph. "Urban Liberalism and the Age of Reform." *The Mississippi Valley Historical Review,* 49 (September, 1962), 231–41.

Jensen, Richard. "Power and Success Scores." *Historical Methods Newsletter,* 1 (June, 1968), 1–6.

Kerr, Thomas J. IV. "The New York Factory Investigating Commission and the Minimum-Wage Movement." *Labor History,* 12 (Summer, 1971), 373–91.

Laslett, John H. M. "Socialism and the American Labor Movement: Some New Reflections." *Labor History,* 8 (Spring, 1967), 135–55.

Lively, Robert A. "The American System: A Review Article." *Business History Review,* 29 (March, 1955), 81–96.

Lubove, Roy. "Workmen's Compensation and the Prerogatives of Voluntarism." *Labor History,* 8 (Fall, 1967), 254–79.

MacRae, Duncan, Jr., and Hugh Price. "Scale Positions and 'Power' in the Senate." *Behavioral Science,* 4 (July, 1959), 212–18.

Nolen, Russell M. "The Labor Movement in St. Louis prior to the Civil War." *Missouri Historical Review,* 34 (October, 1939), 158–81.

Patterson, James T. "The New Deal and the States." *American Historical Review,* 72:1 (October, 1967), 70–84.

Riker, William. "Some Ambiguities in the Notion of Power." *The American Political Science Review,* 58 (June, 1964), 341–49.

Rogin, Michael. "Voluntarism: The Political Functions of an Antipolitical Doctrine." *Industrial and the Labor Relations Review,* 15 (July, 1962), 521–35.

Saposs, David J. "Voluntarism in the American Labor Movement." *The Monthly Labor Review,* 77 (September, 1954), 967–71.

Shover, John L. "The Progressives and the Working Class Vote in California." *Labor History,* 10 (Fall, 1969), 584–601.

Weinstein, James. "Big Business and the Origins of Workmen's Compensation." *Labor History,* 8 (Spring, 1967), 156–74.

Wesser, Robert F. "Conflict and Compromise: The Workmen's Compensation Movement in New York, 1890s–1913." *Labor History,* 12 (Summer, 1971), 345–72.

Yellowitz, Irwin. "The Origins of Unemployment Reform in the United States." *Labor History,* 9 (Fall, 1968), 338–60.

I. UNPUBLISHED STUDIES

Cotter, John C. "The Negro in Music in St. Louis." Master's thesis, Washington University, Saint Louis, 1959.

Fink, Gary M. "The Evolution of Social and Political Attitudes in the Missouri Labor Movement, 1900–1940." Doctoral dissertation, University of Missouri, Columbia, 1968.

Forsythe, Edwin J. "The St. Louis Central Trades and Labor Union, 1887–1945." Doctoral dissertation, University of Missouri, Columbia, 1956.

Gentry, Carl C. "Children's Code of the State of Missouri." Master's thesis, University of Missouri, Columbia, 1925.

Graham, Fred R. "A History of the Missouri State Federation of Labor." Master's thesis, University of Missouri, Columbia, 1934.

Houf, Walter R. "Fifty Years of Missouri Labor, 1820–1870." Master's thesis, University of Missouri, Columbia, 1958.

Lowe, James L. "The Administration of Arthur M. Hyde, Governor of Missouri, 1921–1925." Master's thesis, University of Missouri, Columbia, 1949.

Melom, Halvor G. "The Economic Development of St. Louis, 1803–1846." Doctoral dissertation, University of Missouri, Columbia, 1947.

Miller, William T. "The Progressive Movement in Missouri." Master's thesis, University of Missouri, Columbia, 1927.

Muraskin, Jack D. "Missouri Politics during the Progressive Era, 1896–1916." Doctoral dissertation, University of California, Berkeley, 1969.

Ogilvie, Leon P. "The Development of the Southeast Missouri Lowlands." Doctoral dissertation, University of Missouri, Columbia, 1967.

Porter, Curtis Hunter. "Charter Reform in St. Louis, 1900–1914." Master's thesis, Washington University, Saint Louis, 1966.

Rogge, Edward A. "The Speechmaking of Harry S. Truman." Doctoral dissertation, University of Missouri, Columbia, 1958.

Schmidtlein, Eugene F. "Truman the Senator." Doctoral dissertation, University of Missouri, Columbia, 1962.

Sears, Wilford R. "The Kansas City Building Trades and Trade Unionism." Master's thesis, University of Missouri, Columbia, 1947.

Towne, Ruth W. "The Movement for Workmen's Compensation Legislation in Missouri, 1910–1925." Master's thesis, University of Missouri, Columbia, 1940.

Van Eaton, Anson E. "The Initiative and Referendum in Missouri." Doctoral dissertation, University of Missouri, Columbia, 1954.

Vogt, Herbert J. "Boot and Shoe Industry of St. Louis: Origin, Growth and Causes of Its Development." Master's thesis, Washington University, Saint Louis, 1929.

Worner, Lloyd E., Jr. "The Public Career of Herbert Spencer Hadley." Doctoral dissertation, University of Missouri, Columbia, 1946.

Index

A

Adamson Eight Hour Law, 124
Afro-American Workers, 55, 56, 57n
Allen, Henry J., 103
Amalgamated Association of Street, Electric Railway and Motor Coach Employees of America, 66, 125, 179
American Alliance for Labor and Democracy, 68
American Association for Labor Legislation, 49, 171
American Federation of Labor: institutional character, vii, 165, 180, 181; and Missouri State Federation of Labor, 6; political activities, 12, 14, 15, 16, 19, 22; voluntarism, 12, 162–67; conflict with Socialists, 15, 29, 164; and workmen's compensation, 92, 169, 170; CIO conflict, 143, 144; mentioned, *passim*
American Federation of Musicians, 25
American Labor Party, Saint Louis, 106
American Labor Union, 26
American Plan, 71, 98
Andrew Jackson Democratic Club, 149
Andrews, John P., 49
Anti-injunction legislation, 53, 100, 130, 136, 140, 175, 176, 186, 191
Associated Employers of Missouri, 52
Associated Industries, 85, 87, 91
Atkinson, John M., 95
Audrain County, 196

B

Baker, Sam, 114, 115
Bakers' union, 25
Baltimore Journal, 26
Barbers' Local No. 102, Journeymen Barbers' International Union, 30
Barker, John T., 48, 50
Barkley, J. C., 69n
Barkley, William, 151, 158
Behrens, Edward H., 22, 22n, 27
Bellamy, Edward, 6
Bellamy clubs, 28, 143
Berger, Victor, 6, 27
Big Cinch, 38

Billings, James V., 154, 155
Black, Hugo, 131
Board of Business Agents, Kansas City, 72
Bonne Terre, Mo., 104
Brandt, William, 32, 106, 142n, 158
Brewery workers, 25, 141
Bridge, Structural and Ornamental Iron Workers, International Association of, 151
British Labour party, 95, 105
Brittinghous, Charles G., 50, 95, 100
Brookfield, Mo., 194
Brooklyn (N.Y.) Central Labor Union, 174
Brown, B. F., 150
Brown, W. H., 22n
Brunett Immigration bill, 55
Bryan, William J., 19, 20
Butler, Edward, 20n, 155

C

California State Federation of Labor, 167n
Cannon, Clarence, 116, 123n, 152
Carpenters' District Council, Saint Louis, 25
Carpenters' Local No. 4596, 25
Casey, Michael, 127, 191
Cassidy, Maurice, 146n
Caulfield, Henry, 114, 115, 125
Chaffee, Mo., 102
Chicago *Arbeiter-Zeitung,* 26
Child labor reform, 53, 88, 129, 131, 132, 137, 173, 186
Children's Code Commission, 53
Church, John, 158
Cigarmakers' unions: Socialist influence on, 25, 28; leadership role, 28; declining influence of, 141
Cigarmakers Local No. 44, 25
Civilian Works Administration, 133
Clark, Bennett Champ, 122, 123, 147, 148, 149, 158
Clark, Champ, 18
Clark, Joseph, 158
Cochran, John J., 147, 148, 149
Compulsory arbitration, industrial court, 83, 88, 93, 101, 176, 197
Conference for Progressive Political Action, 99, 104–8
Congress of Industrial Organizations, 143, 144

Helm, Arch, 28, 103, 115
Henderson, Arthur, 105
Hendricks, A. R., 146n, 148, 151
Henry County, 196
Higgins, George G., 164
Hillquit, Morris, 6
Hirth, William, 150
Hoehn, Gottlieb A.: early career, 26, 27; and controversy over Federal Labor Union No. 6482, 30–32; Saint Louis charter reform, 37; racial attitude, 56
Hofher, Phil, 22n
Hoover, Herbert C., 113, 131
Hopkins, Harry, 133, 134, 135
Howell, Charles, 122, 123
Hunt, John T., 17
Hyde, Arthur M.: gubernatorial campaign, 94; railroad shop craft strike, 101; position on open shop, 103; mentioned, 100, 112, 114

I

Ickes, Harold L., 133
Igoe, Richard, 127
Illinois State Federation of Labor, 174
Immigration restriction, 55
Industrial Employers of Missouri, 91
Industrial Progress, 103
Industrial Workers of the World, 15
International Association of Machinists, 25
International Union of Mine, Mill and Smelter Workers, 104

J

Jasper County, 28
Jenkins, E. W., 124
Jennings, O. E., 66n, 124, 124n
Jobbers and Manufacturers' Association, Springfield, 66
Johnson, Jackson, 70
Johnson, Richard, 146n
Joint Conference on Charter Revision, 37, 38
Joint Conference of Non-partisan Committees of the State Federation of Labor, 94
Joplin Trades Assembly, 52
Judson, Frederick N., 80
Juneman, H. A. W., 28

K

Kansas City: character of, 2; streetcar strike, 67, 74–76, 124; police department, 67, 72; general strike, 71–74; drive for open shop, 98

Kansas City Board of Business Agents, 73
Kansas City Building Trades Council: character of, 3; on workmen's compensation, 90, 91; patronage, 146; in 1934 elections, 148
Kansas City Central Labor Union: on workmen's compensation, 86, 87, 90, 91; political activities in 1920, 97, 98; and Pendergast, 122; gubernatorial campaign of 1932, 124, 125, 126; in 1934 elections, 148; mentioned, 120. *See also* Kansas City Industrial Council
Kansas City Commercial Club and Manufacturers Association, 52
Kansas City Cooperative Society, 96
Kansas City Council of National Defense, 72
Kansas City Election Board, 154
Kansas City Employers' Association: general strike, 72; streetcar strike, 75; workmen's compensation, 86, 87, 90
Kansas City Industrial Council: character of, 3; relationship with State Federation, 5; direct legislation, 37, 39; employer liability, 49; workmen's compensation, 51, 52, 85; preparedness, 61; mentioned, 21. *See also* Kansas City Central Labor Union
Kansas City Star, 95
Kansas City Union Labor Democratic Club, 148, 155
Kansas Court of Industrial Relations, 88
Karson, Marc, 164
Kealy, P. J., 75
Kindorf, William, 22n, 82
Kinney, Michael, 127, 191
Kinney, Thomas, 20n
Knefler, Cynthelia, 50n
Knights of Labor, 6, 27, 28, 143
Krauthoff, Edwin, 49
Kreyling, David: association with the Socialists, 26; Conference for Progressive Political Action, 105; American Labor party, 106; mentioned, 142n
Ku Klux Klan, 107

L

Labor, 122
Labor's Bill of Grievances, 15
Labor Education League, Saint Louis, 98
Labor Herald, 55, 74, 86, 92

AFL, 6, 12, 13, 14; Socialist influence, 25, 29; Afro-American workers, 55, 56; immigration restriction,
55; movie censorship, 55; Springfield streetcar strike, 65–67; postwar
reconstruction, 82; Alroy S. Phillips, 83; cooperative movement, 96;
membership, 99n, 144n; changes
during 1930s, 142, 143; on voluntarism, 162; mentioned, 27, 120,
176, *passim*
—in elections: 1906, 18, 19; 1908,
21, 22; 1920, 95; 1932, 123, 126;
1936, 151; 1940, 158
—legislative objectives: direct legislation, 36; workmen's compensation,
51, 87; prohibition, 54, 55; child
labor, 137; anti-injunction law, 140.
See also Labor lobby
—political activities: objectives, 13;
questioning candidates, 14, 47; preferred list, 44, 130; Conference for
Progressive Political Action, 106;
Constitutional Convention, 100,
101; Pendergast's influence, 122;
political patronage, 146
—and World War I: early attitude
toward the war, 61, 62; preparedness, 61; effects of the war, 62,
63; objections to the employment
of women, 71, 72; labor unrest in
Saint Louis, 79
Mitchell, John, 49
Moberly, Mo., 102, 194
Morrin, P. J., 151
Morrison, Frank, 15, 16, 17
Movie censorship, 55
Moyer, Charles H., 104
Mullaney, Edward, 151
Municipal home rule, 168
Murray, Matthew, 155

N

National Association of Manufac-
turers, 77
National Civic Federation, 49
Nationalization of industry, 82, 175
National Labor Relations Act, 136
National Labor Relations Board, 136
National Recovery Administration:
Section 7a, 132; Blue Eagle, 132;
mentioned, 131, 136
National War Labor Board: Kansas
City streetcar strike, 75, 76; labor
unrest in Saint Louis, 80, 81
Nelson, Charles B., 87, 90, 125
Nelson, Daniel, 171n
Nelson, Oscar C., 77

New Constitution Association of Mis-
souri, 100
New Franklin, Mo., 102
New Hampshire State Federation of
Labor, 165
New York State Federation of Labor,
174
Norris, George, 130
Norris–La Guardia Anti-Injunction
Act, 136
North Dakota Non-Partisan League,
95

O

O'Connell, James, 16
Old-age pensions, 53, 82, 100, 127,
129, 131, 138, 139, 140, 172, 186.
See also Labor lobby
O'Malley, Emmett, 153, 154, 155, 157
Open-shop movement: during the
1920s, 98, 99; in Saint Louis, 98;
in Kansas City, 98
Organization for Progressive Political
Action, 118
O'Shea, Frank, 75
Outstate Missouri: character of, 3;
Socialist influence, 27

P

Park, Guy B., 114, 126, 136n, 137,
149
Patterson, James T., 135n
Patterson, Roscoe, 149
Pauls, Otto, 26
Pendergast, Thomas J.: attempts to
win labor support, 120, 121, 122;
and Reuben Wood, 121, 147, 148,
149; in 1932 gubernatorial campaign, 123; patronage, 146, 147;
in 1936 campaigns, 149; relations
with Lloyd Stark, 154–59 *passim;*
mentioned *passim*
Peoples League: charter reform in
Saint Louis, 38
Peterson, Frank, 87, 89, 90
Phillipi, Louis, 25
Phillips, Alroy S., 52, 83
Political reform: direct legislation,
34–41, 44, 45, 93, 101, 169; direct
primaries, 34, 83, 93, 101, 127, 168,
197; direct election of senators, 34,
168; woman suffrage, 34, 168;
municipal home rule, 168
Populist party, Populism, 6, 28, 143
Porter, F. W., 72
Postwar reconstruction, 82, 83
Preparedness: State Federation, 61;
Saint Louis Central Trades, 61;
Kansas City Industrial Council, 61

Private and public housing, 82
Progressive party of 1924, 95
Prohibition: labor's opposition to, 54, 55; Trades Union Liberty League, 54; in 1920 elections, 95; position of Democratic party, 119; in 1932 elections, 122, 123; effect on brewery unions, 142
Public ownership of utilities, 82, 136, 137
Public Works Administration, 133

Q

Quinn, Thomas, 146n

R

Railroad brotherhoods: in 1920 elections, 95; 1932 elections, 122; declining influence in State Federation, 142; in 1936 elections, 151; in 1940 elections, 156; mentioned *passim*
Railroad Labor Board, 101
Railroad shop craft strike, 99, 101–4
Railway Federationist, 27
Railway and Steamship Clerks, Brotherhood of, Hannibal, 157
Railroad Trainmen, Brotherhood of: Conference for Progressive Political Action, 107; Pendergast's influence on, 122; in 1932 elections, 123; relationship with labor lobby, 125n; in 1934 elections, 147; in 1936 elections, 151; mentioned, 157
Randolph County, 196
Ready Mixed Concrete Company, 121
Relief and public works, 82, 107, 132, 172
Republican party: in Constitutional Convention, 100; character of, 112–15; in General Assembly, 185–97; mentioned *passim*
Republican State Central Committee, 125
Retail Merchants Association, Springfield, 66
Richmond, Mo., 147
Rogers, Jesse 'L., 146n
Rogers, William C., 77–78
Rogin, Michael, 163
Romjue, Milton, 123n
Roosevelt, Franklin D., 130, 131, 145, 149, 153, 156
Roosevelt, Theodore, 15, 112
Roosevelt Coalition, 127
Rucker, William, 117, 118
Ryder, Mary, 121, 122, 158

S

Sacks, William, 100
Safety standards on construction, 175. *See also* Scaffold laws
Saint Francois County, 196
Saint Louis: character of, 1; extent of labor organization, 4; municipal elections of 1911, 32; Big Cinch, 34; charter reform, 37, 38, 39; opposition to prohibition, 54; Afro-American workers, 56; unrest during World War I, 76–81; open shop drive, 98; mentioned, *passim*
Saint Louis Building Trades Council: character of, 2; charter reform, 38; Afro-American workers, 56; and World War I, 69; workmen's compensation, 90; Conference for Progressive Political Action, 107; political patronage, 146; mentioned, 158
Saint Louis Board of Aldermen, 55
Saint Louis Bucks Stove and Range Company, 22
Saint Louis Business Men's League, 52
Saint Louis Central Trades and Labor Union: organization, 1; relationship with AFL, 1, 2, 19, 20; relationship with State Federation, 5; political activities, 16, 98, 105, 106, 107; Socialist influence, 25, 26, 29, 30, 31, 32; charter reform, 38; workmen's compensation, 51, 85, 87, 88, 90; Afro-American workers, 56; World War I, 61, 68, 69, 79; postwar reconstruction, 82; cooperative movement, 96; mentioned, 158
Saint Louis Chamber of Commerce, 70
Saint Louis Cigar Makers International Union, Local No. 44, 82
Saint Louis Civic League, 37, 38
Saint Louis Conference for Progressive Political Action, 105
Saint Louis Employers' Association, 80
St. Louis Globe-Democrat, 32
Saint Louis Industrial Council, CIO, 158
St. Louis Labor, 26, 27, 30
St. Louis Post-Dispatch, 38
Saint Louis Shoe Workers Union, 45
St. Louis Tageblatt, 26
St. Louis Union Labor Advocate, 145
Saint Louis Union Workingmen's party, 16
Saint Louis Women's Trade Union League, 50n